The Moment

STUDIES IN SOCIAL AND POLITICAL THOUGHT 4

STUDIES IN SOCIAL AND POLITICAL THOUGHT
Editor: Gerard Delanty, *University of Liverpool*

This series publishes peer-reviewed scholarly books on all aspects of social and political thought. It will be of interest to scholars and advanced students working in the areas of social theory and sociology, the history of ideas, philosophy, political and legal theory, anthropological and cultural theory. Works of individual scholarship will have preference for inclusion in the series, but appropriate co- or multi-authored works and edited volumes of outstanding quality or exceptional merit will also be included. The series will also consider English translations of major works in other languages.

Challenging and intellectually innovative books are particularly welcome on the history of social and political theory; modernity and the social and human sciences; major historical or contemporary thinkers; the philosophy of the social sciences; theoretical issues on the transformation of contemporary society; social change and European societies.

It is not series policy to publish textbooks, research reports, empirical case studies, conference proceedings or books of an essayist or polemical nature.

Discourse and Knowledge: The Making of Enlightenment Sociology
Piet Strydom

Social Theory after the Holocaust
edited by Robert Fine and Charles Turner

The Protestant Ethic Debate: Max Weber's Replies to his Critics, 1907–1910
edited by David Chalcraft and Austin Harrington

Essaying Montaigne
John O'Neill

The Moment: Time and Rupture in Modern Thought
edited by Heidrun Friese

The Moment
Time and Rupture in Modern Thought

Edited by

HEIDRUN FRIESE

LIVERPOOL UNIVERSITY PRESS

First published 2001 by
Liverpool University Press
4 Cambridge Street
Liverpool
L69 7ZU

British Library Cataloguing-in-Publication Data
A British Library CIP record is available

ISBN 0 85323 956 8 cased
ISBN 0 85323 966 5 paperback

Typeset by Freelance Publishing Services, Brinscall, Lancs
www.freelancepublishingservices.co.uk
Printed in Great Britain by
Antony Rowe Ltd, Chippenham, Wiltshire

Contents

Bewußtsein könnte gar nicht über das Grau verzweifeln, hegte es nicht den Begriff von einer verschiedenen Farbe, deren versprengte Spur im negativen Ganzen nicht fehlt.

(Greyness could not fill us with despair if our minds did not harbour the concept of different colours, scattered traces of which are not absent from the negative whole.)

Theodor W. Adorno, *Negative Dialektik*

Acknowledgements

I would like to express my gratitude to the UK Economic and Social Research Council, whose support for the research seminar on Social Theory and Major Social Transformations made possible the discussions at the Social Theory Centre of the University of Warwick on which this book draws, as well as to the European University Institute, Florence for the support provided for the seminar series on The Languages of the Political. A note of thanks is also due to my colleagues at the University of Warwick for the warm interest with which they approached me and my work. Peter Wagner knows what the singular moments of our endless dialogues mean to me.

Heidrun Friese

Introduction

HEIDRUN FRIESE

Were this then this ungraspable something ... the moment ... this ungraspable something that does not belong to any time.

Plato

This gradual crumbling, which did not alter the physiognomy of the whole, is interrupted by the rising that, a lightning flash, creates in one stroke the formation of the new world.

Georg Wilhelm Friedrich Hegel[1]

The 'moment', *Momentum, movere*, that which moves, that which irrefutably vanishes. *Clin d'œil, en un clin d'œil, en un temps très court*, an 'infinitely short space of time', *Augenblick*, the 'blink of an eye', glance, eye, the eyelid, a steady, unperceivable rhythm of opening and closing, the infinitely short interruption of seeing that only allows to see. And, at the same time, an opening glance, by which we are being seen, an open eye that lets the glance abide.

The 'moment', this is a word which addresses particular relations to time and temporality; a word that questions the empty continuity of an infinite linear time in which one moment devours the other one like Chronos devoured his children; a word that asks for fine rifts, sudden fractures and interruptions in such permanence. This is also a double word, since philosophical and scientific traditions linked the eyesight, the glance, the faculty of vision to cognition, knowledge and *theoria*; they have posed an original relation of curiosity, of seeing and knowing, of looking and cognising, of sighting and conceptualising, and have endowed these relations with a specific reference to time.

1

Introduction

The 'Moment', therefore, is a word that has become a central concept in all attempts at questioning the idea of empty, homogeneous and continuous time. The social sciences, in the form in which they emerged at the turn of the nineteenth century, commonly declared time to be a function of structure, continuity and eternity, not least with a view to postulating an ontological stability and a lawlike regularity of social life.[2] Philosophy, in some contrast, avails itself of an old – even if manifold – heritage in thinking the moment, a concept the elaboration of which, within different strands of modern philosophy, reaches from romanticism to Søren Kierkegaard and Friedrich Nietzsche to Edmund Husserl, Martin Heidegger or Walter Benjamin. In these lines of thought, the moment negates the empty continuum of time – and, that is, a view of time as an empty stretch of objective and quantifiable units in which past and future are separated from one another, yet at the same time connected to each other, at the point of the boundary of the 'now'. The moment is the decisive caesura, which bids its farewell to the irrevocable past and opens up towards that which is to come, to the not-yet of the future. The significant, decisive, historic moment – which calls for presence of mind, and needs to be grasped – demonstrates that neither the time of the singular human beings and their – more or less determined – actions[3] nor history and, with it, language unfolds within a continuous and chronological measure of time, but in tremendous disruptions, leaps and breaks. While philosophy remained able to think phenomena from the discontinuity of the moment, the social sciences have banned the interruption, the sudden loss of context, the caesura from their perspectives. They have privileged identity and regularity over singularity and structure over event to be able to establish the temporal tenacity of social institutions, the steadiness of repetitions in routine actions and societal life and, thus, have grandiosely ever again confirmed the continuity of temporal connections.

The moment, therefore, demands the questioning of all too common notions of time, of past, present and future; it demands that we think about uniqueness and repetition, identity and difference, suddenness and duration, rupture and continuity. As the contributions to this volume illustrate, addressing the moment – its inaccessibility and unattainability – inevitably requires us to engage in questions that concern vision, the glance of the eye in its relation to *cognition and theory*. In its complexity, the moment does not just place demands upon the thinking of presence and representation, of temporality and historicity, of the closure or incompleteness of history, *time*, *eternity* and *rupture*, but can open up the question of the relation of *decision*, *event* and *authenticity*.

The following contributions unfold in a complex rhythm created by these aspects and by the paradoxes of the moment. At the same time, they demonstrate how such manifold philosophical and literary heritage can be read today – and be

2

made productive for contemporary theorising of the social. They point to the kairotic moment, the rupture of time, and to the aporias of the moment (Geoffrey Bennington, Maurizio Ferraris). Against the indifference of an empty and homogeneous temporal sequence they open towards the thinking of the existential moment, the sudden event, the moment of decision and its ethical dimensions (Peter Poellner, Heidrun Friese, Simon Critchley). They present the moment in its epiphanic fulfilment and the moments of diminishing representation in literary modernity, the semantic complexity of the moment and the caesura (Karl Heinz Bohrer, Andrew Benjamin). Against the plain infinity of time, they elucidate the 'now' and its relations to historical time and cognition (Werner Hamacher).

Glance, Cognition and Theory

Plato calls moment, or the sudden (*to exaiphnes*), the peculiarity, in which the revulsion from movement to stillness and from stillness to movement occurs, the transition from being to non-being and from non-being to being.[4] This moment is peculiar because it is situated between stillness and movement, belongs to no time, and because the One within it neither rests nor moves, neither is nor is not. Plato grasps the moment as timeless, not as an individualised atom of time but rather as the totality of oppositions. The moment is timeless, negation of time – therefore it is not, in contrast to all temporal being. In its nullity it is that which is discontinuous in the continuity of time; and as the timeless principle of time, it is nevertheless effective 'within time'; as the sudden-discontinuous it is paradoxically the ground of the continuity of time. It occurs suddenly and immediately, and it nevertheless is that which mediates. As timeless, the moment is not, but it nevertheless is that within time which is most time's being.

On the one hand, the moment is determined as transition, as the timeless and moving principle within time; on the other hand, and distinct from such a founding, however, the moment also appears in the beholding of the eternal–beautiful and everlasting – then, namely, when the wise man 'finally, arrived at the end of the path leading towards the lovable, gains sight of a beauty of marvelous nature, precisely that towards which all earlier strivings were directed.'[5] The moment becomes the event of philosophical existence not by the transition between oppositions, steadily performed in time, but as the revulsion from not-knowing to knowing, as the incursion of the timeless moment of sighting, which was prepared for over all the course of life but which occurs unhoped-for and like a strike.

The 'site' of the moment is taken by the 'now', in the thought of Aristotle. The 'now' is – in contrast to the Platonic moment – the indivisible boundary of time but also that which holds time together. Every 'now' is at the same time the end of the past and the beginning of the future in the present. Such present now thus is situated between becoming and passing away and allows for both past and future. While in Plato the moment is determined as the timeless in-between of the times, in Aristotle the timeless being of the 'now' is cast each as the respective in-between of time. Aristotle understands such 'now' thus not as a timeless transition within temporal continuity, but rather as the permanent unfolding of time itself.

The moment, further, entertains a complex relation to the recognising glance. While not immediately linked to the *theorein* of *sophia*, the observing beholding, it is rather connected to practical knowledge (*phronesis*) and the *kairos*. The seeing that is specific to *phronesis* occurs momentarily, as a moment of utmost concretion in which a situation comes to a head and in which the (absolute) *eschaton* is sighted. *Phronesis* sights the present instance, that which is present in the single situation; such glance of the eye regards – in contrast to *sophia* – not the eternal, but the specific situation, which requires particular modes of seeing, not the looking and observing of theoretical seeing, but rather insight, circumspection and respect (*Einsicht, Umsicht, Rücksicht*). *Eschaton* is the farthest boundary of deliberation in a momentary decision, in an appropriate action – which in turn, though, is connected to the good, to ethical action, and thus also to *sophia* and *eudaimonia*. Theoretical knowledge and ethical practice, therefore, are not separated but rather related to one another in a complementary way.

Like praxis, *theorein* is oriented towards *eudaimonia* – such 'happiness', however, is not something that resides outside of action, but it is precisely the activity itself. This specific activity (*energeia*) does not thrive through its results, but through living in this activity. Activity in the sense of *theoria* is the final objective, a self-satisfying purpose, pursued for its own sake, and it does not produce anything beyond itself. *Theorein*, further – in contrast to *phronesis* – aims at the cognition of that which is eternal. As such it is among the human activities the one that is most lasting, since it is autonomous of external changes and participates in the eternal that it regards, recognises and knows.

Even as the highest form of human activity and excellence, *theorein* is tied both to ethos (as a stance, *Haltung*) and to *phronesis*. Theory and praxis, knowing and acting, even though separated, enter into a proximity and share common aspects. *Theorein* – like *eudaimonia* – is not characterised by fleeting momentariness; rather, *theorein* is an activity, the open eye, a 'condition and state, in which one stands and stays',[6] and this state has steadily to be preserved – precisely, in and as such activity. Heidegger will call such conception the authenticity (*Eigentlichkeit*) of *Dasein*, and it is precisely the held moment that becomes characteristic of authentic time, in which *eudaimonia* and the (held) moment are connected to each other.[7]

The moment as transition, the 'now' as the essence of time and point-like boundary and *theorein*, the flashlike-revealing seeing of truth and the active, 'productive' and dwelling glance of the eye, the *Augen-Blick* – within the mixed heritage of thinking the moment, these are the relations that ceaselessly return and will constantly be read anew.

Time, Eternity and Interruption

Moment, 'now' and time – once defined as transition or as point-like boundary and foundation of time – these conceptions become the reigning principle of dialectical movement and of the mediation of its non-identical aspects in Hegel's logic. But against not only the dialectical mediation of contradictions in the idealistic system but also the project of a philosophy of history that theorises a teleologically progressing and meaningful course of history, Kierkegaard's pathos of existence introduces the singular human being, who – indifferent towards that course of history – freely holds his ground. In Kierkegaard, the singular human being and history encounter each other only at singular points. History, which cannot be objectively grasped through concepts, becomes a 'situation', a present proper to the individual, subject to his decision and broken away from historical continuity.

The paradox of the moment, in which Kierkegaard's thinking gets entangled, has different aspects. The moment as cast in Christian theology refers to the – indeed – ungraspable paradox of God's incarnation as a human being by means of the temporalisation of the eternal, of the appearance of the eternal in the temporal, which calls upon the human being to relate to the eternal in time. The intersection of eternity and time occurs in the moment, as the paradox of positing the historical as eternal and the eternal as historical, and as the paradox of the possible and the necessary. As that within time where time and eternity touch each other, the moment appears not as an empty now-point, but rather as fulfilled present. But it is also precisely this moment that permits – and at this point Heidegger's distinction, elaborated against the 'vulgar' concept of successive linear time, is prefigured – a temporality that is temporalised by the future. Only such a view of temporality allows for historicity – 'history commences only in the moment'.[8] Such kairotic unity of finitude and infinity, of eternity and history is, indeed, not speculatively dissolvable; such speaking 'verily' is a truth inaccessible to reason, if not even opposed to it, a truth that reveals itself only in the bond (*religio*) and in the belief of the singular human being. Such 'decisive' moment, laden with meaning, is of a specific kind. As a moment it is transitory, but it is nevertheless filled with eternity. Such moment – abundance of time –[9] strikes from a hidden, invisible place and turns into the fulfilled present; like a disclosing flash, it is 'seen' and 'recognised' as the final truth.

The 'abundance of time' of the New Testament – which has been given an eschatological direction by St Paul as the unavailable moment, 'in the indivisibly brief, in the casting of the eye' – is, however, also an *existential moment*, a moment of decision that returns in the life of the individual and that is also claimed with regard to the ethical 'elaboration of the personality'.[10] In this moment, namely, the singular human being is confronted with the choice to choose himself. Such absolute choice, in which one chooses what has chosen him, namely to become one's own self in its 'eternal validity', the choice of oneself, is an affirmation of one's own history, an avowal of one's own identity, of being oneself.[11] The 'moment of choice' is the moment in which the human being tears away, gives his self to himself as a gift and receives himself as a self – this is the unforgettable, accomplished, happy moment in which the soul sees the divine, sees eternity, and in which the firmament descends on the self:

> When everything around has become silent, solemn as a clear, starlit night, when the soul comes to be alone in the whole world, then before one there appears, not an extraordinary human being, but the eternal power itself, then the heavens seem to open, and the I chooses itself or, more correctly, receives itself. Then the soul has seen the highest, which no mortal eye can see and which can never be forgotten; then the personality receives the accolade of knighthood that ennobles it for an eternity.[11]

That is why the blink of an eye is a term for time, of a time, though, in its 'collision pregnant with fate', in which it is touched by eternity.[12] Such moment 'full of danger',[13] as a rupture that links the glance again to everlasting bliss, permits the emergence of temporality, namely in the becoming of the self, and opens up the dialectic of subjectivity – of the aesthetic, ethical and religious 'spheres' of existence[14] – grounded in the positing, in the act of the leap namely, the leap by which the specific human being inaugurates the self, against the 'hedonistic' aesthetic immediacy of outer reality and its illusions of happiness, and receives himself. By this 'sincere and meaning-laden' act, in which the human being 'brings himself to birth',[15] the individual has not only to face the abyss of absolute solitariness and isolation but also assumes responsibility for himself and 'for all togetherness';[16] his sovereignty is testified in his 'real concrete being', which he sees as 'task, destiny, as end'.[17]

Thus, the moment is quite ambiguously again linked to the glance and to the seeing of the truth. On the one hand, the moment – which is to be separated from the allegedly 'soundless atomistic abstraction'[18] in Plato and professedly gives down-right testimony of Christendom against Greek-pagan thought – does not disap-pear in eternal truth which is always already known and to be remembered. The moment is not merely the appearance of the pre-existing eternal within time but also the starting-point for an eternal which has not been before and is created in this very moment.[19] On the other hand, the moment of choice neither bears the 'now' of transition nor joins the logos of distance, but it posits a specific simulta-neity, a particular closeness of distant times. In the presence of truth, human be-ings become 'transparent to themselves', and the 'profound glance that penetrates transparency without resistance' reveals precisely such transparence.[20] In turn, (self-) knowledge is itself dynamic, and as the choosing-of-oneself it is an unfor-gettable, unlosable action by which a human being enters into life (*existere*) and finally accepts the moment that has to be grasped and carried by responsible ac-tion. Even though Heidegger remarked contra Kierkegaard that nothing can oc-cur or be found 'in' the moment, since the moment as the authentic present only lets *encounter* that which (as ready-to-hand or present-at-hand) can be in time, he nevertheless recognises Kierkegaard as the one – next to Hölderlin and Nietzsche – who was able to think truth as the 'abode of the moment'.[21]

The moment of touch between time and eternity, the moment as the inter-ruption of time, the moment that gives birth to time and temporalises it – that is the moment of choice, the dangerous moment, which has to be carried and en-dured in responsible action, the moment in which the singular human being chooses himself in his specific existence, and the moment of truth. In terms that call upon different traditions and belong to various genealogies, such thinking presents that which the philosophy of modernity attempts to ground anew: the other of time and the other that is not redeemed in chronological time: authen-ticity.

Decision, Event and Authenticity

The meaningful, 'decisive' moment turns the fate of the human being or of his-tory at one stroke, defies any concept of continuous progress and enters into an alliance with the pathos of existence and of the moment. The moment becomes the guarantor of the dissociation of the human being from the steady course of things, his liberation from alienation and mere semblance. The decisive histori-cal moment provides redemption and liberation of the present, a liberation that shows and promises 'true' being. To follow the pointer of the moment means acting to respond to its demands and to direct one's glance not towards that which is (*das Vorkommende*), but towards that which comes (*das Zukommende*). Such sudden moment promises to bring itself out into the free and open of that which is to come, against the bad past and present, those times beyond becoming. It is this suddenness by which, according to Nietzsche, the decisive event is to occur, the 'great separation' of the free spirits, of those who belong to the future and who are only yet to come:

> The great separation comes ... suddenly, like an earth-quake: the young soul is all of a sudden shaken, torn loose, deracinated, – it does not understand what is going on ... A sudden horror and suspicion against That which it loved, a light-ning of contempt against That which meant 'duty' for it, a rebellious, arbitrary, volcanically beating desire for peregrination, strangeness, estrangement.[22]

No present that is squeezed in between the past and the future and decrees the passing away and the becoming, but the true beat of the eyelid, the moment as the glance of the eye and its unknown happiness interrupt time and redeem the unin-terrupted flow of time. Finally blasted away from the duration of time, the power-ful moment that erases that which is past – that demands forgetting[23] – and turns the human being into the rootless wanderer without historical complement, is a non-intentional, an undecided, occurrence just like the revelations of inspiration and cognition,[24] an event that grasps the human being and whose meaning, whose enigma reveals itself only after the fact. It is a steep abyss both sides of which, though, are staked out, since the immediate suddenness, which was in the liberat-ing dissociation still the irrefutable mark of the event, is, once it has become part of a scenario of expectations, deprived of its suddenness and thus of its imponder-ability. But, indissolubly linked to crisis, to the 'decision' without decision, the moment, as it is distinguished by its quality, functions as the opposition both to time and to eternity, since eternity is neither a steady 'now' (*nunc stans*) nor an endless series; rather, such 'now' strikes back on to itself.

The moment thus becomes, on the one hand, a 'time' without time, time with-out chronos, a momentary segment and the time of the Now of precisely this deci-sive occurrence. On the other hand, it becomes the 'time of fulfilled responsibility in the face of the eschatological power that resides in every moment.'[25] The re-demption from time is not negation or sublation of time; it occurs only if it is seen, recognised and grasped in the kairotic moment, in the sudden, happy open-ing of the eye. Such moment is not just happily 'there', accidental event and gift at the behest of goddess Tyche. The abysmal moment and its chance need to be grasped; the moment demands presence of mind, and it vouches for itself in the dangerous leap in which everything is at stake, the abyss of decision, whose deci-sion always also means dissociation, responsibility, authentic being.

This moment, to which the singular human being has been consigned, will become – in various and contradictory intellectual settings – the moment of authentic time, of a time that does not continue the endless proceeding of counted numbers. In the moment, inauthentic time is out of joint; as interruption and standing-out (*Ausstand*), the moment releases time as authentic time. Heidegger distinguishes the 'authentic present' from the now of a chronological series of numbers, since only a present that is held in authentic temporality can be called a moment. Such moment means the 'resolute rapture with which *Dasein* is carried away to whatever possibilities and circumstances are encountered in the situation as possible objects of concern, but a rapture which is *held* in resoluteness' and cannot be derived from the now that belongs to the inner temporality and to the vulgar consciousness of time.[26]

It is predominantly anxiety (*Angst*) that lets the moment come forth – its presence 'holds the moment *in readiness*'.[27] *Angst* leads Heidegger via the analysis of the basic structure of being and via temporality to the concept of 'situation'. Situation means 'being-in-the-position-to', a position that is being opened up (*erschlossen*) when *Dasein* is being called forth (*vorruft*) into the situation by the call of conscience. Resoluteness, resolute openness (*Entschlossenheit*) which belongs to the opening up, the disclosure (*Erschlossenheit*), is action that lies beyond the distinction between the theoretical and the practical faculty. The situation is always a 'specific situation', namely the *Da* (there) of *Dasein*, and it culminates when it turns into a situation at the margins, the limiting situation of death.[28] The limiting situation sets the moment free as much as the moment stems from the situation at the limits. *Dasein*, if it wants to avoid surrendering to the situation, has to tear itself away from 'inauthenticity'. This happens when *Dasein* ecstatically sustains and stands out (*aussteht*) and calls back the dimensions of time, and, as a *held moment* thus opens and accesses the specific situation and, with it, also the limiting situation of being towards death. The moment thus becomes an ecstatic unit that moves forth (*vorlaufen*) towards death. Each moment is unique and only at this particular instance; it mixes with the future, the open possibility, but also with the past which, as that which has been (*Gewesenheit*), is seen from the angle of its *having been possible*. In contrast to the self-forgetful temporalisation of temporality in the mere present, 'authentic time' is assembled in the moment.[29] The present, if fallen to the given, is without sojourn, 'dispersed not-staying, non-dwelling' (*zerstreutes Unverweilen*) and opposed to the moment, a moment in which the resolute surrender (*entschlossenes Sichüberliefern*) to the *Da* becomes the moment of destiny.

The moment vouches for the extreme situation, for the culmination and sharpening in which destiny is sealed. 'Limiting situation', 'danger' and 'presence of mind', 'state of emergency' – time and temporality are no longer grounded in the steady, even pace, in the tenacious proceeding of counted homologous units, in the thinking that reaches from Kierkegaard to Nietzsche, from Karl Jaspers and Martin Heidegger to Carl Schmitt and Walter Benjamin, since time springs off in the leap, as that which interrupts continuity.

Tied to this movement, the epiphanically filled or, in contrast, the 'empty' moment becomes the mark and signature of literary modernity and its various attempts to cope with time, succession and simultaneity, movement and stand-still.[30] In contrast to the vitalistic psychology of Bergson, which denies the moment any distinction in the flow of consciousness, time in literary modernity is neither seen as an endless-persistent and invariable flow nor as an empty continuum that proceeds from past to future in a steady, unchanged and unalterable way. Rather, flash-like raids into the conceptual, which drive thinking and imagination into unforeseeable directions, are experienced and projected as a simultaneous layering of different times. These constellations, like language itself, are a complex formation of distinct and distinguished moments, harsh interruptions and events, which only liberate language and show nothing else than the presencing of language, the moment in which language articulates itself as language. The moment filled by nothing but its emptiness, in which nothing happens that is external to the moment itself, and which, in contrast, shows nothing but itself, its event and its presence: such are moments in which nothing else, no referent, appears, but in and through which nothing but the event of language becomes present.

But even the fulfilled moments, which present themselves in epiphanic immediacy – just like remembrance then remembers not the duration, but nothing but the fulfilled moment[31] – are not any steady transition, no joining of one momentum to another, in which one moment relentlessly replaces the other without ever putting an end to this process. Rather, they appear as formations of single, qualitatively filled sections which, separated by bold leaps and brusque interruptions, become presentable in a quasi-'monadic' way. 'The highest time' (when it is 'high time') appears as the time of the fulfilled moment and 'all these faces of creation (*Schöpfungsgesichte*) were moved or arranged around such opening-up of its sign, around the unloading of its contents, around the utopia of the fully spelled-out now and here', as Ernst Bloch remarks.[32] In the moment of full *Da-Sein*, the moment becomes an *Augen-Blick*, precisely the opening of the eye of the 'world experienced through and through', which inscribes itself indelibly into memory.

The moment, in which the other opens its eyes and in which the other's glance touches and strikes, that is the moment of happiness, of its promises as stored in the inconclusive past;[33] and the moment, in which time lost – as in Marcel Proust – is found again or – as in Walter Benjamin – is to be rescued (*gerettet*) by mindful remembering (*Eingedenken*).

Such moment is, on the one hand, immediate fulfilment, transparent assertion, seen truth and present concretion of existence, but, on the other hand, it is insight as well. The immediacy of – epiphanic – occurrence as well as memory, remembrance, rescue and reflection are present within it. 'True touch of the moment', as Bloch remarks, 'only occurs in strong experiences and at the sharp turning-points of existence, be it one's own or be it the one of time, in as far as they are noticed by the eye that shows presence of mind.'[34]

Whereas on the one hand the moment is considered as the event of immediate being-looked-at, as sudden appearance and revelation of the authentic, as immediate presence of the true in which that which is invisible discloses itself, as a moment that excludes any repetition and in its uniqueness and singularity cannot be ritualised and carried across time or be grasped in concepts, on the other hand the moment can unfold and thus be sustained as experience only in the work of remembering and in the distance of the concept. 'The actor is always without conscience; nobody has conscience but the observer',[35] as Goethe remarks. Action is ethically blind, not determined, undecided and unrecognised. 'The moment is dark', Bloch says, it is always unknown, its meaning is elucidated always only in a posterity (*Nachträglichkeit*) – safeguarded by reflexivity – that turns the moment into experience, as opposed to the living of its immediacy.[36] And Bloch continues by saying that dark remains 'finally the now itself, in which we as those who experience find ourselves ... Thus, that which is right now lived is most immediate, and therefore least already experiencable. Only when the now has just passed or when, and as long as, it is being expected, is it not only lived (*ge-lebt*) but also experienced (*er-lebt*). As long as it is immediately being, it lies in the darkness of the moment.'[37] The lived moment is anything but transparent; it remains invisible, the blind life of the now, that which is 'really most intense', not yet seen, and thus least *Da-Sein* or even revealed being (*Offenbar-Sein*).[38] The aporia of the now that never 'is', but has already lost itself in its identification as that which is past: self-consciousness that has entangled itself irredeemably in the aporia of temporality in the attempt at bringing its own being in front of itself is – not only in Bloch – cast by means of the distinction between immediate living (*Erleben*) and experience (*Erfahrung*). The immediately shining moment and the event of the – epiphanic – now, thus, always remain incomplete and come into being only at a distance. The fulfilled moment shows itself in its heightened momentariness anything else but perfect and complete, and it does not become evident or self-transparent in the immediate event or even in the submerging of feeling. Rather, it comes to be in its experience, in its insight. Insight – that, however, does not only refer to the sighting of the moment in its *Nachträglichkeit*, but also and in particular to an insight in which existence is given away, exposed to the non-givenness of

11

the future and always remains incomplete, distant and inexplicable.

Possibilities of a particular glance, thus, open up; possibilities of a seeing that, as holding, dwelling, tarrying, possibly befits the experience of the moment.[39] Such moment of holding which liberates time from chronology does not mean the contemplation of the eternal, nor is it the result of a synthesising that belongs to the subject and thus becomes masterable; rather, the 'presence of the other', its presencing becomes present in the work of holding. Thus understood, such moment, such unfolding of the moment, would be a productive tarrying, dwelling, would be the work of unfolding the moment, a held moment, emphatic insistence and task. The following reflections aim at contributing to such productive holding, to understanding the moment as the productive 'glance of thought', thus, to 'theory'.

Notes

1 Plato, *Parmenides*, in *Sämtliche Dialoge*, IV (trans. Otto Apelt), Hamburg: Meiner, 1993 [1922²], pp.1–162 (156c 9); Georg Wilhelm Friedrich Hegel, *Phänomenologie des Geistes*, in *Werke*, III, ed. Eva Moldenhauer and Karl Markus Michel, Frankfurt/M.: Suhrkamp, 1973 [1807], pp.18–19. If not indicated otherwise, all translations are mine.

2 The constitutive character of time for social theory has often been invoked. Theories of action, such as those proposed by Pierre Bourdieu and Anthony Giddens in particular, have demanded the inclusion of the temporal dimension in theoretical reflections on society. Even such theories, however, have subordinated the multifarious and contradictory social constructions of time and their practical logics to the discursive organisation of a linear world time. I have tried to identify these academic procedures with a view to elaborating possibilities for using the plurality of social times and its ruptures in social theory. See Heidrun Friese, 'Le temps – discours, les temps – image. Pluralisation et ouverture de l'organisation temporelle de la vie quotidienne', *Politix*, 1997, 39, pp.39–64; 'Die Konstruktion von Zeit: Zum prekären Verhältnis von akademischer "Theorie" und lokaler Praxis', *Zeitschrift für Soziologie*, 1993, 22:5, pp.323–37; 'Bilder der Erinnerung', in Michael Neumann (ed.), *Erzählte Identitäten*, Munich: Fink, 2000, pp.153–77.

3 The moment contradicts any rationalistic-teleological grounding of action in the decision that precedes it and that is to be redeemed and realised by action. Such theory needs to base itself on the assumption of steady time, as the only time that permits the realisation of a predesigned intention. This presupposition, however, does not only assume that action evolves *in* time – time being an empty container of action – but also privileges the alleged continuity of action over the sudden act and therefore can neither think nor admit the moment and the interruption.

4 Plato, *Parmenides*, 155e–157b: for a more detailed account, see Werner Beierwaltes, 'Exephnis oder: Dei Paradoxie des Augenblicks', *Philosophisches Jahrbuch*, 1967, 74:2, pp.271–83, 275.

5 Plato, *Das Gastmahl*, in *Sämtliche Dialoge*, III (trans. Otto Apelt), Hamburg: Meiner, 1993, pp.1–84, 59 (Engl. edn) *The Symposium*, London: Penguin, 1951, p.93. Cf. Plato, *Platons Briefe*, in *Sämtliche Dialoge*, VI (trans. Otto Apelt), Hamburg: Meiner, 1993, pp.1–184, Siebenter Brief 341c, p. 72; see also *Phaedrus*, 210c. Such moment, however, is distinct from the concept of the sudden that proceeds through time as elaborated in *Parmenides*. See Beierwalters, 'Paradoxie', p.275. And of course, within the

Platonic-Aristotelian conceptualisation of *eidos*, the glance is always already linked to knowledge: *theorein*, derived from *thea*, is the 'outward look ... in which something shows itself, the visual appearance in which it offers itself. Plato names this aspect, in which whatever is present shows what it is, the *eidos*. To have seen this look, *eidenai*, is to know' ['dieses Aussehen gesehen zu haben, *eidenai*, ist Wissen']. The second root of theorein, *horao*, means to look at something attentively, to take in its appearance, to look at it closely. Martin Heidegger, *Vorträge und Aufsätze*, Pfullingen: Neske, 1985, p.48: for a more detailed account, see William McNeill, *The Glance of the Eye: Heidegger, Aristotle, and the Ends of Theory*, Albany: State University of New York Press, 1999.

6 Hans-Georg Gadamer, 'Lob der Theorie', in *Gesammelte Werke*, IV, Tübingen: Mohr, 1987, pp.37–51, p.48.

7 Martin Heidegger, *Platon: Sophistes*, in *Gesamtausgabe*, XIX, Frankfurt/M.: Klostermann, 1992 [1924], pp.172–73, 179 (Engl. edn *Plato's Sophist* [trans. Richard Rojcewitz and André Schuwer], Bloomington: Indiana University Press, 1997). See McNeill, *Glance*, p.49.

8 Søren Kierkegaard, *Der Begriff Angst*, in *Gesammelte Werke*, XI, ed. Emanuel Hirsch and Hayo Gerdes, Gütersloh: Gütersloher Verlagshaus, 1995⁴, p.90.

9 Søren Kierkegaard, *Philosophische Brocken*, in *Gesammelte Werke*, X, ed. Emanuel Hirsch and Hayo Gerdes, Gütersloh: Gütersloher Verlagshaus, 1991³, p.16 [B b IV 188].

10 Søren Kierkegaard, *Entweder/Oder, Zweiter Teil*, in *Gesammelte Werke*, III, ed. Emanuel Hirsch and Hayo Gerdes, Gütersloh: Gütersloher Verlagshaus, 1987², pp.167–377.

11 Kierkegaard, *Entweder/Oder*, p.188 [II 160].

12 Kierkegaard, *Der Begriff Angst*, p.89 [IV 357]. See Karl Jaspers, *Psychologie der Weltanschauungen*, Munich: Piper, 1994² [1919], pp.109–11 and 419–32.

13 Kierkegaard, *Entweder/Oder*, p.247 [II 208].

14 Adorno already pointed to the dependence of Kierkegaard's system on the existence of Hegel's systematics. Theodor W. Adorno, *Kierkegaard. Konstruktion des Ästhetischen*, in *Gesammelte Schriften*, II, ed. Rolf Tiedemann, Frankfurt/M.: Suhrkamp, 1997, pp.124–50 (ch. V).

15 Kierkegaard, *Entweder/Oder*, p.219 [II 185].

16 Kierkegaard, *Entweder/Oder*, p.268 [II 226].

17 Kierkegaard, *Entweder/Oder*, p.268 [II 226].

18 Kierkegaard, *Der Begriff Angst*, p.85 (note).

19 Kierkegaard, *Philosophische Brocken*, p.11 [B IV 183].

20 Adorno, *Kierkegaard*, p.104, ch. IV.

21 Martin Heidegger, *Sein und Zeit*, Tübingen: Max Niemeyer Verlag, 1984 [1927], §68a, p.338 (Engl. edn *Being and Time* [trans. John Macquarrie and Edward Robinson], Oxford: Blackwell, 1995¹²); and Martin Heidegger, *Beiträge zur Philosophie*, in *Gesamtausgabe*, LXV, Frankfurt/M.: Klostermann, 1989, p.204.

22 Friedrich Nietzsche, *Menschliches, Allzumenschliches*, in *Kritische Studienausgabe*, II, ed. Giorgio Colli and Mazzino Montinari, Munich/Berlin/New York: DTV/de Gruyter, 1993³, pp.9–408, *Vorrede*, 2, p.15 and *Vorrede*, 3, p.16.

23 'And it is a matter for wonder: a moment, now here and then gone, nothing before it came, again nothing after it has gone, nonetheless returns as a ghost and disturbs the peace of a later moment. A leaf flutters from the scroll of time, floats away – and suddenly floats back again and falls into the man's lap. Then the man says "I remember" and envies the animal, who at once forgets and for whom every moment really dies, sinks back into night and fog and is extinguished for ever.' Friedrich Nietzsche, *Unzeitgemässe Betrachtungen, Zweites Stück. Vom Nutzen und Nachteil der Historie für das Leben*, in *Kritische Studienausgabe*, I, ed. Giorgio Colli and Mazzino Montinari, Munich/Berlin/New York: DTV/

de Gruyter, 1988² [1874], pp.243–334, *Abschnitt* 1, pp.248–49 ('On the uses and disadvantages of history for life', in *Untimely Meditations*, Cambridge: Cambridge University Press, 1997, pp.59–123, p.61). 'Historical meaning', this sleeplessness, turns into the antipode of life; action needs forgetting: 'He who cannot sink down on the threshold of the moment and forget all the past, who cannot stand balanced like a goddess of victory without growing dizzy and afraid, will never know what happiness is – worse, he will never do anything to make others happy' (p.250/Engl. edn p.62). Nietzsche emphasises the social importance of remembering, which alone permits promising and assuming of responsibility, guilt and conscience, calculable stability of behaviour as the basis for sociality, a memory that has to be burnt into 'the intellect of the now', into 'bodily forgetfulness' through torture and through the use of pain as a mnemotechnique. Friedrich Nietzsche, *Zur Genealogie der Moral*, in *Kritische Studienausgabe*, V, ed. Giorgio Colli and Mazzino Montinari, Munich/Berlin/New York: DTV/de Gruyter, 1988², pp.245–412, *Zweite Abhandlung*, esp. pp.1–4, 291–98.

24 'The concept of revelation, in the sense that something suddenly, with unspeakable certainty and subtlety, becomes *visible*, audible, something that shakes and overturns one to the depths, simply describes the fact. One hears, one does not seek; one takes, one does not ask who gives; a thought flashes up like lightning, with necessity, unfalteringly formed – I have never had any choice.' Friedrich Nietzsche, (Engl. edn *Ecce Homo. Wie man wird, was man ist*, in *Kritische Studienausgabe*, VI, ed. Giorgio Colli and Mazzino Montinari, Munich/Berlin/New York: DTV/de Gruyter, 1988² pp.255–374, 339 (Engl. edn *Ecce Homo*, trans. R.J. Hollingdale, London: Penguin, 1992, pp.102–03).

25 Massimo Cacciari, *Zeit ohne Kronos. Essays* (trans. Reinhard Kacianka), Klagenfurt: Ritter, 1986, p.11.

26 Heidegger, *Sein und Zeit*, §68a, p.338.

27 Heidegger, *Sein und Zeit*, §68b, p.344.

28 Cf. Jaspers, *Psychologie*, pp.229–80. Otto Pöggeler, 'Destruktion und Augenblick', in Thomas Buchheim (ed.), *Destruktion und Übersetzung: Zu den Aufgaben von Philosophiegeschichte nach Martin Heidegger*, Weinheim: VCH, Acta humanoria, 1989, p.19.

29 Heidegger, *Sein und Zeit*, §68c, p.347.

30 See Karl Heinz Bohrer, *Plötzlichkeit: Zum Augenblick des ästhetischen Scheins*, Frankfurt/M.: Suhrkamp, 1981 (Engl. edn *Suddenness: On the Moment of Aesthetic Appearance*, New York: Columbia University Press, 1994).

31 Following Roupnel (*Siloë*, 1927), see Gaston Bachelard, *L'intuition de l'instant*, Paris: Gonthier, 1966 [1932].

32 Ernst Bloch, *Das Prinzip Hoffnung*, in *Werkausgabe*, V:2, Frankfurt/M.: Suhrkamp, 1993⁴ [1938–47], p.1154. See Remo Bodei, *Multiversum: tempo e storia in Ernst Bloch*, Naples: Bibliopolis, 1982.

33 And this was precisely Horkheimer's objection to Bergson's *durée* – 'Bergson's metaphysics suppresses death' – and Benjamin's notion of the inconclusiveness, the lack of closure (*Unabgeschlossenheit*) of history. Max Horkheimer, 'Bergsons Metaphysik der Zeit', *Zeitschrift für Sozialforschung*, 3, 1934, p.332. See Walter Benjamin, *Das Passagen-Werk*, in *Gesammelte Schriften*, V:1, 2, ed. Rolf Tiedemann and Hermann Schweppenhäuser, Frankfurt/M.: Suhrkamp, 1991 [1927–], pp.588–59, n.8, 1.

34 Bloch, *Das Prinzip Hoffnung*, 5:1, p.342 (ch. 20).

35 'Der Handelnde ist immer gewissenlos; es hat niemand Gewissen als der Betrachtende', Johann Wolfgang von Goethe, *Maximen und Reflexionen*, in *Werke*, Hamburger Ausgabe, XII, Munich: DTV, 1998, p.399.

36 See Jaspers, *Psychologie*, pp.108–17.

37 Bloch, *Das Prinzip Hoffnung*, 5:1, p.334 (ch. 20).

38 Bloch, *Das Prinzip Hoffnung*, 5:1, p.341 (ch. 20).
39 See Michael Theunissen, *Negative Theologie der Zeit*, Frankfurt/M.: Suhrkamp, 1991, pp.291–95.

CHAPTER 1

Is it Time?

GEOFFREY BENNINGTON

'The time has come', the Walrus said,
'To talk of many things:
Of shoes – and ships – and sealing-wax –
Of cabbages – and kings –
And why the sea is boiling hot –
And whether pigs have wings.'

Lewis Carroll[1]

No *différance* without alterity, no alterity without singularity, no singularity without here and now.

Jacques Derrida[2]

Blessed *is* he that readeth, and they that hear the words of this prophecy, and keep those things which are written therein: for the time *is* at hand.

Revelation[3]

Is it time?[4] It's *about* time. Just a moment. Any moment now. But the moment or the time in the sense I shall be discussing it has a curious and difficult relation to time in general. In English, at least, it is difficult to separate questions about time in general in all its complexity (cosmological time, psychological time, the phenomenology of internal time consciousness and so on) from questions about the time, the time that might have come, the right time, the moment as appropriate moment, not the moment as just *now* or as *present*, but as the *right* moment, *le bon moment*, the moment as *kairos* rather than as *nun*. This thought of the moment as the *right* moment, the moment whose moment has come, for which the time is ripe, the time whose time it is, the time that must accordingly be grasped or seized[5] before it has gone, the time as opportunity not to be missed, is, or so it would appear, *itself* a thought whose time has come. The time has come to talk of many things, but among those many things the thing whose time has *most* come is, apparently (blame the millennium) the thought *of* the time's having come. And the proof of that is given among many other signs (including a flurry of recent French philosophical interest in St Paul, messianism and eschatology)[6] by the fact of the conference for which this paper was written,[7] which could not but invite the reflection that it had been organised at the right moment, that this indeed was the moment to talk about the moment. And it seems that any attempt to think about the moment as right or appropriate moment has to accept this reflexive paradox from the start. Whatever I talk about, I implicitly claim that it is the right moment to talk about it – *any* speech act, however mistakenly or apologetically, lays claim, usually tacitly, to its own timeliness: and a speech act concerning the question of the moment, the time, or timeliness in general leads to a potentially paradoxical reflection of that structure. Any talk about the moment suggests that it really is the right moment to talk about the right moment, that its time has come – and explicit claims to untimeliness or intempestivity are, one might suspect, no more than a further twist of this structure. For there is nothing for which the time has come so much as for the very thing no one is now talking about, nothing hopes to be more timely than meditations which proudly claim to be untimely. The proud or apologetic claim to untimeliness is just a claim that the timeliness of what is being presented as untimely is not obvious or widely perceived, and it thereby adds a supplement of timeliness to the untimely. Fashion, which will return as a question in a moment, is a helpful way of thinking about this link of the timely and the untimely: timing in fashion is all about the timeliness of the untimely, choosing the right moment to go against the present moment, and apparently modest claims to be unfashionable, to be refusing fashion, quite common in academic discourse, always hope to set the trend again.

But if the untimely can in this way always claim to be the most timely, the gesture that reverses appearances and renders the fashionable dated and instantaneously makes the unfashionable into the *dernier cri*, then the apparent reflexivity of the relation of the right moment to itself is disturbed in some way. If the most apparently untimely *always might* be the most timely, then the timeliness of the timely is no longer so secure. The untimely can turn out to be timely only to the extent that there is at least the suspicion of a non-coincidence between the time that has come and the time *in* which it comes, between the moment as container and the moment as arrival. If I need to say or to announce that the time has come to talk of shoes or ships or sealing-wax, then I imply that in some way that necessity, the having-come of the time that has come, is not so obvious, not so present. If I need to tell you that the time has come, then this implies that you hadn't noticed, or might not have noticed, if I hadn't told you. The arrival of the right moment is in this sense always at least potentially not synchronised with the time in which that moment arrives: it is time *only when* in some sense it is untimely. Nietzsche's *Untimely Meditations* of course present themselves as arriving at just the wrong – and therefore right – time,[8] and the same can be said for Derrida's book on Marx – *just because* everything suggests that the time is wrong, then maybe in truth it is right. The time is *always* ripe just for the untimely. The chance of the right moment's really being the right moment is given only by its discordance with the time in which it arrives. The moment, in its arrival, its event, has to arrive in a moment of time; the *kairos* has to present itself as a *nun*, so that it can, 'by extension', according to the dictionary, signify also just 'the present time' or 'the times'. But the possibility of the moment's being the right moment depends on an at least possible (and in fact necessary) dissonance between the moment as event and the moment as the time of its arrival: and this dissonance then opens the possibility that *any* moment could be the moment, that the question 'Is it time?' can be asked of *any* time. We might speculate that the experience of time is always the experience of a more or less muted expectation that any moment be *the* moment, and that the various fantasies we may have as to just what any moment might be the moment for are secondary to this fundamental structure of the relation between time and event. If I am right that this is just an analytical consequence of the concept of *kairos*, then we could link it rapidly to the famous Benjaminian notion of the *Jetztzeit*, the thought, itself as timely as it is untimely, with which, according to Benjamin, historical materialism 'cuts through' historicism (*kairos*, from the verb *keirein*, to cut or shear). The chance of a moment's being the right moment, given by its interruptive untimeliness with respect to the present, generates in Benjamin the thought of messianic time (which is famously also a cessation or interruption of time, a revolutionary moment), whereby, in the Jewish tradition on which Benjamin is drawing, 'every second of time [is] the strait gate through which the Messiah might enter'.[9]

I want to suggest that it is time today, the right moment, to think about two broad ways of dealing with this situation. The first, which is massively dominant in the metaphysical tradition (and especially perhaps the Christian tradition), attempts to map the apparent untimeliness of the time in its arrival on to a truer timeliness, giving rise (or birth) to a metaphorics of ripeness and fruition, pregnancy and childbirth. The second, traces of which can be found no doubt throughout that same tradition, but which might be seen more obviously in, say, Stendhal, Kierkegaard or Benjamin, accentuates the irruptive or interruptive temporality of the moment in its intempestive arrival.[10] I want to suggest that the function of the first type of view is, to state it rather bluntly, to resolve contradiction. If there is a time for every purpose under heaven, as Ecclesiastes affirms, then the various contradictory activities the passage goes on to list are no longer contradictory: war and peace, for example, both have their right moment or right moments, and this rightness is the sign of the overall prospect of the resolution of contradictory predicates in the mind of God: no one *in the world* (i.e. 'under the heaven' [3:1]; 'under the sun' [3:16]) can 'find out the work that God maketh from the beginning to the end' (3:11). The temporal world unfolds puzzling contradictions, but the puzzle is not insurmountable if it is thought that each element is right for its time, its *appointed* time, even if the detail of that appointment remains a mystery to us. Of course not all biblical texts encourage the type of languid contemplative acceptance of this structure that this passage from Ecclesiastes might seem to promote: St Paul, famously the thinker of the *kairos* in a more urgent sense,[11] thinks of it more as a moment of awakening from the type of slumber Ecclesiastes might be taken to encourage: 'And that, knowing the time [*ton kairon*], that now it *is* high time [*ede hora*] to awake out of sleep: for now [*nun*] is our salvation nearer than when we believed' (Rom. 13:11); but this awakening still, of course, brings a promise of reconciliation and redemption (I Cor. 4:5: 'Therefore judge nothing before the time [*pro kairou*], until the Lord come, who both will bring to light the hidden things of darkness, and will make manifest the counsels of the hearts: and then shall every man have praise of God', or II Cor. 6:2: 'Behold, now is the acceptable time [*nun kairos euprosdektos*]; now is the day of salvation').[12] And this urgency brings out another feature of the thought of the time as the right time – it is, typically, referred to the question of *judgement*, the moment of separation of the good from the bad, the moment at which all becomes clear, at which the temporal resolves into the eternal. On this view, the right moment not only cuts into the flow of time, but it is the *end* of time – time as such will be revealed on the Day of Judgement to have been only for the sake of that Day of Judgement: the whole of time is the ripening of the *kairos*, the *point* of time, which will put time to an end in a definitive moment of judgement and redemption.[13] My further unresolved question will be that of whether it is possible to think the interruptive force of messianic time without being committed to the thought of a rebirth, or the thought of the end of time, of time having an end in *parousia* or epiphany, the thought of *telos* or *eskhaton*; and, relatedly, whether it is possible to think of a judgement that is not more or less surreptitiously mortgaged to a thought of the Last Judgement.

In order to keep things relatively simple, I shall concentrate for this first type of thinking about the moment on Hegel,[14] and for the second on Derrida. It will rapidly become clear that I do not think that the relationship between these two types of thought is simply oppositional or contradictory, nor indeed that there is, under heaven, a time for one and a time for the other. With luck, *si ça tombe*, we may hope to understand a little more clearly how and why deconstruction, as deconstruction of *presence*, is also, and thereby, affirmative of the here and now.[15]

In a very famous passage in the Introduction to the *Philosophy of History*, Hegel is discussing 'world-historical individuals'.[16] History is the sphere in which collisions between existing ethical systems (States as ethical totalities) appear as contingencies which disrupt and unsettle such systems. Only such disruptive contingencies (most typically in the form of war, that agent of ethical health for the State) prevent States from achieving the somnolent repetitive permanence that would otherwise be their goal (and simultaneously their collapse back first into the merely worldly concerns of civil society, and ultimately into nature), and world-historical individuals are the agents of such contingencies – contingencies which are, of course, according to the general rule of Hegelian thought, to be grasped as necessities at a different level of description.[17] For that to be possible, the contingencies in question cannot be simply random or irrational, and it is to a version of the thought of the *kairos* that Hegel will appeal, as to a 'general principle' to operate the required conversion of contingency into necessity.[18] It is a crucial feature of Hegel's account that such individuals (Caesar being his prime example) are not *conscious* of pursuing any goal other than an essentially particular, passionate and even selfish one – Caesar acts against the established legality of the Roman constitution and turns it in his own interests into an autocracy, but that shift was, says Hegel,

> an independently necessary feature in the history of Rome and of the world. It was not, then, his private gain merely, but an unconscious impulse that occasioned the accomplishment of that for which the time was ripe. Such are all great historical men – whose own particular aims involve those large issues which are the will of the World-Spirit.[19]

The temporality of this 'ripeness' is complex. According to the paradoxical structure I sketched out at the beginning, the timeliness of the world-historical individual's action depends, at least in part, on the *untimeliness* of the action, as measured by the time in which it takes place. Hegel says:

> Such individuals had no consciousness of the general Idea they were unfolding, while prosecuting those aims of theirs; on the contrary, they were practical, political men. But at the same time they were thinking men, who had an insight into the requirements of the time – *what was ripe for development*. This was the very Truth for their age, for their world; the species next in order, so to speak, and which was already formed in the womb of time. It was theirs to know this nascent principle; the necessary, directly sequent step in progress, which the world was to take; to make this their aim, and to expend their energy in promoting it.[20]

That for which the time is ripe, on this description, is precisely not what is coincident with the time in which the actions take place, but what disrupts and disturbs that time. The time *in* which the world-historical individual acts is the time of the tendential permanence of the State: the act itself cuts into and disrupts that time, and if it is none the less *time for* this other, disruptive, time, it is time for it in that the *proper* time for that time (the time in which the action in question will in some way coincide with itself) is still to come. The time is ripe, but its ripeness is not a self-coincidence – ripeness here is rather an anticipation of such a coincidence. This anticipatory gesture is itself complex: the event anticipates a time in which it will turn out to be right or appropriate, it will drag the time in which it occurs along to the stage which it already represents, ahead of its time; but it also anticipates a time in which it will be possible to see that it *always was* going to turn out to be appropriate, that the next stage already was 'formed in the womb of time', as its very appearance will have proved. The metaphorics of ripeness or of pregnancy mean that the appearance of the fruit or the child is an event whose absoluteness is immediately compromised by its necessary earlier preparation or anticipation.[21] This way of thinking the moment gathers up past, present and future in a way that is entirely consistent through the tradition: in the same chapter of Ecclesiastes quoted above, for example, the 'time' or 'season' for every purpose *under* heaven is guaranteed by a divine time in which 'That which hath been is now; and that which is to be hath already been' (3:15).[22] The adventurous and passionate unconsciousness of the world-historical individual achieves its rational character from the point of view of Spirit having come to knowledge of itself as a result of the sequence of ripe times in which the world-historical individuals played their part. And just this is the operation of reason as essentially cunning, that is, dialectical.

Which seems to confirm that the very thought of a right moment or a *kairos* entails some thought of a temporal dislocation or non-coincidence. The *kairos* is always *another time* appearing in *the present* time: its *own* time is never that of the present, and to that extent is arguably not 'in' time at all. The rightness of that other time is asserted through an anticipation of the knowledge of its past: the right moment *will have been* right because, its structure implies, we will be able to see that it was always going to (have) be(en) right. Figures of ripeness, maturation and especially childbirth carry this complex recognition and denial of the otherness of the moment: the appearance of the new is thereby retrospectively presented as, if not exactly always *planned*, then at least explicable by the retrospective assumption of a causal sequence with its own laws.

It is, then, perhaps not surprising to find Derrida himself making a curious and displaced use of this figure of childbirth in one of his earliest essays. In 'Structure,

Sign and Play in the Discourse of the Human Sciences',[23] in the context of the famous explanation of why the 'two interpretations of interpretation' cannot be the object of a *choice*, we find this:

> And because this is a type of question [i.e. a question as to the common ground of those two irreducibly different interpretations of interpretation] – let's call it historical still – whose *conception, formation, gestation, labour*, we can today only glimpse. And I say these words with my eyes turned, certainly, towards the operations of childbirth; but turned too towards those who, in a society from which I do not exclude myself, are still turning them away before the still unnameable which is looming (*qui s'annonce*)[24] and which can only do so, as is necessary every time a birth is at work, in the species of the non-species, the formless, mute, infant and terrifying form of monstrosity.[25]

This rather less reassuring view of the figure of childbirth as giving rise to the terrifying and the monstrous is, or so it seems to me, announcing already in Derrida the theme of the 'out-of-jointness' of time which is arguably already the central point of his early analyses of phenomenology, but which becomes explicitly formulated – and is explicitly given the ethico-political resonance the notion of the *right* moment cannot fail to provoke[26] – only much more recently, most notably at the beginning of *Specters of Marx*, where a certain 'non-contemporaneity of the living present with itself' is presented as a condition of possibility of responsibility and justice.[27] And, as is quite often the case in Derrida, such a non-contemporaneity is explicitly presented as non-dialectical:

> To hold together what does not hang together, and the disparity itself, the same disparity, can only be thought – we shall ceaselessly return to this as to the spectrality of the spectre – in a dislocated present time [or tense], at the jointing of a radically dis-joined time, with no assured conjunction. Not a time whose jointings would be denied, broken, ill-treated, dysfunctioning, ill-fitting, according to a *dys* of negative opposition and dialectical disjunction, but a time without *assured* jointing nor *determinable* conjunction. What is said here of time also goes, consequently or concurrently [*du même coup*] for history, even if this latter can consist in repairing, in conjunctural effects, temporal disjuncture: 'The time is out of joint', the time is *disarticulated*, put out, unhinged, dislocated, the time is unbalanced, hunted down and unbalanced [*traqué et détraqué*], both broken and crazy.[28]

Our exegetical problem will be to understand this out-of-jointness in its non-oppositional difference from the dialectical understanding of the moment we have briefly seen in Hegel; and the challenge it will lay down to us will be that of seeing how this non-dialectical disjointing is in fact already at work *in* Hegel's understanding of the moment, as an 'earlier' and more powerful quasi-temporal dispensation.

Derrida himself first discusses this motif of the time being 'out of joint' in the context of discussing the difficulty of translating that idiom into French: the translations are *themselves*, he says, out of joint, depending on their understanding of the word 'time' here as meaning temporality in general, the times in which we live, or the world itself in its actuality. (This difficulty of translation is of course rendered even more serious when Derrida's work is translated back into English: Derrida says that the translations, in their irreducible inadequacy, can only aggravate or confirm the inaccessibility of the other language. When all of this is translated back into that other language, the effect is less to render familiar the Shakespearean idiom and more or less laughable the French versions rendered back into 'the language of Shakespeare', where their unavoidable inadequacy shows up all the more starkly just because of the still-ready availability of the idiom Shakespeare actually used, so that the need for the English translator to avoid it in rendering the different French versions make them look curiously blind or perverse – less that, than to open up the out-of-jointness of English itself with respect to itself, so that these retranslated translations stand for and provoke different possibilities of reading the English (even if we are reading in English as competent anglophones): the expression 'out of joint' *itself* is thereby out of joint with itself. A little later I'll be suggesting that the constitutive (and still temporal) out-of-jointness of reading is a promising way of understanding the structure of the moment we are trying to unpack, and a good way of attacking its relation to Hegel.)

We might in any case wonder if it is by chance that Derrida goes on from his remarks about the dislocation of time from itself to an incisive reflection on the timeliness or untimeliness of his reading of Marx. (And indeed the blurb on the back cover, which I would imagine was written by Derrida himself, brings this out quite explicitly: 'Distinguishing between justice and right, crossing the themes of inheritance and messianism, *Specters of Marx* is above all the *gage* – or the untimely wager – of a position taken up: here, now, tomorrow'). That (un)timeliness depends on an attempted cutting intervention into what is seen as a 'fashion or coquetry'[29] that 'one feels coming', namely the fashion for now treating Marx as a mere object for scholarship, a philosopher among others, in other words for treating Marx as fundamentally non-political, as having no bearing on the urgency that the dislocation of the present generates in the thought of the here and now. That dislocation should also bear on the way in which we have seen past, present and future being knotted together in the Christian-Hegelian version of the *kairos*. Derrida is commenting on a 1959 text of Blanchot on the end of philosophy:

We do not know if expectation prepares the coming of the to-come or if it recalls the repetition of the same, of the thing itself as ghost ... This non-knowledge is not a lacuna. No progress of knowledge could saturate an opening which must have nothing to do with knowledge. And therefore not with ignorance either. This opening must preserve this heterogeneity as the only chance of a future affirmed or rather re-affirmed. It is the future itself, it comes from the future. The future is its memory. In the experience of the end, in its insistent, instant coming, always imminently eschatological, at the extremity of the extreme to-day would be announced in this way the future of what is coming. More than ever, for the to-come can only be announced as such and in its purity from a *past end*: beyond, *if it is possible*, the last extremity. If it is possible, *if there is any*, future, but how to suspend such a question or deprive oneself of such a reserve without *concluding in advance*, without reducing in advance both the future and its chance? Without totalizing in advance? We must here discern between eschatology and teleology, even if the stake of such a difference constantly risks being erased in the most fragile or the slightest inconsistency – and will in some sense always and necessarily be deprived of an assurance against this risk. Is there not a messianic extremity, an *eskhaton* whose ultimate event (immediate rupture, unheard-of interruption, untimeliness of infinite surprise, heterogeneity without accomplishment) can exceed, *at each moment*, the final term of a *physis*, and the labor, production and *telos* of any history?[30]

This affirmation of untimeliness, out-of-jointness of time, involves, then, a certain eschatological affirmation against its teleological recovery. This is a refined distinction in view of a more general 'post-structural' (and indeed earlier Derridean) tendency to identify the eschatological and the teleological, or at least to treat them as in some way equivalent metaphysical closures. This eschatological affirmation is what Derrida also calls a 'messianic without messianism', or a *formal* messianicity which cannot project any content or specificity whatsoever into the advent or coming it none the less affirms. So where Benjamin, in the 'Theses on the Philosophy of History', invokes the Judaic thought whereby 'every second of time was the strait gate through which the Messiah might enter',[31] Derrida's attempt to radicalise this[32] involves the affirmative maintenance of the strictly messianic *moment*, not only short of any predictive *when* (for that is already the case with the Judaic construal to which Benjamin refers), but of any content and axiological determination whatsoever. The event of the coming of the other is 'properly' (i.e. formally) eschatological to the extent that its *what* is radically indeterminable, and so cannot confidently be called the Messiah, for example.[33] Derrida points out that this would already make his version of the messianic unacceptable to any messianism whatsoever, depriving it of what it would have to think of as the essential point, i.e. the Messiah himself whose coming is promised. The Messiah is the first casualty of this construal of the messianic, which is why the word 'messianic' can seem a risky or unduly provocative term for Derrida to use in these contexts, a perhaps extreme form of the familiar deconstructive strategy of paleonymy, the use of old names. Derrida's point, then, is to radicalise the messianic motif beyond the tendency of messianism to map it on to a teleological schema – and just this is what we were seeing in the biblical and Hegelian passages we were considering earlier. The moment the moment is figured as occurring *on time*, in due time, at the right time, in the ripeness or fullness of time, then we can conclude that the radically disruptive thought of the event as absolutely unpredictable arrival of the other, for which no amount of preparation could prepare, in other words the thought of the future as such, has been written back down into a teleological structure, which is most clearly evidenced by the figures of ripeness or pregnancy that we have picked out. The here and now which allows for the thought of singularity as alterity in its arrival requires a thought of the moment that is not only not simply present to itself in the presence of the present, but which is not recoverable as the *telos* of any natural or institutional process whatsoever, an *eskhaton* without salvation or redemption.

I would like to conclude by trying to relate this structure, from which Derrida's thinking about what is traditionally called 'ethics' and/or 'politics' explicitly flows, to the question of reading. The point of doing this is not to fold back this complex thinking about time on to a 'merely literary' problematic, but to try to show how it must be presupposed by all attempts to refute it. I want to say that Derrida's affirmation of the messianic without messianism is also an affirmation of reading, and that the metaphysics of presence, dominated by the interpretation of time as deriving from the presence of the present moment, necessarily entails the foreclosure of the moment of reading. I would like to suggest, for example, that the experience of reading is a salient and familiar experience of the non-coincidence of the present with itself. The simplest way to argue this is to point out that reading is necessarily in a relation of *delay* with respect to the text read: however minimal that delay, reading always *comes after* the writing it reads. But that irreducible belatedness goes along with a sort of internal dislocation whereby reading is always remembering and anticipating reading in order to function. My reading can never coincide with the present moments of its activity (can never simply read one word after another, one at a time, for example), but must recall and anticipate other reading moments at every moment. As Derrida points out at the beginning of *Glas*, we cannot form the project of reading Hegel *in order*, from the first word of the first text onwards, because at the very least we should have to 'anticipate, if only the end of the first sentence of the first text'. In that context, Derrida goes on as follows: 'Genealogy cannot begin with the father. Anticipation or precipitation (risk of precipice and fall) is an irreducible structure of reading. And teleology does only or always have the appeasing character people wish to give it.'[34]

If this is so, then it is because teleology cannot ever quite reduce the moment we are calling, on the basis of *Spectres de Marx*, the messianic, and to that extent can never quite be teleological, so that the programmed ends do not quite come out at the appointed time, so that it is never quite time. It is no accident that Hegel should appear as a test case for this type of argument (though it is certainly possible to run it through the teleology of Kant, too, not to speak of Aristotle), both in the earlier account I gave of the moment, and in Derrida's remarks here about reading, because Hegel represents the most complete and thorough attempt to reduce reading altogether. One description of Hegel's writing is just that it is an attempt to be its own reading, or to read itself so exhaustively that there is no opening for reading left, and therefore no chance of that text's having a future other than one of confirmatory coincidence, on the part of competent readers, with the reading the text is already dictating to them. Hegel's text is calculated to account for and include within itself all the readings to which it might be open, including bad ones, as Derrida also discusses in *Glas*.[35] Which is why reading Hegel turns one into a Hegelian. But in order to be read at all, Hegel's text, like any other, must in principle be *open* to reading, and thereby open to a reading it cannot entirely predict and dictate in advance. It would not be hard to show that any reading worthy of its name *must depart from* the text it reads, meaning both that it must begin with it, but also that it cannot just stay with it – if Hegel is to be read rather than simply repeated, then the *chance* of a radically unpredictable reading must be left open even in this text which is entirely written in order to *prévenir* (forestall) any such reading.[36] And once we have shown that reading must in principle be subject to a pre-teleological principle in this way, to a moment of 'pure reading' prior to, and making possible, any subsequent issue about correct or incorrect reading, respectful or disrespectful reading, then we have *already* dislocated reading's moments beyond the grasp of a teleology read merely respectfully (i.e. not read at all). To this extent, *any reading of Hegel* is already, as I suggested at the start, in a relation of structural disagreement with the text read, and the most Hegelian reading must somewhere and somehow be marked by this non-Hegelian moment.

And just this is the point of Derrida's remarks in *Spectres de Marx* about inheritance. Inheritance as a relation of indebtedness to the traditionality which makes it possible to speak and think at all must involve, if it is to be worth its name, a moment of possible infidelity with respect to what it inherits. An inheritance that was always completely faithful would not inherit from the earlier moment, but would merely be a causal outcome of it. According to a familiar form of Derridean argument, the *necessary possibility* of infidelity to the tradition is a positive condition of the chance of being faithful to it – implying that fidelity is always marked by, or tormented by, infidelity. This is a general structure of Derrida's thought, and part of what it has become common to call the 'quasi-transcendental': what might look like a negative contingency which might affect or compromise the ideal purity of an event is integrated into the description of that event as a condition of possibility which is simultaneously the condition of the a priori impossibility of the event's ever achieving that ideal purity. And this structure of inheritance is insistent in *Specters of Marx:*

> Let us consider first the radical and necessary *heterogeneity* of an inheritance, the difference without opposition that must mark it, a 'disparateness' and a quasi-juxtaposition without dialectic (the very plural of what further on we shall call Marx's spirits). An inheritance is never gathered, it is never one with itself. Its presumed unity, if there is one, can only consist in the *injunction* to *reaffirm by choosing. You must* [*il faut*] means you must filter, select, criticize, you must sort out among several of the possibilities which inhabit the same injunction. And inhabit it in contradictory fashion around a secret. If the legibility of a legacy were given, natural, transparent, univocal, if it did not simultaneously call for and defy interpretation, one would never have to inherit from it. One would be affected by it as by a cause – natural or genetic. One always inherits a secret, which says 'Read me, will you ever be up to it?'[37]

And, a little later:

> Inheritance is never a given, it is always a task. It remains before us, as incontestably as the fact that, before even wanting it or refusing it, we are inheritors, and inheritors in mourning, like all inheritors. In particular for what is called Marxism. *To be ...* means *... to inherit.* All questions about being or what one is to be (or not to be) are questions of inheritance. There is no backward-looking fervor involved in recalling this fact, no traditionalist flavor. Reaction, reactionary or reactive are only interpretations of the structure of inheritance. We *are* inheritors, which does not mean that we *have* or that we *receive* this or that, that a given inheritance enriches us one day with this or that, but that the *being* we are *is* first of all inheritance, like it or not, know it or not.[38]

This scene suggests a rather different gathering of past, present and future to the one we noted in the biblical construal of the *kairos*. The structure of inheritance commits us to a view of the here and now as a moment when the past always still remains before us as an endless task. The chance of the moment is that it is

28

never a moment of Last Judgement (in which the eschatology is gathered up by a teleology), but a moment of judgement in the radical absence of last judgement, an eschatology without end. This would mean that we could never really know – even after the event – whether or not the time was ripe for this or that, just because any judgement to that effect would itself be subject to the same structure of uncertainty. The absence of a Last Judgement liberates judgement from its traditional status as a provisional anticipation of a Last Judgement to come. The out-of-jointness of the time dislocates it across its responsibility towards the past in the form of the inheritance it cannot simply accept and the concomitant futural task which, however, commits it here and now.

Is it time? It is now. It's time.

Notes

1 Lewis Carroll, *Through the Looking-Glass: and what Alice found there*, London: The Folio Society, 1962, p.47.

2 Jacques Derrida, *Spectres de Marx*, Paris: Galilée, 1994, p.60 (Engl. edn *Specters of Marx: The State of the Debt, the Work of Mourning, and the New International*, trans. Peggy Kamuf, New York: Routledge, 1994, p.31). All references are to the original text followed by the translation reference.

3 Rev. 1:3.

4 A slightly different version of this chapter has been published in my *Interrupting Derrida*, London: Routledge, 2000.

5 According to Diogenes Laertes, the notion of seizing or grasping time goes back to Pittacos of Mitylene, one of the so-called seven sages.

6 Giorgio Agamben, Alain Badiou, Jean-François Lyotard and Jacques Derrida all have recent work on St Paul; see Agamben's seminar series at the Collège international de philosophie, Paris, 1998–99; Alain Badiou, *Saint Paul, la fondation de l'universalisme*, Paris: PUF, 1997; Jean-François Lyotard, *D'un trait d'union*, Sainte-Foy/Quebec: Les presses du griffon d'argile and Presses Universitaires de Grenoble, 1993, trans. Pascale-Anne Brault and Michael Naas with other texts by Jean-François Lyotard and Eberhard Gruber as *The Hyphen: Between Judaism and Christianity*, Amherst, NY: Humanity Books, 1999; this nexus, and the very different versions of Paul that emerge from it, would merit a separate discussion.

7 'The Moment', University of Warwick, November 1998.

8 'This meditation too is untimely, because I am here attempting to look afresh at something of which our time is rightly proud – its cultivation of history – as being injurious to it, a defect and a deficiency in it; because I believe that we are all suffering from a consuming fever of history and ought at least to recognise that we are suffering from it ... it is only to the extent that I am a pupil of earlier times, especially the Hellenic, that though a child of the present time I was able to acquire such untimely experiences. That much, however, I must concede to myself on account of my profession as a classicist: for I do not know what meaning classical studies could have for our time if they were not untimely – that is to say, acting counter to our time and thereby acting on our time and, let us hope, for the benefit of time to come' (Friedrich Nietzsche, in David Breazeale [ed.], *Untimely Meditations*, trans. R.J. Hollingdale, Cambridge: Cambridge University Press, 1997, p.60).

9 Walter Benjamin, 'Theses on the Philosophy of History' (trans. Harry Zohn), in

Illuminations, London: Fontana, 1992, p.255, XVIII B. Derrida quotes from this in *Spectres*, pp.95–96, n.1 [180–81 n.2].

10 A properly careful typology of thoughts of 'the moment' would of course need to be much more differentiated than I can attempt to be here: for example, it would have to distinguish this interruptive moment from the sort of totalising or epiphanic moments found in, for example, Virginia Woolf and James Joyce. See Bohrer in this volume.

11 And also, of course, inheriting something of his eschatology from a Judaic tradition. See, for example, William David Davies, *Paul and Rabbinic Judaism*, London: SPCK, 1955².

12 In context: 'For he saith, I have heard thee in a time accepted [*kairos dektos*], and in the day of salvation have I succoured thee: behold, now *is* the accepted time; behold, now *is* the day of salvation.' Naturally enough, if the thematics of the *kairos* are inseparable from the language of fruition, pregnancy and childbirth, it is not surprising that the birth of Christ should be the best example of the *kairos*: 'when the fullness of the time [*pleroma kronos*] was come, God sent forth his Son, made of a woman, made under the law' (Gal. 4:4). Cf. too Eph. 1:9–10: 'Having made known unto us the mystery of his will, according to his good pleasure which he hath purposed in himself:/ That in the dispensation of the fullness of times [*ekonomian tou pleromatos ton kairon*] he might gather together in one all things in Christ, both which are in heaven and which are on earth.' Also I Tim. 2:6 and 6:14–15, where the expression *kairois idiois*, the proper time or its own time, can, according to Herman Ridderbos, be taken as synonymous with the expressions for 'fullness of time [*pleroma tou chronou*]' or just 'the moment [*ton kairon*]'. See Herman Ridderbos, *Paul: An Outline of his Theology* (trans. J.R. de Witt), Grand Rapids, MI: Wm. B. Eerdmans Publishing Company, 1975 [1966], p.47, n. 12. It is striking that there is always a moment of repetition in this thought of the moment: in separating the Old from the New, the *kairos* always makes the New into some form of repetition of the Old, and the Old some form of anticipation of the New (see Heb. 8 and 9, and of course the whole thematic of rebirth in e.g. John 3:3–8, where Jesus is answering Nicodemus: 'Jesus answered and said unto him, Verily, verily, I say unto thee, Except a man be born again, he cannot see the kingdom of God. Nicodemus saith unto him, How can a man be born when he is old? can he enter the second time into his mother's womb, and be born? Jesus answered, Verily, verily, I say unto thee, Except a man be born of water and of the Spirit, he cannot enter into the kingdom of God. That which is born of the flesh is flesh; and that which is born of the Spirit is spirit. Marvel not that I said unto thee, Ye must be born again'). And of course if the presence of the *kairos* is determined as always-going-to-have-been, then it is in some sense *already* a repetition ... We would need to explore carefully the relationship of this thinking with that of Walter Benjamin, for whom the *Jetztzeit* emerges from a sort of non-linear superimposition (a 'constellation', 'Theses', XVIII A, p.255) of past and present, a nonidentical repetition, and in which the figure of redemption is difficult to separate from this thematic of rebirth. We should also point out a further ambivalence in Paul's thought of the moment, which is also often the 'now' of worldly existence as opposed to the 'now' of salvation: see Ridderbos, *Paul*, p.52: 'It is this remarkable ambivalence of the "now", which can have the sense of the "*already* now" of the time of salvation that has been entered upon as well as of the "*even* now" of the world time that still continues, which imparts to Paul's eschatology its wholly distinctive character.'; and cf. Ridderbos, *Paul*, pp.487ff. on the future this opens up: the first coming is the moment of fulfilment of time, but it opens up the perspective of the need for a second coming to fully achieve that fulfilment. This complication of the 'now' is increased if we take into account more than does Ridderbos the reflexive or auto-graphical 'now' through which the text refers to its own enunciation or inscription – this *textual* now that contaminates any other 'nows' and opens the text to its own future reading is something we shall pursue a little later. It is perhaps worth pointing out that these temporal expressions

occur much more frequently in the epistles of Paul than in other parts of the Bible.

13 Cf. II Thess. 2:6–8: 'And now [*nun*] ye know what withholdeth that he might be revealed in his time [*en tou autou kairo*]./For the mystery of iniquity doth already work: only he who now letteth *will let*, until he be taken out of the way./And then shall that Wicked be revealed, whom the Lord shall consume with the spirit of his mouth, and shall destroy with the brightness of his coming [*epiphaneia tes parousias autou*].' It is this feature of the *kairos* that justifies the appeal to the prophetic character of the Old Testament, and the thought that this is the prepared fulfilment of God's promise made 'before the world began' (Tit. 1:2).

14 The choice of Hegel here is of course overdetermined, but we might attempt to summarise that overdetermination by saying that the specifically Hegelian concept of 'moment' as a specific stage in a dialectical process has *already* gathered up the more interruptive sense we are also trying to understand. It goes without saying that the 'Hegel' presented here is the Hegel of the 'official' version, and makes no attempt to do more than posit as inevitable that another, more interruptive thought of the moment could also be found inhabiting his text. For some sense of that other thought, see Catherine Malabou, *L'Avenir de Hegel: Plasticité, temporalité, dialectique*, Paris: Vrin, 1996, and Derrida's remarks in 'Le temps des Adieux: Heidegger (lu par) Hegel (lu par) Malabou', *Revue philosophique*, 1998, 1, pp.3–47.

15 This would then be the taking up again of the *gage* or wager laid down ten years ago in 'Deconstruction and the Philosophers', where I propose to 'argue against anybody that deconstruction really is a thinking of and for the present, for now, *en ce moment même*' (*Legislations: The Politics of Deconstruction*, London: Verso, 1994, p.44.) Cf. on the same page the argument that the 'old names' deconstruction uses 'are not provisional stand-ins in view of a perfected language to come: the necessary imperfection of these words means they are just fine as they are, nothing could do better *this time...*'

16 Georg Wilhelm Friedrich Hegel, *Introduction to the Philosophy of History* (trans. J. Sibree), New York: Dover Books, 1956.

17 See, among many references, the remark to §146 of the *Encyclopedia*, where Hegel says straightforwardly enough, 'the problem of science, and especially of philosophy, undoubtedly consists in eliciting the necessity concealed under the semblance of contingency' (*Encyclopedia of the Philosophical Sciences in Outline, and Critical Writings*, ed. Ernst Behler, New York: Continuum, 1990). The fact that contingency in Hegel is *sublated* rather than simply denied or abolished again suggests the necessity of a more complex account of their relation than the 'official' words of Hegelianism might suggest. Cf. Jean Marie Lardic, *La contingence chez Hegel*, Arles: Actes Sud, 1989; Malabou, *L'Avenir de Hegel*; and Bernard Mabille, *Hegel: l'épreuve de la contingence*, Paris: Aubier, 1999.

18 Hegel, *Introduction*, p.29.

19 Hegel, *Introduction*, p.30.

20 Hegel, *Introduction*, p.30.

21 Whence Hegel's persistent illustrative use of the figures of seed and plant to expound the movement of spirit, in, for one example among many, the *Lectures on the History of Philosophy*: 'The seed is simple, almost a point; even the microscope cannot discover much in it; but this simplicity is large with all the qualities of the tree ... This evolution comprises a succession. The root, the trunk, the branches, the leaves and flowers ... all these determinations, all these moments are absolutely necessary and have as their aim the fruit, the product of all these moments and the new seed.' (*Lectures on the History of Philosophy* [trans. E.S. Haldane], Lincoln: University of Nebraska Press, 1996, p.66).

22 This motif of tying together past, present and future would be worth pursuing as a rhetorical figure, often in surprising places. See the passage from Nietzsche quoted above, n.8. See too Rev. 1:8, 'I am Alpha and Omega, the beginning and the ending, saith the

Lord, which is, and which was, and which is to come, the Almighty'; cf also 1:18–19: 'I am he that liveth, and was dead; and, behold, I am alive for evermore, Amen; and have the keys of hell and death;/ Write the things which thou hast seen, and the things which are, and the things which shall be hereafter.'

23 In Jacques Derrida, *L'écriture et la différence*, Paris: Seuil, 1967 [1966] (Engl. edn *Writing and Difference* [trans. Allan Bass], London: Routledge, 1978).

24 Cf. the return of this verb in the review of Malabou, *L'Avenir de Hegel*, p.10.

25 Derrida, *L'écriture*, p.428. See my discussion of this passage in a different context in 'R.I.P', ch. 5, *Interrupting Derrida*, pp.61–75.

26 The place for this explicit development is none the less already given by the earlier identification in *La voix et le phénomène*, Paris: PUF, 1967 (Engl. edn *Speech and Phenomena* [trans. David Allison], Evanston: Northwestern UP, 1973) of Husserl's determination of being as presence as an 'ethico-theoretical' act or decision (p.59 [53]; cf. too p.6 [7]).

27 Derrida, *Spectres*, p.16 [xix]; see too p.44 [19–20] and pp.55–56 [27–28].

28 Derrida, *Spectres*, pp.41–42 [17–18].

29 Cf. Benjamin: 'Fashion has a flair for the topical, no matter where it stirs in the thickets of long ago; it is a tiger's leap into the past. This jump, however, takes place in an arena where the ruling class gives the commands. The same leap in the open air of history is a dialectical one, which is how Marx understood the revolution' ('Theses', XIV, p.253). Compare Derrida's remarks about fashion at the beginning of 'Force and Signification' (*L'écriture*, p. 10; *Writing and Difference*, p.14).

30 Derrida, *Spectres*, pp.68–69 [36–37].

31 Benjamin, 'Theses', p.255, XVIIIB.

32 Derrida quotes this text in *Spectres*, pp.95–96, n.1 [180–81 n.2], and elsewhere in the book is prepared to claim that deconstruction only ever made sense to him as a radicalisation of Marxism (p.151 [92]); see p.152, n.1 [184 n.9] for a thematisation of the word 'radicalise' and its insufficiencies (tied to the motif of the 'root' which inhabits it, and the tendency of that motif to assume a root that is, at root, unified and singular).

33 Derrida, *Spectres*, p.102 [59]

34 Jacques Derrida, *Glas*, Paris: Galilée, 1974 (Engl. edn trans. J.P. Leavey Jr and Richard Rand, Lincoln: University of Nebraska Press, 1986), p.7a.

35 Derrida, *Glas*, pp.258a–60a [231a–33a].

36 Cf. the reflections on 'inventive' reading in the Malabou review, *L'Avenir de Hegel*, p.14.

37 Derrida, *Spectres*, p.40 [16].

38 Derrida, *Spectres*, p.94 [54].

CHAPTER 2

The Aporia of the Instant in Derrida's Reading of Husserl

MAURIZIO FERRARIS

Socr. You know, Phaedrus, there is a strange thing about writing which makes it analogous to painting. The painter's products stand before us as though they were alive: but if you question them, they maintain a most majestic silence. It is the same with written words: they seem to talk to you as though they have something in mind but if you ask them anything about what they say, from a desire to be instructed, they go on telling you just the same thing for ever. And once a thing is put in writing, the composition, whatever it may be, drifts all over the place, getting into the hands not only of those who understand it, but equally of those who have no business with it; it doesn't know how to address the right people, and not address the wrong. And when it is ill-treated and unfairly abused it always needs its parent to come to its help, being unable to defend or help itself.

Plato[1]

What You Rightly Doubt

At a culminating point in *Speech and Phenomena* Derrida writes that phenomenology, whether it wishes so or not, knows so or not, is always a phenomenology of perception. The irony of this remark is not difficult to grasp: indeed, what is it that phenomenology deals with, if not that which appears to our senses as phenomenon? The trouble, however, is that perception as such is strictly speaking impossible since what appears to us as phenomenon, immanent to our consciousness, is not being 'as such' which remains assigned to a transcendent realm; and indeed this is the fundamental problem for Husserl who is well aware that all that appears to be immanent to our consciousness reveals itself to be surrounded by all sorts of transcendences after a deeper examination. Thus the issue is not to deny the world but rather to ask to what extent perception may be justified, namely how one may get perception 'as such'; nor is the issue to abolish presence but rather to question why – ultimately – there is so little presence. When I touch an object, what is deposited in my soul is its form and not its matter; I shall never have but forms (therefore, I shall never have matter), yet I know, with an odd kind of certainty which is not merely empirical, that the same path which entitles me to scepticism (we have but forms) leads me by the same token to a naïve although institutive faith in the reality of the outer world.

Now, the shibboleth of phenomenology consists precisely in this question. Phenomena are not shadows, or appearances, or figures of speech: they are as hard to remove as the tree stumps in the snow which Kafka talks about, which look as if you could kick them away like pieces in the game of draughts and yet it turns out they are stuck there. And if the world is to be turned into the realm of the will-to-power it has to be postulated (or, more ponderously, to be shown) that the world is available to us as such, a possibility which Derrida resolutely excludes. Jews, Kierkegaard wrote, are the most unfortunate of peoples because they are situated between memory and waiting, namely between two unfulfilled presences which, however, appear to be the condition of phenomena. We may here recognise the reason for the hyperbolic loyalty which binds deconstruction to phenomenology: for both, the phenomenon is not to be transcended, yet at the same time the phenomenon is not everything. Derrida maintains, just like both Kant and Husserl, two philosophers who programmatically opposed dogmatic idealism as well as nihilism, that the present presupposes two non-presences, i.e. past and future, which define the present as such, and that there must be something somewhere (following Kant let us call it the synthetic unity of apperception) which, by retaining the past and by anticipating the future, allows for the possibility of the present, the evidence and the phenomenon. Such 'something', however, does not phenomenise itself as such, it is not itself the subject matter of representation which allows for the possibility of something to present itself as being (as present being, that is) while not appearing in turn. As in Kant,[2] the noumenal hypothesis – i.e. the hypothesis that not everything is phenomenon – rules out any reduction of being to pure perception, namely – in the last instance – to pure thought and to the realm of some sceptical phenomenalism resting on dogmatic idealism:

> To utter force as the origin of phenomenon is doubtlessly to utter nothing. Once uttered, force is already phenomenon. Hegel had already shown that the explanation of a phenomenon through a force is a tautology. When uttering this, however, one should bear in mind a certain incapacity of language to reach

out of itself to utter its origin, and not the *thought* of force. Force is the other of language, without which language would not be what it is.[3]

That not everything is phenomenon, namely that things are not *entirely* present to us, is therefore the best proof that something exists beyond the realm of that which is defined – altogether presumptively – as the realm of our inner representations; in this sense, Derrida's critique of empiricism – I will come back to this in a moment – is not to be taken as demoting experience, but rather, if anything, as acknowledging that the claim of a totally present presence, of a completely internalised outer world, would be tantamount to annihilating the world. The double register Derrida uses in his writing consists in a double gesture in which the very movement (idealisation) which constitutes presence by rescuing it from the ephemeral character of the certainty of the senses, is precisely what destitutes it by shaking the distinction between perception and retention; such predicament, it should be noted, has nothing to do with the features of some historically produced (therefore historically amendable) metaphysics, it rather belongs to the standard situation of perception. To tell the truth at all costs means then to keep two hyperboles simultaneously standing: both the certainty of the senses and hyperbolic doubt, absolute immediacy and infinite mediation.

In fact, Derrida's early philosophical curiosities pointed at Rousseau and Nietzsche. Retrospectively, such choice appears prophetic: in Rousseau's philosophy immediacy hides within itself a laboured mediation, and nature reveals itself at bottom as culture; in Nietzsche the dogmatic denying of the subsistence of facts *vis-à-vis* interpretations, practising the hermeneutics of suspicion and the genealogy of morals, coexists with the paradoxical seeking for the ultimate, positive, immediate truth. Here, then, are the two hyperboles: the appeal to the most sensible of certainties as well as to the most methodical of doubts; or, in other words, here are the two authors in whom that specific taste for hyperbole is channelled, a preference that Derrida diagnosed as being valid for himself: 'Exaggerated hyperbolism. In the end, I exaggerate. I always do.'[4]

It is not, however, a purely idiosyncratic pathology, like the prosopagnosia which Derrida accounted for in *Carte postale*. Grimm's tale, revived by both Heidegger and Derrida, points out the problems immanent in such a hyperbole. A hedgehog enters into a race with a hare, but has the she-hedgehog posted at the finishing-line; so, no matter how fast the hare runs, the she-hedgehog is always already there, at the finishing-line, and says 'I'm here already'. The she-hedgehog saying 'I'm here already' is perception making fun of dialectic, because it has always already begun, before any dialectic, in the same way as time has already settled in when we start reasoning about time and its original constitution; still, in perception there is dialectic, namely *Aufhebung*, the act whereby matter is known only through its exact antithesis, namely form. One should not rush, however, to resolve everything into a universal mediation that constitutes the closest antecedent first of hyperbolic doubt and second of dogmatic idealism. In fact, the certainty of the senses which remains, as Hegel writes, the *richest* of all cognitions, is not as naïve as one might think. It is from such certainty (namely, from that which Heidegger qualified as *Dasein*'s thrownness, i.e. the fact that I am in a world which has begun before me and to which my reflection is inevitably secondary), that I get my standards of reality, adequacy, existence and presence; they, in turn, cater to the doubt, which is always *derivative*, for it grafts on to an experience, like the one of time, which surprises and anticipates a questioning that by definition will appear as subsequent. If this is true, then, just as in Pascal's fragment, we always find ourselves both in excess of and in need of certainty. In fact, on the one hand, all the things we do, doubt included, presuppose a world; on the other hand, just because they are part of this world, they will never be able fully to decide upon their own validity. Which amounts to saying that *radical* alterity is impossible, therefore one cannot conclusively distinguish waking from dreaming.

As Derrida makes explicit in *Cogito and the History of Madness*[5] – in his exchange with Foucault concerning *Madness and Civilization*, particularly Foucault's reading of the Cartesian doubt – it is not only that the project to write a history of the other of reason is highly problematic given that the other would be assimilated to the same the very moment it entered any history; rather, and furthermore, it is at bottom impossible to rule out the hypothesis of madness waking at the heart of reason, because precisely the doubt implied by madness is not the most extreme of all experiences, but only a secondary and derivative version of an all too common uncertainty, namely the check one suffers when attempting to ground in reason the difference between dreaming and waking. Leibniz wrote that metaphysically speaking a lifelong dream cannot be ruled out; and Schopenhauer – who did not doubt the outer world practically, but rather claimed that such a scepticism could only take hold over a mind marred by sophistry – maintained that there is no difference between sleeping and waking except for the following: while awake we read the pages of the book of life one after the other, while in sleep we skim through it in a disorderly way. The difficulty lies precisely here: if it is reason (order) to tell us whether we are dreaming or awake, then such principle cannot be grounded in reason, for reason itself might be a dream.

There is not just a gnoseological relationship between doubt and certainty, there is also a chronological relationship between a copy and its original, so that the two levels inevitably get mixed up. The distinction between dream and waking, as well as the one between appearance and reality, between copy and original, postulates an access to that which is 'as-such', an access which is highly problematic. After all, if Plato argues against mimesis, it is not because of a generic and anachronistic disapproval of art, but rather – as we shall see, for the same reasons which lead him to condemn writing in the *Phaedrus* – because on the one hand art pragmatically questions the relationship between original and copy, while on the other hand, and most importantly, art thematises the genesis of idea from iteration. What are ideas but *eide*, namely pictures organised by a visual code and related to both painting and imitation but also to the matterless phantoms that are everything we have? A good mimesis is one which takes us along the thread of a good memory from the empirical world of repetitions to the transcendental or a priori-like world of simple essences, so as to build up a demarcating line in which what is repeated lies on our side, whereas on the other side the originary is situated. It does not seem to be irrelevant, though, that such originary, that is, the world of ideas, occurs as representation and therefore, again, as mimesis and repetition. Hence the need for a transcendental questioning: 'We ought to venture further, reconsider all that might have been conceived as origin so far, return to this side of the basic principles, that is of the opposition between paradigm and its copy.'[6]

The pre-philosophical man who believes in what lies in front of him, however, is not simply naïve. From the very beginning it becomes clear that some experience of temporality and spatiality has been at work in the moment of the 'this' of sense certainty (which indeed is precisely the '*da*' of *Dasein*); an experience which is not self-evident since it vanishes in the phenomenon that it gave rise to, but an experience representing itself according to that very retaining which in the realm of reflection is assigned the task of contesting the alleged immediacy of sense certainty. The relationship between immediacy and mediation thus traditionally constitutes the fundamental problem of perception: if perception implies a mediation as its basis, how can we distinguish between two kinds of repetition, namely, the ideal and the real one? From Socrates onwards, many philosophers have maintained that nothing exists outside the text. From *Theaetetus* to Hegel's *Phenomenology* the simple or immediate identification of sensation with knowledge has been questioned: if knowledge really consisted in sensation, then we should not even be aware of perceiving and therefore we would not perceive at all; but if, vice versa, perception requires (in fact, it presupposes) retention, then retention makes perception possible by safeguarding it and yet destitutes it, for what is retained as ideality – due to the passing of time – appears different from what was once perceived in the present impression. This is the argument instituting the critique of sense certainty at the outset of Hegel's *Phenomenology*: if one says 'it is night now', relying on the evidence of the senses, and takes a written note of such alleged truth, one will find that hours later this sentence is no longer true. In this sense the safety of perception, its true objectivity lies not in the present sensation but in an idealisation which is equivalent to an interiorisation.

Such shift from perception to interiorisation and hence to idealisation is inevitable as soon as one pauses to consider sensation. Sense certainty, which is the *form* of all presence (iterating and altering itself in intelligible presence) is also the most fragile among all presences because it is ephemeral. From Plato to Descartes, from Locke to Husserl, true presence is not the mirage of the senses, but presence inscribed in the soul: 'objectivity and innerness ... only appear to be opposites, since the meaning of idealization (from Plato to Husserl) is to confirm them simultaneously, one through the other. Ideal objectivity preserves its self-identity, its integrity and resistance, because it no longer depends on a sensible empirical presence.'[7] The form of truth does lie in sensible presence, but since it is a transient *hic et nunc*, it will have to be fastened into something more lasting, namely idea, which – on this level – will be nothing but the outcome of a retention occurring within the possibility of indefinite iteration. That is why *Aufhebung* – whose instituting role Derrida underscored already at the level of perception – is so central and why Hegel concludes that language 'constitutes a higher truth'. Within consciousness we own a reality that is still there at the end of the day, for it constitutes itself as ideality; in it, what may appear perishable or fallacious outside keeps its full certainty (even Hume's scepticism of the outer world spared mathematic idealities, and Descartes could question them only through the hypothesis of the evil spirit). Since the opening of the game therefore – and it is certainly not we who started it, since it takes place long before we begin to reflect upon it – we find ourselves in an embarrassing predicament, for that which ensures presence, namely the form of something under our senses, is also that which destitutes it, because form lends itself to iteration, therefore to shift from an intuitionistic to a formalistic paradigm and, furthermore, from a seemingly immediate presence to an *indefinite* (that is, iterative) number of either reproductions or simulations of presence. These insights however do not follow straightforwardly from a sceptical intent but are the result of the thematisation and exploration of certainty.

Circle

What are the *impasses* in which even the most well-meaning and least sceptical research exhausts itself? First of all, that which looks like a bothersome but apparently harmless circularity: on the one hand, all concepts whereby form could be determined refer to presence, beginning with the instituting concept of 'living present' in Husserl;[8] on the other hand, and reciprocally, presence is form, and that constitutes the very evidence through which past and future cannot ever be thought otherwise than in the form of either a past present or a future present.[9] Through a telling criss-cross, logic takes its model from aesthetics, while at the same time aesthetics finds in logic its own safety and certainty. The unheard-of privilege of the present (Hegel), the present as *Urform* preserving itself for ever-new matters, the very notion of 'logical form' in Wittgenstein, are the product of a deep-seated solidarity. There is nothing but the present, which means that there is nothing but forms, namely that *hyle*, as such, never occurs. Most notably, this is not simply a historical decision, it is rather a phenomenological constraint (and a resource as well).

What do we mean by 'form'? The *pointe* of Husserl's reflection, as well as the critical site of phenomenology, lies precisely – according to Derrida's analysis, first offered in *Speech and Phenomena* – in identifying the peculiar features of form as ideality. Metaphysics is fallen and degenerated if it is blind towards an ideality as the possibility of indefinite repetition, a repetition of that which has been in-vented rather than fallen from the sky, of that whose conservation is guaranteed by the present, by the presence of the living present. However, this living present – that is, a present present to itself and intentionally animated, a full presence and condition of ideality – is *from the beginning* haunted by two elements: the shift from retention to representation (as though an instant-like diastem occurred be-tween presence and re-presentation as constitution of ideality), and the necessity of appresentation, namely of the transmission to others and its traditionalisation. At the very moment in which *Urform* must be able to preserve itself beyond the punctuality of an instant, it will have to call for mechanisms of retention and protention that are not structurally present. That is, it will have to employ signs and traces, languages and inscriptions, in just the same way in which Thales's invention, no less than Theaetetus's perception, would have remained a secret had it not been recorded on a *tabula*, later deposited into a language, and still later traditionalised in a writing. That is why a non-presence in its apparently firmest and most certain form originally troubles the present, for it is precisely in living present that presence appears to be determined by sign (retention, in the percep-tion of matterless form; appresentation, in the form of expression; the teleological projection of the text, in traditionalisation); and the sign is understood within language, which is a logical a priori that – paradoxically by now – constitutes itself in view of presence.

The point where the circle turns into aporia is not difficult to identify. As we have just begun to see, what is inherent to this process is precisely the circumstance that ideality sets itself as a possibility of indefinite repetition, in a way that *the determination of being as presence gets confused with the determination of being as ideality*. Thus, on the one hand, if idealisation is possible, it is because it has already taken place in perception which grasped a matterless form, so that the diastem between ideal and real is from its very beginning hard to find and problematic, in principle at least. On the other hand, however, ideal presence (the perfection of presence) is troubled by two non-presences – analytically, because of its connection with temporality (which in Husserl is configured as the constitution of the present through retention and protention). First, form carries *archaeologically* within itself its own matter, its own genesis. Form is form-of; we do not have pictures, rather matterless forms, although we never access *hyle* as such. Form always has a past and that is its matter (this is what both Schelling and Levinas hint at when they talk about 'a past which has never been present', that is precisely the *dynamis* which, although never present as such, must be thought of as implied by *energhēia*). Second, and most importantly – because the interiorised ideal form, the perfection of *morphē* is essentially concerned – form constantly carries within itself its own *teleology*, namely its future. If it is to be an ideal form, a perfect structure, then it must be possible to repeat it infinitely. This teleology which exceeds form, introduces a non-presence, a not-yet, at the heart of the present, a present which appears to be constituted and therefore not entirely present, a present which comes from some past and anticipates some future (as we shall see, if there weren't a future, time would be defluxion rather than fluxion).

Aporia

Here then is the aporia: on the one hand, presence is self-presence of consciousness in a living present, that is, an instantaneity unmediated by either retentions or protentions, an instantaneity precisely which constitutes the *telos* of every sign, and the sign is defined in turn as provisional reference to some presence; yet, on the other hand, the living present, as possibility of indefinite repetition, turns out to be determined by that very non-presence (sign, retention, protention) which would merely be its own vicarious, provisional or supplemental structure. Such substitution is not accidental, for it proves constitutive of the notion of 'presence' designating a possibility of repetition which is capable of surviving the disappearance of the empirical living. If that proves to be the case, the originary point from which Husserl derives his analysis – living present as unity of form and matter – cannot be identified as such, and not be distinguished from ideality and iterability, because the distinction between originary and derivative, between presence and representation, is compromised as a matter of principle. The principles underlying the criss-crossing of presentation and representation are indeed spelled out by Derrida when describing the movement of temporality and the constitution of intersubjectivity. Let us examine them in detail.

As to the problem of *temporalisation*, the aporia can briefly be described as follows: presence is as such something instantaneous, and – through the very notion of living present – Husserl aims at making it the source of any other form of presence. What is present, however? It is simply the limit between past and future, nothing in itself, and if it is something, it is so only insofar as it is the outcome of something which is no longer and of something which is not yet. Since Husserl's 1923–24 lectures on First Philosophy, 'things' do not only have an inner, but also an outer horizon which is made up by past and future. This is not accidental, since if the past did not constitute the premise of the present, then we would not be able to identify the present as such, and if the present did not constantly orient itself towards the not-yet of the future, then we would not have time, which is phenomenologically perceived not just as movement from past to present, but as flux coming to the present from the past and orienting itself towards the future. Therefore, the very first and ultimate fundamental of presence turns out to be but the limit between two non-presences. Instead of thinking of the past and the future as two alterations of the present, the present has to be thought as a determined alteration of two non-presences (and the living present has to be conceived not as an originary point from where forms and matters will be drawn but, to the contrary, has to be seen as the junction of matterless forms with formless matters).

By introducing retention and teleology, however, we have now touched upon the problem of the *constitution of intersubjectivity*. As we have already seen, perception is nothing unless it is first retained by the subject, then linguistically deposited, next dialogically transmitted to others and lastly traditionalised through writing. True enough, from the linguistic deposit onwards we are not dealing with something inherent in all perceptions, but only with a principle which proves to be teleologically involved in perceiving. Even in the case of the solitary self-relationship of the soul, however, the latter cannot operate in the absence of a scriptural deposit, as is traditionally indicated by the picture of the soul as *tabula rasa*.

It is just in order to remedy this situation and to let the present be something more than a breath that Husserl, in the *The Phenomenology of Internal Time Consciousness* (1928), is forced to assert the phenomenological validity of retention. Within phenomenology, which rests on the principle of evidence, something has to be assumed which is not immediately evident: namely that the past is retained and that the present is defined by its difference from the past. Evidence, in this sense, is not so much perception but rather the fact that retention has been preceded

41

by a perception: indeed, in this sense we may see what ultimately motivates Derrida to turn to the notion of *trace*, namely to that which, in the present, refers to something which is not present (typically – as we have seen, the punctual instant would not be fully present, but would appear to be present, or better still, would offer itself as the very form of presence – only to the extent to which it would refer to a past preceding it and to a future towards which it is heading). At the same time, certainty would not lie in the living present, which would appear as a surface effect, but rather in something which in the strict sense is neither present not living, a sheer resource of retention in which amorphous matters and anhyletic forms weld together.

It is not difficult to find the common root of these difficulties. If full presence is 'not susceptible to be exhibited phenomenologically',[10] this very impossibility is not due to some immaterialistic whim, but because 'the idea of pure presence is contested by phenomenological descriptions referring to the movement of temporalization and to the constitution of intersubjectivity'.[12] The paradox therefore is that presence, which appears to be the clearest thing, is nothing but a mirage. The problem that tormented Husserl was in fact to define that which distinguishes a hallucination from an actual perception, and what holds for the presence of the object also holds for the self-presence of the subject, namely that it should be a guarantee against the uncertainties from the outside. There is no need to go back to the ancient questions concerning the distinction between being and phenomenon. It will suffice to consider that Kant underlined that imagination *already* intervenes in perception,[12] first of all because the grasping of an event as such presupposes the retention of past events as well as those of the present one. Thus, traditional criteria employed to distinguish reality from hallucination, namely constancy and consistence of representation, turn out to be the same as those involved in the genesis of hallucination.

We understand why the risk of total madness in Descartes does not consist in the rather rare experience of feeling naked or of believing oneself to be a king, but rather in an ordinary one, namely of being a human who dreams every night. Against the objection that hallucination (or dream) is less constant than perception, it is easy to see that here we are dealing with a purely empirical fact, while *as a matter of right* (as Leibniz replied to Locke, and as Derrida will remark in his reading of Austin)[13] we have no criteria to distinguish the veridical picture from the hallucinated one. What is real is evident only from the viewpoint of naïve understanding (*as a matter of fact* from this viewpoint we have no problem); as retention, however, ideality defines both ideal and real, and it is at this level that the distinction appears problematic. In fact, it is just at the level of either right or ideality that the question of discriminating between two representations, the ideal and the real one, arises. Téniers's painting discussed by Husserl in *Ideen* and placed by Derrida at the beginning of *Speech and Phenomena* epitomises the situation. Let us suppose, Husserl suggests, that the paintings in the gallery represent in turn other paintings, which in turn represent 'inscriptions which can be deciphered', according to an unstoppable *mise en abîme*, which is not just a matter of pictures but of traces and writings, namely all that in the presence refers to something else. At this point the question arises: how to distinguish presentation from representation, simple presence from all its iterations on the one hand and, on the other hand, from the chain of references which it may give rise to? This *mise en abîme* is to a certain extent the standard condition of perception. It is not owed to a decision, but to a lack of criteria to distinguish the ideal from the real and to the circumstance that these difficulties may only be encountered at the level of right and ideality and not at the level of fact and therefore cannot be exorcised by shrugging one's shoulders and saying: 'but these people are crazy, and I would be just as crazy if I acted following their example'.[14] In fact, what would happen if instead of acting like madmen we tried to follow the example of the sane? To perceive means to make notes, which amounts to saying that perception is conceived from its beginning as matterless form (*eidos aneu tes hyles*).[15] Husserl's aporias, therefore, take up and summarise a long tradition.

First, there is the aporetics of *presence*. The first and most apparent problem is that no distinction is secured between aesthetics and logic (both sensations and thoughts are impressed on the *tabula* and both share a purely formal character, namely that of form as form of presence). The second problem is that from this perspective it seems to be very difficult to distinguish perception from memory. In *Philebus*,[16] after memory has been defined as the 'safeguard of sensation' (in fact, as we are beginning to realise, memory is at the same time the *possibility* of sensation), the soul is described as a book in which an internal scribe writes down speeches; when 'this comprehensive process of affection writes the truth', then speeches and opinions (*doxai*) turn out to be true or false. If we are always dealing with forms, the criterion to distinguish true from false opinions cannot easily be determined. This difficulty reappears in *De anima* when Aristotle states that the difference between *doxa* and *phantasia* lies in the fact that the former may be either true or false, while in the latter case we are free to deliberately invent. Here the problem seems to be that on this basis there are no criteria to distinguish between veridical impression and imagination, just as, logically (following Wittgenstein), the discrimination between following a rule and *thinking* of following a rule is more than complicated. The third problem, following from the difficulty immanent in the distinction between perception and memory, concerns the difficulty of distinguishing between simple presence (presentation) and representation. Once fully developed, this argument leads to the difficulty of distinguishing between presence and absence. At this point it is not difficult to see why the problem of writing is so central: in *Phaedrus* writing is condemned, but only because it spoils memory, namely 'the discourse that is *written* … in the soul of the learner'.[17] The bifidity of this approach, thematised in *Plato's Pharmacy*,[18] consists, however, in the fact that the soul (the inside) seems to draw its model from the outside (which on the other hand is repressed and condemned, namely demoted to imitation), and the possibility of something's presence to someone's soul in the end coincides with the possibility of an absence, since the character of writing lies in its capacity to function even in the absence of the original intentionality as well as of the addressee.

There is a second family of aporias, which concern *the present*. These aporias – we have seen them in Husserl as well – have already been pointed out by Aristotle in the fourth book of the *Physics*, and are again thematised in Derrida's *Ousìa et grammé*.[19] In fact, what appears to be present, namely the instant, the exact moment from which the *'there'* of Being-there and the *this* of sense certainty are thought, cannot be as such, for if presence were not simply a limit between past and future, but had a density of its own, then things from ten thousand years ago would be contemporary with things of today, and time would not be, but would turn into space (that is, it would shift from the order of succession to that of coexistence). On the other hand, if time is made up by non-beings (namely if present is simply a limit and not a being), it is not clear at all how things which are in time may have any density at all. We thus have two versions. Either the moment is something, and therefore time as the sum of moments, is not, for it becomes an order of coexistences rather than an order of successions; or the moment is not (namely it is only a limit between past and future), but then it is impossible to see how time, which is made up by non-beings, may have a being of its own. Hence, Aristotle concludes, time is not, or hardly is. The difficulty arising from this situation therefore is that what allows for the experience of beings as beings (i.e. that they are present and in present, in space and in time) eludes ontological thematisation.

Pharmakon

Within this framework, *first*, Derrida confines himself to summming up. If we are looking for true presence, we are certainly going to find it, if only as an ideal presence which means that our certainties lose the ground on which they rest: 'Ideality is either salvation or mastery of presence in repetition. In its purity, such presence is not presence of anything *existing* in the world, it is correlated with *acts of repetition which are in themselves ideal'*.[20] How to distinguish, as soon as one reaches ideality (which happens right away), between retention (primary memory) and recollection (secondary memory), namely, in Aristotelian terms, between *mneme* and *anamnesis* or, in Hegelian terms, between *Erinnerung* and *Gedächtnis*? Psychologically, such a distinction appears very problematic.[21] The issue is not to reduce the abyss separating retention and recollection,[22] but rather to consider that if a certain absence were lacking, it would be impossible even to define retained presence, in the same way that language works as a system of differences, and we would not be able to talk properly about a colour if there were one colour only. Still more seriously, can we really set aside the most hyperbolic hypothesis, consisting not so much in the factual difficulty of distinguishing between dreaming and waking but rather in the theoretical evidence which conceives both waking and the vigilance of living present as the secondary outcome of iteration? This question is not raised against Husserl but complies with his own analyses, which in this case contradict his intentions: 'Against Husserl's expressed intention one arrives to let "representation" (*Vorstellung*) itself depend on the possibility of repetition, and to let the simplest "*Vorstellung*", namely presentation ("*Gegenwärtigung*") depend on the possibility of re-presentation ("*Vergegenwärtigung*"). The presence-of-present is derived from repetition, not vice versa.'[23] Living present – and, more globally, the notion of life lying at the very heart of it – appears to be divided in itself and determined by something which appears neither present nor alive:

> Presence is therefore posited – and particularly consciousness, the being-by-itself of consciousness – not as that which forms being, but as a 'determination' and as an 'effect'; either determination or effect inside a system which is no longer the system of presence but of difference, which no longer tolerates the opposition between activity and passivity, nor that between cause and effect or determination and indetermination, etc.[24]

It is on the basis of these remarks that many have wished to see in Derrida a sceptic, a postmodernist, in short, a 'charlatan' hiding behind a smoke screen, and did not consider that smoke is always sign of something, although not currently present or not so easy to determine.

Second (as we shall see, this is the general method ruling Derrida's work), the aporia – which was neither wished for nor invented, but handed down and justified by tradition – is to be turned into an asset, although not a merely speculative one, since there is no doubt – sense certainty testifies to this – that the present is there. We just cannot prove it, no more than Baron Munchausen could get himself out of the pond by pulling the nape of his own neck. In fact, we are facing the typical transcendental problem: how can you give what you do not have? Scholastics employed the formula: *forma dat esse rei*, and after all Derrida merely underscores that by giving being to a thing, form (that is, presence and retention together) posits the premises to revoke it. Yet that which, with the one hand, is summoned as destituting presence, also appears as the way through which another hand might proceed to constituting it. The duplicity of *pharmakon*, both poison and remedy, begins its therapeutic action. In a different register – that of dialectics, which Derrida thinks to have at least partly abandoned – what is at stake is making contradiction productive. The original synthesis giving rise to perception and to idealisation is synthesis of matter and form, outside and inside, originary and constituted temporality.[25] Like all syntheses, this one too is an *impure* one in which we mix together perceptual faith and uncertainty concerning sense testimony generally.

Given that we are in such impure mix, there is no need to assume a primary evidence, immanent to consciousness, which might be counterposed *at a later time* by some faith in the outer existence of intuition qualifying it as sensation: faith comes before consciousness, just as sensation precedes the reflection questioning it; the originary presenting of sensation to consciousness is characteristically a sensation of something; by itself, the sheer circumstance that such presenting takes place in a present, in time that is, shows that outside there is something, although not necessarily what we want or, more seriously, see. As Derrida remarks, in both Aristotle and Heidegger *the sense of being precedes the notion of being*.[26] Be it the sense of the word 'being' (as in Heidegger) or the sense as sensation (there is nothing in the understanding that has not earlier been in the senses) we enter a circle emptying a priori all possible ontological radicalness of the hyperbolic doubt, while obviously leaving intact all its legitimate gnoseological claims or precautions. We do not in any way doubt that beings, if they were there, would be existing; yet, if we know what is existing (if therefore we must have had some experience of it), then not only do we assume some existence, we also have already experienced it. Just because of this, sense certainty is not a mere inaugural fiction, the false belief which shall have to be refuted so that a different truth comes in. It is true that *as a matter of right*, reality and representation cannot be distinguished from one another, precisely because we always grasp forms, never matters. It is a fact, however, that they are distinct from one another, and that the task as well as the soundness of an ontology rests with the right which is granted to that fact. Now, if someone argued that nothing is, there would be no room for the hyperbole either; sense certainty then inhabits the centre of the hyperbolic doubt. Do we not already possess some experience of that which we question through the critique of sense certainty and more globally (literally) of the existence of the outer world?

If this is the case, then the impossibility of grounding this certainty is not enough to justify hyperbolic doubt; the latter remains a shadow of things. That the difference between retention and reproduction is not a distinction between perception and non-perception, but between two modifications of non-perception, is similar to a hyperbole and essentially brings back God's viewpoint; it is to this viewpoint that Descartes refers in the hyperbolic doubt, which in fact he can ground in its ultimate consequences only thanks to the fiction – unthinkable before Ockham – of an all-powerful demon capable of deceiving on even the most evident matters. Viewed from another perspective this means that if it is necessary to call upon God to defeat the evidence of the senses, the significance of this evidence is no less hyperbolic than the one of the doubt.

Following this line of reasoning one has to realise that, as Derrida has often insisted, only failures are productive. In the case under consideration here, the opposing hypotheses of *pure* empiricism and *pure* idealism annul one another. If we take the idealistic hypothesis as dogmatic idealism, it is worth nothing. As critical idealism, in contrast, it is, as Kant remarked, 'in accordance with a thorough mode of thought'.[27] This is the case precisely because thought carries within itself something spurious, for in the Cartesian hypothesis sensible reality had already been introduced (the *cogito* is a phenomenon and precisely a temporal one); and together with an inside, a *tabula* has been postulated in which the temporalisation may take place. The meaning of the hyperbole of sense certainty is to be situated here: the object (let it even be the subject as phenomenon for itself) is given before the law and any sort of doubt is given. Let us now consider the hypothesis of pure empiricism. Without the alterity of bodies not even the alterity of the *alter ego* could arise,[28] yet the very experience of other bodies and other selves testifies to the impossibility of wholly transposing oneself into the other, namely of achieving pure empiricism. When Levinas, with regard to death, talks about an 'empiricism that has in itself nothing positivistic', Derrida wonders whether it is generally possible to talk about 'an *experience* of the other or of difference'.[29] In fact, if the concept of experience is determined as present experience (that is, present to a consciousness), then a contradiction opens up between presence and experience, if 'experience' is meant to refer to some alterity. Empiricism would therefore represent the complete 'inclination of thought in front of the Other', a 'resolute acceptance of inconsistent inconsistency, inspired by some truth deeper than the "logic" of philosophical discourse', insofar as it is a '*resignation* of concept, of *apriori* and of the transcendental horizons of language'.[30] The mistake of radical empiricism would lie in 'presenting itself as a philosophy', while on the contrary it presents itself as 'the *dream* of a thought which is purely *heterologic* in its origin. *Pure* thought of *pure* difference. Empiricism is its philosophical name, its metaphysical claim or modesty. We say *dream* because it vanishes *in the light* and since the dawn of language.'[31] Experience of that which is 'as-such', or experience as such is impossible, just as a radically alienated look at the world which we always already inhabit is impossible. Yet by the very impossibility of reaching certainty a certainty is achieved.

In fact, it is the unfeasibility of a total phenomenisation, namely the defeat of empiricism, which, far from corroborating hyperbolic doubt, lends a decisive hand to sense certainty. That not just persons, but in the first place things and bodies, hide something which can be simply anticipated by way of analogy (for instance, the unseen faces of a die) reveals that alterity belongs to ontology in general. What is hiding in the empiristic *dream* is thus the other hyperbole represented by the Cartesian *dream*: in fact, 'self-presence ... has never been given but rather dreamed of'.[32] In order to be able to annul the outside, the *cogito* has to be entirely certain of itself, but that would in turn require the certainty that what is seen is entirely immanent and without any residue or transcendence. Yet this is something the critical idealist cannot prove (isn't that the reason why he doubts?), and he could certainly not be satisfied with the convictions of dogmatic idealism. On the other side, if it is problematic to hold the position of hyperbolic doubt in its absolute claim to ontologically revoke the world, the demand of an absolute empiricism aiming to a philosophical access to the other as such, namely to a full presence 'for-itself' which were at the same time not also a 'for-us' is equally hyperbolic, because it wishes to penetrate the world not just as representation but also as will. In short, the very fact that I know myself only through others, that is that I know myself as other and as phenomenon, implies an underlying realistic faith. *Alterity is always already at the heart of ipseity, just because the latter is not present to itself.* In this way, that which interrupted the self-presence of the *cogito* in the living present ends up providing the proof of the outer world. In other words, the proof we possess of the outer world derives just from our very incapacity of ultimately founding experience, including of course the instituting experience that is *cogito's* self-intuition. This is why for Husserl, and Heidegger in his sway,[33] the demand for the proof of the outer world was unmotivated. Unlike Moore's argument, this rejection was not due to the 'evidence' of the outside world, but resides in the fact that the object's as well as the world's sense of being is supplied within an impure framework, that is, within a temporal synthesis which we cannot grasp as given in an unmediated way.

This is the reasoning developed in the Kantian refutation of Descartes.[34] The *cogito* perceives itself as temporal flux but, in order for the flux to recognise itself as such, there ought to be something stable outside to ensure the flowing of the *cogito*. If this argument sounds formal, it may be better to draw on a second argument, less evident but exactly to the point, which refers not to the temporalisation of the *cogito* but rather to a certain intentional relation which links us to the world.

Can we really doubt that something is there? Where would we get the feeling of this lack from? (This is the core of Descartes' argument for the ontological proof of the existence of God, stripped of the objectivist element.) Assuming that one may imagine feeling joy, and that such imagination be different from joy, why on earth would one imagine suffering? In Locke's argument in favour of the outer world,[35] reference is made to this specific point: we may well think that there is no difference between burning and dreaming of burning, but at that point arguments are of no use. In other words, although one might find the Kantian proof of the existence of the outer world in the first *Critique* insufficient, the true proof is rather that which Kant, in the *Critique of Judgement*, had used as an argument for aesthetic disinterestedness *vis-à-vis* the existence of the objects. The analysis of feelings, namely the critique of judgement which doesn't concern the existence of the objects but rather examines the effect they exert upon us, reveals feeling as a self-affection which, just as temporality, is to be considered as a hetero-affection.[36] That is indeed the meaning of time as self-affection which acknowledges itself to be both internal and external, insofar as it presupposes that something exists as the cause of sensation, and proves its existence in the very moment in which it estimates the effects of the outside on the inside. In the judgement of taste we do not care whether things are there or not, we are only interested in the effects of pleasure and displeasure. Even if we doubt about everything, even if we have suspended any reference to the object as a matter of principle, the object still keeps generating a feeling of pleasure and displeasure. In phenomenological terms this allows us to say that alterity has already constituted ipseity, and that such constitution fails neither in the sceptical hyperbole nor in the aesthetic *epochē*. And yet, is this not precisely the moment when the two hyperboles join, when the sense certainty of naïve physics and hyperbolic doubt come together? Within us we carry the traces of the outside, which means that we cannot wholly interiorise (that is phenomenise) the outside, and that our doubt will never really be able to hit the question of being but only that of the veracity of representation.

Something is present (*pharmakon* as a remedy) only to the extent that it is not entirely present (*pharmakon* as poison). We do not have experience as such, the other remains transcendent and therefore consistent. Given these premises, the proof of the outer world would be a variation of the Freudian theme of mourning.[37] Mourning can never succeed: either the other is left alone and therefore it is not brought back to the ego; or it is incorporated in order to bring it back to the ego, but then mourning has failed. Just as mourning can never succeed because it either leads to integral extraneity or to integral identity, the constitution of subjectivity appears itself determined by an outside which it cannot grasp as such but which none the less has necessarily to be presupposed. It is clear that we are dealing with a recurring structure which consists, according to the first gesture of deconstruction, in hyperbolising traditional counterpositions (for instance and typically, the one between sense certainty and hyperbolic doubt) and, according to the second gesture of deconstruction, in bringing a third element out of this tension which suspends the validity of traditional pairs or oppositions.

This procedure is made possible by recurring to that hyperdialectic performance which Derrida named 'logic of supplement' (which in fact can be recognised in the bifidity of writing as *pharmakon*, the *double bind* and in all double figures thematised by deconstruction). On the one hand, what ensures presence (the possibility of retention) is that which destitutes it (because of the permanent chance of confusion between retention, idealisation and iteration). On the other hand, the very fact that this *impasse* is inherent in form, and that form is never entirely present, testifies to the fact that not everything is phenomenon and, indeed, that something exists, although as reference, namely as a supplement which both reveals how presence is not fully present and allows for the becoming-present of presence. At the origin, then, there is not simple presence but rather a reference which Derrida characterises by the figure of the 'supplement', which

> takes the place of something that gave in, a non-meaning or a non-represented, a non-presence. There is no present before it, therefore it is only preceded by itself, that is by another supplement. Supplement is always the supplement's supplement. If one wishes to go back from the *supplement to the source*, one must acknowledge that there is some *supplement at the source*.[39]

Notes

1 Plato, *Phaedrus*, 275 d–e, ed. C. J. Rowe, Cambridge: Cambridge University Press, 1993.

2 Immanuel Kant, *Kritik der reinen Vernunft*, 1–2, in *Werkausgabe*, III/IV, ed. W. Weischedel, Frankfurt/M.: Suhrkamp, 1974 [1781A/1787B], A 267–68; B 322–24.

3 J. Derrida, *L'écriture et la différence*, Paris: Seuil, 1967, p.34.

4 J. Derrida, *Monolinguisme de l'autre*, Paris: Galilée, 1996, p.81.

5 J. Derrida, 'Cogito et histoire de la folie', in *L'écriture*, pp.51–97.

6 J. Derrida, *Khôra*, Paris: Galilée, 1993, p.93.

7 J. Derrida, *Marges de la philosophie*, Paris: Minuit, 1972, p.108n.

8 Derrida, *Marges*, p.188.

9 Derrida, *Marges*, p.37.

10 R. Bernet, 'Differenz und Abwesenheit. Derridas und Husserls Phänomenologie der Sprache, der Zeit, der Geschichte, der wissenschaftlichen Rationalität', in *Studien zur neueren französischen Phänomenologie*, Phänomenologische Forschungen, XVIII, Freiburg/Munich, 1986, p.54.

11 V. Costa, *La generazione della forma. La fenomenologia e il problema della genesi in Husserl e in Derrida*, Milano: Jaca Book, 1996, p.21.

12 Kant, *Kritik der reinen Vernunft*, A 120n.

13 Derrida, *Marges*, pp.367–93.

14 J. Derrida, *La voix et le phénomène. Introduction au problème du signe dans la phénonoménologie de Husserl*, Paris: PUF, 1967, p.64.

15 Cf. Aristotle, *De anima* (trans. Hugh Lawson-Tancred), Harmondsworth: Penguin, 1986, 424a, p.17 and *De memoria* (ed. and trans. Richard Sorabji), London: Duckworth, 1972, 450a, pp.31–32.

16 Plato, *Philebus*, 38e–39a.

17 Plato, *Phaedrus*, 275c–276b.

18 J. Derrida, *La dissémination*, Paris: Minuit, 1972, pp.101–97.

19 J. Derrida, *Ousìa et grammé*, in *Marges*, pp.31–78.

20 Derrida, *La voix*, p.114.

21 Derrida, *La voix*, p.73.

22 Derrida, *La voix*, pp.103–5.

23 Derrida, *La voix*, p.58.

24 Derrida, *Marges*, p.17.

25 J. Derrida, *Le problème de la genèse dans la philosophie de Husserl*, Paris: PUF, 1990 [1953–54], pp.155–56.

26 Derrida, *La voix*, pp.82–83.

27 'Problematic', as translates N. Kemp Smith.

28 Derrida, *L'écriture*, pp.157–58.

29 Derrida, *L'écriture*, p.195.

30 Derrida, *L'écriture*, pp.194–95.

31 Derrida, *L'écriture*, p.84.

32 J. Derrida, *De la grammatologie*, Paris: Minuit, 1969, p.131.

33 M. Heidegger, *Sein und Zeit*, Tübingen: Max Niemeyer Verlag, 1984 [1927], pp.202–8, § 43a.

34 Kant, *Kritik der reinen Vernunft*, B 275–76.

35 J. Locke, *An Essay Concerning Human Understanding*, ed. Peter H. Nidditch, Oxford: Clarendon Press, 1979, IV, II, 14.

36 J. Derrida, *La vérité en peinture*, Paris: Flammarion, 1978, p.55.

37 S. Freud, 'Trauer und Melancholie', in *Das Ich und das Es: Metapsychologische Schriften*, Frankfurt/M.: Fischer, 1992, pp.171–89.

38 Derrida, *De la grammatologie*, pp.342–43.

CHAPTER 3

Existential Moments

PETER POELLNER

Within the philosophical and broader cultural discourse of modernism, 'the moment' occupies a position of elevated significance. This valorisation of the moment is by itself not new. Traditionally, a certain self-conscious, emphatic concern with the moment is predominantly associated with two contexts, both of which broadly speaking are religious ones: first, the context of conversion and, second, the context of eschatology, more specifically, the moment of vision. 'On the day of the Lord I was taken by the Spirit and I heard behind me a voice loud as a trumpet', we read at the beginning of the Revelation of St John (1:10). Perhaps most famous of all, the first letter to the Corinthians (15:52) prophesies that at the end of history 'we shall all be changed, in a moment, in the twinkling of an eye'. Luther's translation of the expression which the King James Bible then translates as 'twinkling of an eye' is *Augenblick*, and this has remained the standard German expression for the moment or instant. In the Gnostic traditions, the moment also takes on a special significance as the sudden, violent irruption of the wholly other which breaks up or ruptures the context of worldly illusion and frees the self in the rapturous vision from its imprisonment in the material world: 'My spirit ... *tore* me away ... taking me to the summit of the world which is in proximity to the light ... And my spirit separated itself from the body of darkness as if it had fallen into a trance.'[1] This is how the moment of vision is described in a hermetic tract from the Library of Nag Hammadi.

Even in these traditional contexts of conversion and revelatory vision, the moment is thus the mode of temporality in which *a radical break* is effected. It contrasts both with conceptualisations of temporality which emphasise patterns of *cyclical repetition* – as for instance in Greek myth and many other polytheistic frameworks, but also in some aspects of Christianity (the cycle of sin and repentance;

the Catholic interpretation of the Eucharist as literal repetition) – and on the other hand with the pattern of linear and essentially *continuous progression* of or towards increasing perfection or sanctification, characteristic especially of the soteriology of ascetic Protestantism and still lying behind Kant's thinking in the postulate of immortality in the *Critique of Practical Reason*.

It is therefore not surprising that the 'moment' comes to be a form or aspect of temporality frequently made the focus of thematic attention in the era of modernism or High Modernity (by which I intend to refer to roughly the period between the 1880s and 1950s). In this chapter I want to look at two particularly influential manifestations of this concern in the work of Nietzsche and of the early Heidegger. My interest here is not primarily in the philosophy of time *per se*, but rather in uncovering a certain complex nexus of thought, a *Denkfigur*, characteristically associated with the privileging of the 'moment' in central currents of modernist thinking; to this extent, the reflections that follow fall perhaps under the rubric 'cultural hermeneutics'.

The choice of Nietzsche rather than, say, Kierkegaard as a particularly important figure in the emerging of the modernist preoccupation with the moment is at first sight perhaps surprising. Isn't Nietzsche the philosopher of the 'eternal recurrence', on the face of it reintroducing into modernity an essentially pre-modern conception of time derived from the Greeks? As Karl Löwith showed quite a long time ago, such apparent affinities are in fact quite superficial, even on a conventional reading of the eternal recurrence doctrine.[2] In fact, of course, as everyone familiar with Nietzsche and Nietzsche-interpretation knows, there is no *one* orthodox reading of the eternal recurrence. In order to grasp the specificity of the Nietzschean moment, some detailed attention to the perplexities engendered by the thought of the eternal recurrence is indispensable.

Eternal Recurrence: Nietzsche's Moment of Self-Revelation

The most prominent and detailed 'official' exposition of the doctrine in the section 'The Convalescent' in *Thus Spoke Zarathustra* presents it cryptically as a 'prophecy', thus leaving its status, and hence its significance, somewhat opaque. Elsewhere Nietzsche states his idea of an eternal recurrence in different ways which suggest radically divergent interpretations. In the notebook entries published posthumously as *The Will to Power* he speaks of it as the 'most scientific of all possible hypotheses'[3] and presents it by way of an a priori cosmological argument:

If the world may be thought of as a certain definite number of centers of force – and every other representation remains indefinite and therefore useless – it follows that, in the great dice game of existence, it must pass through a calculable number of combinations. In infinite time, every possible combination would at one time or another be realized; more: it would be realized an infinite number of times. And since between every combination and its next recurrence all other possible combinations would have to take place, and each of these combinations conditions the entire sequence of combinations in the same series, a circular movement of absolutely identical series is thus demonstrated.[4]

One thing that is clear from this passage, as indeed from the statement in *Thus Spoke Zarathustra*, is that Nietzsche is indeed speaking about an eternal recurrence *of the same*:[5] identical collocations of force-constituted physical states or events are to repeat themselves 'eternally', that is, properly speaking, without end or sempiternally. Criticisms of Nietzsche's arguments, beginning with Georg Simmel's in the early 1900s, were quick to object that the argument works only if one ignores infinitesimals.[6] If there can be infinitesimal differences, geometrically representable by asymptotes, either between the temporal intervals occupied by any two distinct physical states or between the respective quantities of force constituting two distinct physical states, then Nietzsche's conclusion does not follow even if one grants his premises. In other words, the endless recurrence 'within' an infinite time of absolutely type-identical states of affairs remains, even on Nietzsche's problematic assumption of a quasi-objective, quasi-substantial infinite time of homogeneous instants within which things happen, no more than at best a possibility. Given that few serious interpreters of Nietzsche have been prepared to challenge the logic of Simmel's objection – which, incidentally, they could have found already in Leibniz – alternative readings soon came to prevail. Rather than a theoretical or scientific doctrine, which Nietzsche supposedly considered true on independent grounds and to which, *therefore*, he thought a certain practical response was required or appropriate, might not rather the practical concern in some sense come first? This is the general thought underlying the various 'existential' readings of the eternal recurrence. And indeed, there is no shortage of passages in his corpus of writings which encourage this hermeneutic approach. Perhaps the most striking of these was written before *Zarathustra* and occurs at the end of the fourth book of the *Gay Science*:

> *The greatest weight* – What if, some day or night, a demon were to steal after you into your loneliest loneliness and say to you: 'This life as you now live it and have lived it, you will have to live once more and innumerable times more; and there will be nothing new in it, but every pain and every joy and every sigh and everything unutterably small or great in your life will have to return to you, all in the same succession and sequence – even this spider and this moonlight

between the trees, and even this moment and I myself. The eternal hourglass of existence is turned upside down again and again, and you with it, speck of dust!' Would you not throw yourself down and gnash your teeth and curse the demon who spoke thus? Or have you once experienced a tremendous moment when you would have answered him: 'You are a god and never have I heard anything more divine.' If this thought gained possession of you, it would change you as you are or perhaps crush you. The question in each and everything, 'Do you desire this once more and innumerable times more?' would lie upon your actions as the greatest weight. Or how well disposed would you have to become to yourself and to life to crave nothing more fervently than this ultimate confirmation and seal?[7]

One aspect of this passage to which I should like to draw attention straightaway, although I want to leave its more detailed discussion until later, is the *two* temporal orders in it which are equally significant. First, there is the order of temporality spoken about by the demon: the infinite repetition of the same, that is, of a type-identical sequence of events. But there is also in this dramatisation a temporality of reception which is a *moment of radical transformation*: 'If this thought gained possession of you it would change you as you are or perhaps crush you.' This is a crucial point which we shall need to come back to. In any case, the passage shows no interest in the *truth* of the cosmology of recurrence. Here, as in some of the fragments in the notebooks, the emphasis lies very clearly on certain practical psychological effects associated with it. What would be required, however, for the idea to have a profound practical import for the recipient – to crush us or to change us? The problematic to which I am alluding becomes quite apparent if one considers, by way of a representative example, and summarising the voluminous and lengthy discussion among Nietzsche scholars, the conclusion of Bernd Magnus's 'existential' interpretation of the eternal recurrence.[8] According to Magnus, the practical significance of the idea of an eternal recurrence lies in its countering nihilism, essentially by intensifying the dynamics of choice: it *matters* infinitely more what you do because what you do you will have to do again for ever. Now, it is fairly evident that the vivifying or intensifying practical effect Magnus ascribes to the doctrine is predicated on the doctrine's being believed. Thus, its existential import, on this interpretation, is obviously *not* independent of belief in its truth as a cosmological theory, and can therefore not be indifferent to the circumstance that there *are* no good independent reasons to believe in the cosmology of eternal recurrence. If, on the other hand, the idea is rather that the reasons for accepting the cosmology of recurrence are not expected to be independent reasons, but rather to include the affective relation to the world made possible by accepting the cosmology – perhaps in a manner reminiscent of William James's 'will to believe' – then we obviously can no longer speak of a transformative *effect* of the doctrine: rather, acceptance of the doctrine then becomes one *manifestation* of an affective pattern which cannot be described as being based on the doctrine, but which rather expresses itself in this way (among others, presumably).

There is another reason why one should be wary of this kind of interpretation. This becomes evident if we ask ourselves why even the truth of eternal recurrence should be a matter of concern for the individual. The answers often given to this question tend to be premised on the rather simple idea that eternal recurrence increases something *within one's life* (for example suffering or joy) infinitely many times – but this idea is of course illusory; for it would require the individual to see herself (*qua* personal self-consciousness) as identical across different temporal cycles, but since there can be no continuity of self-consciousness between earlier and later instantiations of 'myself', the idea of recurrence as adding suffering or joy to one's own personal life is necessarily illusory.[9]

The thought that the doctrine of eternal recurrence could have a radical transformative *effect* on a lucid consciousness is therefore one that ought to be abandoned. Yet it is clear that Nietzsche conceives of the moment of its revelation, especially in the *Gay Science*, as a moment of transformation: '... have you once experienced a tremendous moment when you would have answered him: "You are a god and never have I heard anything more divine." If this thought gained possession of you, it would change you ... or perhaps crush you.' In all of Nietzsche's formulations, the revelation of eternal recurrence is presented as associated with, or constituting, a moment of radical discontinuity or rupture, and it is very clear that it is precisely this circumstance, and only this, which gives it its importance for Nietzsche. In a manuscript containing a section plan for a book to be entitled *The Eternal Recurrence* (which remained unwritten), he muses about the 'probable consequences of its being *believed* (it makes everything *break open*)'.[10] The question I have been pursuing here is whether this 'everything breaking open' should really be seen in the terms in which Nietzsche himself presents it in this manuscript passage.

Arguably, the most fruitful alternative reading, which in fact captures Nietzsche's manifest concerns in this respect, conceptualises the breaking open, the transformation in question, not as the effect of a newly acquired belief about the world or about the individual's personal future – we have seen why these traditional interpretations fail – but rather as a consequence of the explication of the mode of comportment towards one's life and the world which one *already has*. In other words, the confrontation with the idea of eternal recurrence reveals, makes explicit, and thereby also *intensifies*, the recipient's actual *Befindlichkeit*, 'how it is with' her, her previously unthematic or covered-up understanding of herself. The idea then is, I am suggesting, contrary to first appearances, not of a sudden break being effected by the acquisition of some new belief about the world, but rather about the radically transformative character of self-explication or self-transparency. It is this feature of the eternal recurrence which brings it in close proximity not so much to the standard project of 'Enlightenment', that of dispelling superstition and false belief about 'objective reality' ('what is really out there, and what is merely subjective, within the mind?' being one of the most characteristic questions of Enlightenment thinkers), but to one of the primary motifs of *modernist* thought: the transformations consequent upon a self-transparency not simply given, but to be *achieved*, either by going deeper than consciousness *tout court*, as in Freudian depth psychology, or by making explicit what is in some way implicit within consciousness but ordinarily 'covered up' (as in the existential variants of phenomenology, most importantly of course early Heidegger and Sartre).

But there is a further aspect to the moment of revelation and self-revelation which is highly significant: it is a moment of polarisation and thus of *extremity*. For what are the possible responses to it? 'Would you not throw yourself down and gnash your teeth and curse the demon who spoke thus?' or would you answer 'You are a god and never have I heard anything more divine ... how well disposed would you have to become to yourself to crave nothing more fervently ...'.[11] There are, it seems, no intermediate possibilities between despair and ecstatic affirmation, and it is clear that the moment of revelation of the recurrence does not reflect an explicit antecedent extremity of this kind, but rather is intended to produce it, to make it appear inevitable. An important part of the rhetorical strategy which is intended to produce this extremity (and the sense of its inevitability) lies in the decentring effected by the image of the eternal recurrence; it compels the recipient to thematise, to focus on, in the end, not the *individual's* life in its particularity, but the natural nexus in its totality: *deus sive natura*. This is also the reason why the question of whether or how the individual might coherently regard herself as identical across different cycles of the recurrence is ultimately irrelevant – for the point of the idea of recurrence is above all to direct the view beyond merely the individual's own particular life or lives, and, second, to 'remove the idea of a goal from the process'. Some of Nietzsche's formulations are more successful in producing this decentring shift than others.

The mode of comportment privileged by Nietzsche, presented as one pole of the either/or effected, or rather uncovered, by the moment of revelation, is of course what he calls 'affirmation'. In one of his working notes, which are often especially interesting because his writing here is generally probing, tentative and less governed by persuasive design, he asks himself: 'can we remove the idea of a goal from the process and then affirm the process in spite of this? – This would be the case if something were attained at *every moment* within this process ... Spinoza reached such an affirmative position ...'[12] 'Affirmation', according to this particular trajectory in Nietzsche's thinking – and one should emphasise that it is only one of several – is thus total affirmation; this follows from Nietzsche's dignifying of *every* moment with the status of a *telos*, an end in itself. Thus the polarisation which Nietzsche intends to make inescapable in the moment of revelation of the eternal recurrence is a radical either/or: *either* despair *or* what he comes to call *amor fati*, the love of fate:

> My formula for greatness in a human being is *amor fati*: that one wants nothing to be different, not forward, not backward, not in all eternity. Not merely bear what is necessary, still less conceal it – all idealism is mendaciousness in the face of the necessary – but *love* it.[13]

The Spinozist resonances of Nietzschean *amor fati* are probably too obvious to need drawing attention to. But I want to highlight here some of its consequences as well as some significant differences from the Spinozist vision. To begin with, it emerges from our analysis so far that there seems to be a connection between the emphasis on a moment of rupture and a radical or *total* polarity and transformation, rather than a partial or gradual one. In Nietzsche this connection is very clear and we shall find it even more explicitly in early Heidegger. In the moment, the *Augenblick* in the emphatic sense, it is not some intraworldly aspect or part of the world that is modified, improves or gets worse, increases or decreases, but rather the world in its totality is changed. This tendency, which might be called a totalising one, is related to another aspect of Nietzsche's work which has often perplexed readers. It is the peculiar apparent contentlessness of Nietzsche's ideal subject of *amor fati*, the *Übermensch*. What goods or values does the *Übermensch* recognise, what virtues does he embody? Conspicuously, every axiological content which Nietzsche specifies in this context here or there is revoked elsewhere. The conclusion strongly suggests itself that the *Übermensch* is not characterised in terms of any intraworldly evaluative orientation – any particular conception of intrinsic value *within* the world – at all. And indeed, if the notion of *amor fati* is to be taken seriously, he cannot be. For the essence of *amor fati* is precisely 'that one wants nothing to be different ... not merely bear what is necessary – but *love* it'. But since, according to this strand of thought in Nietzsche, as for Spinoza, everything actual is necessary, *amor fati* means to love whatever happens, and thus does not and cannot allow for evaluative distinctions among intraworldly non-instrumental goods or values. Spinoza therefore quite consistently advises the reader of his *Ethics* to overcome the passions or affects, precisely because they involve a passivity *vis-à-vis* things in the world. Since any acknowledgement of a particular thing (a mode, in Spinoza's terminology) as having intrinsic value involves affectivity, hence passivity, the free person, according to Spinoza, cannot form any attachments to particular or specific intraworldly objects for their own sake – all value has to be referred to, and thus ultimately vested in, the totality, God or nature. In Spinoza's texts the logical link between *amor fati* (or rather, *amor intellectualis dei*) and an ideal of *pure activity* is thus very clear.

For Nietzsche, this connection must be far more problematic. Many of his texts not only manifest, but seek to induce, what one might call a heightened affectivity. The Spinozist sage is literally impassive, he quite literally lacks all passion, but few would be prepared to say this about whatever ideal is at work in Nietzsche's thinking. *Amor fati*, the radical transformation ideally to be effected by the idea of the eternal recurrence, remains thus an element of Nietzsche's thought in logical tension with much else in his *œuvre*. But this perhaps only confirms that Nietzsche, unlike many philosophers, cannot be reduced to a univocal position or doctrine, as Karl Jaspers noted many years ago.

Time and Consciousness: Husserl's Ecstatic Now

For Nietzsche the concept of time itself and its conditions of possibility do not constitute the subject matter of serious and sustained enquiry. But in the following decades it is precisely this concept which became the focus of attention for a number of major thinkers: Brentano, Bergson, McTaggart, Husserl and Heidegger. It is particularly Husserl's *Lectures on the Phenomenology of Internal Time Consciousness* which lie in the background of Heidegger's reflections on temporality in *Being and Time*, and often are the unspoken target of his criticisms. These so-called lectures are a strange work with a perhaps even stranger history, about which I will add a few words, although this may not at first sight appear relevant to our topic. In fact, the text as we now have it is largely the product of Husserl's *Assistentin* at Freiburg and one of his most gifted pupils, Edith Stein. As Husserl's assistant, Stein was in charge of ordering his voluminous manuscripts between 1916 and 1918. But she went far beyond this humble role in constantly trying to bring Husserl's often fragmentary notes into some kind of publishable form through what she called *Ausarbeitung* – elaborating them. When she came across a pile of manuscripts entitled 'time consciousness' she enthusiastically set to 'elaborating' them on her own initiative. In 1917 she wrote to her friend, the Polish phenomenologist Roman Ingarden: 'Have spent the last couple of months elaborating Husserl's notes on time – some nice things there, but not quite matured yet.'[14] In another letter she wrote to Ingarden that 'to this work I have authorised myself, without meeting any resistance' [from Husserl, that is].[15] It is therefore clear not only that the final result published as Husserl's lectures is really the product of a collaboration between Husserl and Stein (although eventually authorised by Husserl as his) but also that the work would quite possibly not have been published in Husserl's lifetime – and thus could not have had the remarkable impact it had – without Stein's original initiative. Stein, whose own doctoral thesis on intersubjectivity had been published in 1917, later tried to obtain a position at a German university but, despite her submissions to the state ministry responsible, she was prevented from gaining the formal qualification for a professorship, the *Habilitation*, because she was a woman. Thus she was forced to leave the university and became a schoolteacher. In 1926, when the young Martin Heidegger had succeeded in obtaining Husserl's favour, partly, one may suppose, as a result of Stein's having had to abandon her academic career, Husserl asked Heidegger to take care of the manuscript that had been produced by Stein from his notes nearly ten years earlier. Thus the *Lectures* appeared finally in print in 1928, edited by Martin Heidegger. In the editor's introductory remarks, Stein's role is referred to as follows: 'the division into chapters and paragraphs was made by *Fräulein* Dr Stein when transcribing the shorthand manuscript, partly in accordance with the author's marginal notes'.[16] Heidegger, as we know, went on to great things and even greater ambitions in Freiburg a few years later. *Fräulein* Dr Stein died in 1942 in Auschwitz.

Let me return to the content of the *Lectures*. There are at least two theses in it which came to be of crucial importance for both Heidegger's, and later Sartre's, reflections on original temporality. First, the experience of time, and thus, it turns out, experience *überhaupt*, involves a particular complex structure in the apparent simplicity of every Now. The content of any current experience has as one of its components the temporal content Now. The Now is literally intuited or perceived as part of the content of every current experience. Yet the experience of Now is dependent on its being interwoven with the experiential contents 'having just been' and 'is about to be', in which, according to Husserl, the past and future are given in an originary way. By 'originary' Husserl always means the self-givenness of whatever it is that an intentional experience is about. For example, when I perceive a physical object, it is directly given to me *itself*, hence in an originary way, but when I merely imagine it, or think about it by means of linguistic symbols, it is not given originarily. According to Husserl, the proximally past phases of a temporal object – for example of a melody I am listening to – are part of the content of what I hear Now, and similarly the proximally future phases of the melody are also part of the content of my current experience of the melody. Thus both immediate past and anticipated future are part of what is perceived as it is perceived in any given moment. Another way of putting this is to say that what I perceive now is only what it is for me, or only has the sense it has for me, because the immediate past is still present in what Husserl calls primary memory or retention, and the immediate future is unthematically anticipated by me in what Husserl call protentions. In the example of the melody which I hear, what I hear in the present moment is only as it is for me because of retentions of the melody phases that have just been, and anticipations of what is about to follow. Neither retentive nor protentive intentional contents are of course usually thematised, that is, explicitly attended to. Just as part of the content of my current experience is the temporal content Now, so part of the content of my retentions is 'has just been' and part of the content of my protentions is 'is about to be'. Husserl claims that the past as past is *only* given originarily in retention or primary memory, and the future as future is only thus given in protention or primary expectation. Since Husserl also believes that the meaning of an expression is only understood adequately by someone who knows what it would be for the referent of the expression (i.e. what it is about) to be given itself, in person as it were, it follows that we only understand the expressions 'past' and 'future' because our experience has the complex structure it has in which the past and the future inhabit every moment, every Now. But, similarly, the Now is not only contingently inhabited by the past and the present; rather, without the protentive-retentive structure the content of the present phase of consciousness could not be given either, and since the 'now' is only in principle realisable as a dependent aspect of whatever other, non-temporal content is experienced currently, and the latter is dependent on protentions and retentions, Husserl concludes that:

> the now-phase is only conceivable as the limit of a continuity of retentions ... Every phase of the flow [of consciousness] modifies itself into a retention ... and so forth. Without this a content as experience would not be possible, an experience could not be presented and presentable to the subject as unified and would thus be nothing.[17]

Thus not only the *contents* of experiences require the structure described, the experiences themselves constitutively require it as well. This structure, in which every instantiation of one temporal modality necessarily implies the instantiation of the others is what Heidegger will call the *ecstatic* structure of temporality. Each temporal modality is 'outside itself' in the sense that it requires, and intrinsically refers to, all the others.

The second main aspect of Husserl's analysis of time consciousness which was to become of central importance for Heidegger and later existential thinkers is the *derivative* nature of the objective time series, conceived as an irreversible sequence of homogeneous Now-points in which physical and psychical events happen. This conception of time – what Heidegger is going to call the 'vulgar understanding of time' – seems quite unreflectively assumed in some of Nietzsche's notes, for instance when he says, in the context of eternal recurrence, that 'in infinite time, every possible combination would at some time or another be realised'.[18] The idea of time here is somewhat analogous to Newton's conception of space as a kind of quasi-substantial but immaterial container of physical or psychic objects and processes.

Husserl's analysis of time consciousness, in conjunction with his theory of meaning, implies that the objective time series cannot be given a realist interpretation. (Although early Husserlian phenomenology is supposed to be neutral with respect to metaphysics – it intends to suspend metaphysical assumptions in the εποχη or 'bracketing' – this is in fact not the case.) Husserl says that pastness, and by implication futurity, can *only* be originarily given in retentional and, respectively, protentional consciousness. Hence past and future, and thus also the present moment, in other words temporal succession *tout court*, can only be thought in relation to a consciousness of them.

And indeed Husserl speaks quite explicitly of consciousness as time-constituting. But conversely, of course, time also constitutes, makes possible, consciousness. The time which constitutes consciousness is the original flow (*Fluß*) of necessarily pre-reflective consciousness, which consists in Now-phases continuously arising and continuously modifying themselves into retentional phases. This flow, which Stein describes in one of her paragraph headings as the 'time-constituting flow of absolute subjectivity',[19] cannot be said to be *within time*, for it constitutes the time in which temporal objects as lasting unities may then be found. It cannot strictly even be said to be a process (*Vorgang*), because the concept of a process presupposes that of permanence (there are echoes of Kant's first analogy from experience here), and there is no permanence in the original time-constituting consciousness, the 'absolute timeless consciousness which is not an object'. 'Timeless' here means 'not an object within time'. Husserl struggles to describe this original flow adequately:

> It therefore cannot make sense to say of [the time-constituting phenomena] that they are in the Now or that they were earlier, or that they succeed each other temporally or are simultaneous, etc. But isn't the flow a one-after-another, doesn't it have a Now, a phase of actuality, and a continuity of pasts, conscious now in retentions? We cannot say more than this: the flow is something which we call after that which is constituted by it ... It is absolute subjectivity and has the absolute properties of something metaphorically describable

as a 'flow', originating in an actuality-point, an original source point, a Now, and having a continuity of lingering resonances [*Nachhallmomenten*]. For all this we lack names.[20]

The idea of an 'inner time consciousness', a subjective time series within which temporal objects, happenings, have a determinate position, is a derivative phenomenon, presupposing this absolute flow and also requiring secondary memory (what we ordinarily call memory) which, unlike primary memory, is not passive, but spontaneous, and allows us to re-identify something as the same even when it is no longer itself present to us in current experience. Re-identifiability as the same through numerically distinct acts is constitutive of what it is to be an object. At one further remove is the idea of an objective time series, the one world-time in which all objective events, as well as all 'streams' of natural consciousnesses of animals and people, have a position. To repeat, this idea cannot, on Husserl's analysis, be given a realist metaphysical interpretation.

Heidegger's Authentic Moment

Both the idea of the reciprocal implication of the three modalities of experienced time and the notion of a non-objectifiable 'original time' are taken up, yet given a significantly different slant, by the early Heidegger in *Being and Time*. As for the former, Heidegger states that:

> future, having-been-ness and present display [respectively] the phenomenal characteristics of 'towards oneself', 'back to' and 'letting show up with'. The phenomena of towards ... back to ... with ... reveal temporality as the εκστατικον par excellence. *Temporality is the original 'outside-itself'* ... The characteristic feature of the 'time' which is accessible to the vulgar understanding lies among other things in the fact that in it, as a pure succession of nows without beginning or end, this ecstatic character of original temporality has been leveled out.[21]

For Husserl, original temporality *is* the 'flow' of pre-reflective, non-objectified consciousness. Since, for Heidegger, the being of human 'consciousness' always and indeed necessarily involves an engagement in and with the world, that is, a particular, usually unthematic, project or ability-to-be of *Dasein*, the investigation of original temporality for him becomes an investigation of the ways in which time shows up pre-reflectively in this engagement, an engagement he calls being-in-the-world. Rather than examine Heidegger's complex exposition of the temporal characteristics of each of the structural aspects of being-in-the-world in which the world is disclosed to *Dasein* – understanding, affective condition (*Befindlichkeit*), and telling or discourse (*Rede*) – interesting though this would be, I want to focus on just one very prominent, indeed crucial element of his analysis: the role of the moment or *Augenblick*: 'the … *authentic* present we call the *Augenblick* … by contrast to the *Augenblick* as authentic present we call the inauthentic one *presencing*. Formally speaking, every present is a presencing, but not every present is *augenblicklich*.'[22] We shall see that the *Augenblick* in Heidegger is defined as a transformative rupture or break, a radical discontinuity in original temporality. We might say that the *Augenblick* is the mode of encountering the present *as* radically discontinuous. What effects this discontinuity, this leap or metamorphosis into authenticity, is of course the call of conscience. The 'call' (*Ruf*) is Heidegger's name – derived from the Gnostic tradition like much of his 'existential' vocabulary – for that phenomenon which tears *Dasein*, the human being, out of its everyday absorption and dispersion in the world. Heidegger is explicit about the violent character of this happening which brings *Dasein* back to itself: 'in the disclosing tendency of the call lies something of a jolt, of a discontinuous shaking-up'.[23] Later he speaks rather revealingly of the *Einschlagsrichtung*, the direction of impact, of the call.[24] This is an expression normally only used for things like bombs or artillery shells. The call comes to us, if it comes, 'never planned by ourselves, nor prepared, nor willed by us. "It" calls, against expectation and even against one's will.'[25] The human being is, in its average everydayness, absorbed in the world (*benommen von der Welt*), in the sense that it un-self-consciously finds itself dealing with usable stuff (*Zeug*) which constitutes contexts of significance – for example, at work, or in one's 'leisure' – which are neither made nor explicitly chosen by it but pre-given to it by the public world into which it is 'thrown'. *Dasein* is, in the first place and for the most part, dispersed in and preoccupied by the world (*zerstreut* means both of these), precisely because it finds itself in a being-with-others, a public world (*das Man*), such that this public world has already constituted its contexts of significance for it:[26]

> With the lostness into the Public the primary factical ability-to-be of *Dasein* – the tasks, rules, standards, the urgency and the scope of its … being-in-the-world – has in each case already been decided upon. *Dasein* has always already been relieved by the Public of taking hold of these possibilities of being. The Public even covers up this tacit unburdening from any explicit *choice* of these possibilities. It remains indeterminate who 'really' chooses. This choice-less being-taken-along by nobody in particular, whereby *Dasein* entangles itself in inauthenticity, can only be reversed by *Dasein*'s bringing itself back to itself from its lostness in the Public.[27]

It is this bringing back of *Dasein* from its lostness in the public self, where it unreflectively does what *one* does, desires what *one* desires, and so forth, to its own self which requires the jolt (*Stoß*) of the call of conscience. But what really is the content of the call? Or, to put it differently, what is this 'own self' or 'very own ability-to-be' (*eigenstes Seinkönnen*) to which it calls back? Partly it is simply the double finitude of *Dasein*. First, in the sense that *Dasein* is thrown into the world, not being *causa sui*, and, second, that it is free in the sense of having to choose and thus to exclude: 'freedom is only in the choice of one possibility, that is, in the taking up [the burden] of not having-chosen or not-being-able-also-to-choose the other'.[28] Thus the call of conscience unsettles *Dasein*, tearing it away from its tranquilised state *qua* public self, jolting it into self-transparency as finite. But there is a second aspect often ignored in Heidegger's description of this phenomenon:

> *Dasein*, when it understands the call, *is listening to and in thrall to* [*hörig* here means both of these] *its very own possibility of existence*. It has chosen itself.[29]

> The bringing oneself back from the Public, that is, the existential modification of the public self to authentic selfhood must occur as the belated performance [*Nachholen*] of a choice. Belated performance of the choice means *choosing of that choice*.[30]

This means that the call jolts *Dasein* not so much into making new or different choices as explicitly, thematically affirming whatever possibilities, pre-given by the public world, he or she has already *qua* inauthentic public self tacitly decided upon. This is why Heidegger always emphasises that authentic *Dasein* cannot escape its public world, it can only existentially modify its public self.[31] After the transformation to authenticity, 'the available "world" does not become another one "in terms of its content", nor does the circle of others [which *Dasein* finds itself with] get exchanged for a new one'.[32] The conversion to authenticity thus involves a transformation not in the *content* of what I do – hence it has nothing to do with any re-evaluation of particular or specific intraworldly entities – but rather in the *form* of my engagement with the world *as a whole*. 'Authenticity', at the existentiell level, ultimately means a kind of lucid, self-transparent affirmation of whatever it may be that one has already willed *qua* member of a particular public world, a particular 'culture' if you like.

This interpretation is also confirmed by Heidegger's later adding that the mood of *anxiety* is an essential characteristic of the *Augenblick* in which the call of conscience is heard and understood,[33] for anxiety is precisely the mood in which 'the world in which I exist has sunk into insignificance':[34] 'In anxiety the usable stuff in the environment, and in general all intraworldly entities go under. The "world" has nothing to offer any more … Everyday familiarity collapses. *Dasein* becomes individualized, but *as* being-in-the-world. Being-in acquires the mode of not-being-at-home.'[35]

Since the unsettling onset of anxiety is part of what is essentially involved in understanding the call of conscience which *is* the moment of transformation to authenticity, it follows that the authentic self is not only radically individualised, thrown back on to itself, but that – crucially – nothing *within* the world qua intraworldly entity, nothing available or occurrent, no other *Dasein*, can have any *intrinsic* significance for the authentic self. This is how Heidegger summarises the mode of being of the authentic self: 'This privileged authentic disclosedness … – the silent, anxiously ready self-projecting towards one's very own being guilty – is what we call *resoluteness*'.[36] Resoluteness would appear on the face of it (i.e. to the public self) a rather miserable condition, but far from it:

> Wanting-to-have-conscience, determined as being-towards-death … brings one without illusions into the resoluteness of 'action'. Anticipating resoluteness … originates in a sober understanding of the basic factical possibilities of a *Dasein*. The sober anxiety which brings us face-to-face with our individualized ability-to-be is accompanied by a joyful fortitude [*gerüstete Freude*] in relation to this possibility. In it *Dasein* becomes free of the 'accidents' of being entertained, which busy curiosity procures for itself primarily from worldly events.[37]

In this passage we find virtually all the key terms governing the existentialist writings of the modernist period from Ernst Jünger to Albert Camus. Much could be said about its rhetoric of illusionless, sober, lucid, virile toughness, but I shall forgo this temptation here. Rather, I wish to conclude by raising just one question about the Heideggerian moment and, in doing so, establish a link between it and what I earlier said about the quasi-Spinozist strand in Nietzsche's thought. The question is a familiar one: how does Heidegger's characterisation of the authenticity of the *Augenblick* on the one hand, and inauthentic lostness and dispersion on the other, relate to more familiar classifications of human comportment in terms of the ethical (in the broadest sense)? Or: what is the relation between what Heidegger calls 'authenticity' and what the tradition calls 'the good'? In one sense it is of course clear that Heidegger's analysis of the way of being of *Dasein*, the human being, cannot be a neutral one if he is to be consistent. Since *Dasein* is essentially and constitutively engaged in some project, its understanding of this project will determine how the world, or worldliness as such, are pre-ontologically disclosed, and this will in turn necessarily affect the second-order project of fundamental ontology. Hence it would be naïve to expect a 'neutral' presentation of the various possibilities – authentic and inauthentic – of being human.[38] In fact, within Heidegger's scheme, such 'neutrality', if it was a genuine refusal to choose between possibilities, would of course itself be a manifestation of 'irresoluteness', hence of inauthenticity. Thus the strongly pejorative, indeed often clearly contemptuous, vocabulary employed for characterising the inauthentic modifications of the various existential categories is not inconsistent with the project of a fundamental ontology which has as its prolegomenon the elucidation of the way of being of *Dasein*, that is, of the entity who has an understanding of being. (Although one should not ignore the fact that Heidegger, even in this context, usually cannot bring himself to bypass the opportunity of disingenuously protesting innocence:[39] 'The expression "chatter" [*Gerede* – and thus presumably also "scribbling": *Geschreibe*] is here not used in a derogatory sense.' In any case, the important point, it may be said, is that Heidegger's existential analytic of *Dasein* can still be understood, and in principle be understood as *adequate* or not, by a reader who does not share his existentiell commitments, although such a reader will probably take exception to much of Heidegger's vocabulary and indeed to the expository preference accorded to certain possibilities of existence, such as 'resoluteness' over others.

There is, however, another and more fundamental way of understanding our question. Is Heidegger's distinction between the authentic moment and inauthenticity 'neutral' in the sense of being compatible with different ethical contents – different specific understandings of 'good' and 'bad' – or is it rather in competition, and thus incompatible, with 'ethics' in a more traditional sense? Heidegger seems to claim the former, although not without some ambiguity:

> *Understanding the call* means: *wanting to have conscience … Wanting to have conscience is … the most primordial existentiell presupposition for the possibility of factically becoming guilty* [i.e. of what is usually meant by 'guilty'] … Only thus can [*Dasein*] *be* responsible … Thus wanting to have conscience becomes the taking over of the essential consciencelessness, within which alone there obtains the existentiell possibility of being 'good'.[40]

Heidegger seems to say that fundamental ethical concepts like 'responsibility', 'guilt' and, indeed, 'good', as applied to actions or character, only find proper application where the call has been understood. A residual ambiguity remains with respect to 'good', since the relative prepositional phrase 'within which' could in theory also refer, not to 'taking over', but to 'consciencelessness'. (The fact that Heidegger chose to retain this syntactic ambiguity in such a central passage is itself significant.) But the general point of the passage seems clear: understanding the call, which is the *augenblickliche* conversion to authenticity, is a *condition of possibility* for ethics, rather than itself implying a particular ethics at the existentiell level, or even foreclosing particular ethical possibilities.

But let us briefly look more closely at the crucial discussion of conscience, which occupies the whole of sections 54 to 59 of *Being and Time*. Especially in section 59, Heidegger criticises more familiar interpretations of conscience – what he predictably calls 'the vulgar interpretation of conscience' – as without exception originating in the inauthentic possibilities that constitute the public self. Any interpretation of conscience which relates conscience to particular intraworldly actions or specific types of actions which should or should not be done, any such 'vulgar' understanding originates in and expresses the inauthentic self. Heidegger mentions explicitly in this connection the imperativistic morality of duty of the Kantian tradition and also any ethics of value-contents, i.e. Aristotelian ethics and the neo-Aristotelian approaches of influential contemporaries of his, in particular Nicolai Hartmann and Max Scheler. In *all* these approaches and in the interpretations of conscience associated with them, '*Dasein* appears as an entity which is to be manipulated [*zu besorgen ist*], which manipulation has the sense of a "realization of value" or, respectively, the fulfilling of a norm.'[41] Within this horizon of experience 'conscience shows up as a judge or a warner with whom *Dasein* negotiates in a calculating way [*rechnend verhandelt*]. What are expected and demanded within this horizon are "univocal calculable maxims".'[42] 'The everyday interpretation remains within the dimension of a manipulating counting up and balancing of "guilt" and "innocence".'[43]

We cannot occupy ourselves here in detail with the question of the adequacy of Heidegger's description of the 'everyday interpretation' of conscience and its philosophical representatives. But it is clear that neither of them requires *essentially* an explicit weighing or balancing from the individual agent (e.g. a weighing of alternative courses of action, or of guilt and expected retribution or such like). Yet they do essentially involve the idea of determinable and practically highly significant *differences* among intraworldly entities and courses of action. Thus they also imply the *possibility* of a weighing or comparing goods, actions, etc., although this does not mean, as Heidegger strongly insinuates, that such differentiating must necessarily be a self-interested one ('negotiates in a calculating way'). In any case, it seems that any horizon of significance determined or constituted by the possibility of such differentiations is, for Heidegger, necessarily *uneigentlich*. Thus both the morality of law (Kant) and what might be called the ethics of *eros* – the love of particular intraworldly goods – are quite unmistakably assigned to the sphere of fallen inauthenticity, the covering-up absorption in the world of usable stuff (*Zeug*) and of being-with in the mode of the Public. It follows from this that it is by no means the case that the dichotomy between the moment of authenticity and its other does not prejudge existentiell ethical commitments. To the extent that authenticity *matters* – which it very clearly does in Heidegger's vision – it is not a condition of the possibility of ethics, but rather delineates an ethics of its own which is in competition with other understandings of ethics or of the moral.

If any further confirmation of this should be needed, let us recall that the *Stimmung* of anxiety is essential to the authentic moment, and in anxiety all intraworldly entities collapse into insignificance. Thus, an ethics of wordly goods, for instance, or of gradated, hierarchically structured value-contents is by virtue of this alone necessarily condemned to inauthenticity. Instead of any such ethics of gradations, the ethics of Heideggerian authenticity introduces a stark either/or. And this radical dichotomy has its origin in the call which, if it is hearkened to, thereby inaugurates an absolute discontinuity, the *Augenblick*, in which the world *as a whole* changes for *Dasein*, while nothing *within* the world has changed at all.

In this indifference to any mundane differences, this levelling of anything within the world, the ethics of authenticity recalls the *amor fati* of the quasi-Spinozist strand of Nietzsche's thinking. The 'tremendous moment' of *The Gay Science*, section 341, is also one of absolute polarisation and, simultaneously, of a levelling of differences among particulars. In both Nietzsche and Heidegger there is thus a concomitance, which it is difficult to interpret as fortuitous, between an emphatic concern with the moment of rupture on the one hand and the de-particularising stark polarity of affirmation, either total or 'resolute', versus desperate dispersion on the other.

Notes

1 NHC XII 1, 1–16 (my translation and emphasis). Cited in M. Pauen, *Dithyrambiker des Untergangs: Gnostizismus in Ästhetik und Philosophie der Moderne*, Berlin: Akademie Verlag, 1994, pp.39–40.

2 K. Löwith, *Nietzsches Philosophie der ewigen Wiederkehr des Gleichen*, Stuttgart: Kohlhammer, 1956.

3 F. Nietzsche, *The Will to Power*, ed. W. Kaufmann and trans. W. Kaufmann and R. J. Hollingdale, New York: Vintage Books, 1968, fragment 55, p.36.

4 Nietzsche, *Will*, fragment 1066, p.549.

5 The influential interpretation of the eternal recurrence by Gilles Deleuze is therefore incompatible with the explicit wording of Nietzsche's own statement of it. See Gilles Deleuze, *Nietzsche and Philosophy*, London: Athlone Press, 1983.

6 G. Simmel, 'Schopenhauer und Nietzsche', in *Gesamtausgabe*, ed O. Rammstedt, X, ed. M. Behr, V. Krech and G. Schmidt, Frankfurt/M.: Suhrkamp, 1995 [1907], pp.167–408.

7 F. Nietzsche, *The Gay Science* (trans. W. Kaufmann), New York: Vintage Books, 1974, section 341.

8 B. Magnus, *Nietzsche's Existential Imperative*, Bloomington: University of Indiana Press, 1978.

9 Cf. I. Soll, 'Reflections on Recurrence', in R. Solomon (ed.), *Nietzsche: A Collection of Critical Essays*, New York: Anchor Books, 1973, pp.322–42.

10 Nietzsche, *Will*, fragment 1057, p.544; Nietzsche's emphasis.

11 Nietzsche, *Gay Science*, section 341.

12 Nietzsche, *Will*, fragment 55, p.36.

13 F. Nietzsche, *Ecce Homo*, 'Why I am so clever', section 10, in *Basic Writings of Nietzsche*, ed. and trans. W. Kaufmann, New York: Vintage Books, 1968.

14 Cited in the editor's introduction to E. Husserl, *Zur Phänomenologie des inneren Zeitbewußtseins*, ed. R. Boehm, The Hague: Martinus Nijhoff, 1966, p.xxi. This and all subsequent translations from this text are mine.

15 Husserl, *Zur Phänomenologie*, p.xxvii.

16 Husserl, *Zur Phänomenologie*, p.xxv.

17 Husserl, *Zur Phänomenologie*, pp.33, 117.

18 Nietzsche, *Will*, fragment 1066, p.549.

19 Husserl, *Zur Phänomenologie*, p.74.

20 Husserl, *Zur Phänomenologie*, p.75.

21 'Zukunft, Gewesenheit, Gegenwart zeigen die phänomenalen Charktere des "Auf-sich-zu", des "Zurück auf", des "Begegnenlassens von". Die Phänomene des zu ... auf ... bei ... offenbaren die Zeitlichkeit als das εκστατικον schlechthin. *Zeitlichkeit ist das ursprüngliche "Außer-sich" an und für sich selbst* ... Das Charakteristische der dem vulgären Verständnis zugänglichen "Zeit" besteht u.a. gerade darin, daß in ihr als einer puren, anfangs- und endlosen Jetzt-folge der ekstatische Charakter der ursprünglichen Zeitlichkeit nivelliert ist.' (Martin Heidegger, *Sein und Zeit*, Tübingen: Max Niemeyer, 1986[16], pp. 328–29). All subsequent page references are to this standard German edition. Translations are my own. The page numbers of the German edition are also given on the margins of the standard English edition: *Being and Time*, trans. J. Macquarrie and E. Robinson, Oxford: Blackwell, 1995.

22 'Die ... *eigentliche* Gegenwart nennen wir den Augenblick ... Im Unterschied vom Augenblick als eigentlicher Gegenwart nennen wir die uneigentliche das *Gegenwärtigen*. Formal verstanden ist jede Gegenwart gegenwärtigend, aber nicht jede "augenblicklich".' (Heidegger, *Sein und Zeit*, p.338).

23 Heidegger, *Sein und Zeit*, p.271.

24 Heidegger, *Sein und Zeit*, p.274.

25 Heidegger, *Sein und Zeit*, p.275.

26 I shall from here on translate *das Man* simply as 'the Public', and *man-selbst* as 'the public self'. While this translation erases some of the oddity of Heidegger's neologism, it does not distort his fundamental point and, indeed, makes it clearer.

27 Heidegger, *Sein und Zeit*, p.268.

28 Heidegger, *Sein und Zeit*, p.285.

29 Heidegger, *Sein und Zeit*, p.287.

30 Heidegger, *Sein und Zeit*, p.268.

31 Heidegger, *Sein und Zeit*, p.267.

32 Heidegger, *Sein und Zeit*, pp.297–98.

33 Heidegger, *Sein und Zeit*, pp.296, 344. 'Which mood corresponds to such understanding? Understanding the call discloses one's own being-there in the unsettledness of its individuation. The unsettledness co-revealed in this understanding is genuinely disclosed in the affective condition [*Befindlichkeit*] of anxiety which belongs to it' (Heidegger, *Sein und Zeit*, pp.295–96).

34 Heidegger, *Sein und Zeit*, p.343.

35 Heidegger, *Sein und Zeit*, pp.188–89.

36 Heidegger, *Sein und Zeit*, pp.296–97.

37 Heidegger, *Sein und Zeit*, p.310.

38 In one passage Heidegger makes this entirely explicit: 'But is there not a particular ontic conception of authentic existence, a factical ideal of *Dasein*, lying at the basis of the

ontological interpretation of existence developed here? This is indeed so. This fact must not only not be denied, or only admitted under duress, it must be comprehended in its *positive necessity* from the point of view of the thematic object of the investigation' (p.310).

39 Heidegger, *Sein und Zeit*, p.167.
40 Heidegger, *Sein und Zeit*, p.288.
41 Heidegger, *Sein und Zeit*, p.293.
42 Heidegger, *Sein und Zeit*, p.294.
43 Heidegger, *Sein und Zeit*, p.292.

CHAPTER 4

Augen-Blicke

HEIDRUN FRIESE

Und plötzlich in diesem mühsamen Nirgends, plötzlich
die unsägliche Stelle, wo sich das reine Zuwenig
unbegreiflich verwandelt –, umspringt
in jenes leere Zuviel.
Wo die vielstellige Rechnung
zahlenlos aufgeht.

Rainer Maria Rilke[1]

What an astounding gesture – someone calls my name and I turn my head.

This is a moment of an abrupt invocation to which I immediately respond; I respond without hesitation. I respond without will; I respond without having reflected about responding. I respond to the occurrence of a glance and a call – two moments maybe, which arise in one moment, are assembled to arise in the present. They are presenced as in a single stroke, in a single breath, in the same Now. I am exposed to this occurrence which takes me by chance. This call is the irruption of an act outside of prediction, suddenly I am addressed, unexpectedly, *extempore* – out of the time, at the moment, without premeditation or preparation; at first sight – and I respond without intention. I have to respond. It responds.

I cannot escape it. I cannot escape a response.

Is this, my responding, a response to a name – but why should I respond to a name? – or a response to an invocation, a call, a demand which calls me – and precisely me – to respond – or even to the responsibility of a response?

This moment, a sudden stroke that cannot be derived from any foresight, this incalculable call interrupts my time and turns it around; I am given to this moment of being-turned-towards, I am submitted to this moment. This sudden uniqueness occurs now. And nothing could be more momentous than this encounter – an encounter that occurs now and is at the same time always about to occur. This response is always already marked by a presence of time, as time will have been marked by the *Augen-Blick*, by the glance of the eye.[2]

The moment, in its sudden arrival, portrays itself as the open possibility of an *Augenblick*, and it is – to become an *Augenblick* and to become datable – dependent on a reply. The moment does not happen as an *Augenblick*, it turns into (the *maybe* of) an *Augenblick* not simply because it appears in its sudden givenness, but also because it is to occur in the in-between of a call and reply. The reply is thus neither the repetition of the possible nor a return of that which is past, it provides no link of the present to the past. Rather, the response responds to the possibility of a moment. The *Augenblick* depends on, it demands this undecided and never-decidable decision, this response. The moment, to become an *Augenblick*, needs to be replied to; for it to occur, it requires this in-between of its possibility and a response to this possibility. And the answer is only made possible by the possibility of an *Augenblick* – that which brings something forth, is at the same time brought forth by its own creation. An *Augenblick* would remain a mere moment, if the possibility provided by the moment – as the possibility of an *Augenblick* – were not responded to.

This *Augenblick* breaks the mere succession of 'no longer' and 'not yet'; it interrupts continuity. It does not come forth as a joint of time, of chronological linearity and eternal duration, that bad infinity, in which one instance persistently follows another, in which single moments emerge just to be swallowed by other moments and are to disappear again (*chronos*). Instead it comes forth in its possibility and in the response – brought forth by this possibility – and only then unfolds as an *Augenblick*.

In this disruptive force, it presents itself as an intensity. An intense presence that does not just occur in, and out of the joint of, time, but a presence as the opening of the moment to the occurrence of time and of the *Augenblick*. Not a moment of timeless eternity, stagnation, standing still, or a present that drags itself towards the future, but an *Augenblick* that becomes temporalised by its possibility. An *Augenblick*, in and for which time does not remain the same and which is not left indifferent by time – a moment marked by the presence of time, by time's presentation, and time affected by this unique occurrence. An *Augenblick* as presence of time and simultaneously as the other of time.

This unique *Augenblick*, which resists any repetition or iteration, is not writeable, it lacks words; the *Augenblick* is not describable, but language nevertheless comes forth in this relation, in and through the encounter, in the answer. And what else is writing if not an answer by words to words, the counter-words, the answer by writing to that which is written?

Eyes, glance, the glance of the eye, *Augenblick* – this compound word relates to various and complex moments, which I want to address in the following from three different angles: the moment of the response; the event of seeing (*Ereignis/ Eräugnis*); and the held moment. These are to be considered instances, interventions of the glance, in which interruption and the caring turn towards one another (*Zu-Wendung*), in which the glance given and the response intersect with the unique event and thus turn the moment into an *Augenblick*.

Augen-Blicke: The Response

I have been seen, at first sight, a name is being called. 'He recognised me': is this everyday turn of expression, which refers to that inconspicuous scene, the reassuring repatriation of the unknown into the realm of the known? Such a move would then not only determine the familiar routine of everyday life, but also the concept of cognition. Thus, one would always already have failed to recognise that that which is close is most alien and farthest away.[3] A glance touches, a name is being called (have I been recognised?). My body is in the reach of a glance, exposed, and I respond to this touch by the glance and the call of the name in one and the same breath. Neither observed nor watched, I have suddenly been seen, all of a sudden I am looked at, and I grasp this being looked-at and respond within a blink of an eye (*augenblicklich*) to this entirely unexpected being-called, to this call, and I turn my sight.[4] I come into being in this interwovenness, in the countless interfaces and margins of seeing, in this space of seeing. The glance towards one another (*hergewandt*), from the other to me (*hingewandt*), from me to the other, the glance turned towards (*zugewandt*) refers to a distance and at the same time to a closeness, which itself only emerges from this distance. The turning eyes thus entail not only a temporal, but also a spatial, relation, since I am positioned by the glance and the call. However, in the in-between of that which positions and that which is positioned, as the response to the response, an always vague and uncertain possibility opens. A possibility that opens the moment as the *Augenblick*. A possibility that demands the labour of its unfolding, a work that comes to be the signature of the unique *Augenblick*.

Martin Buber regards a similar scene – glances that meet in the crowd of the metropolis, a crucial scene for modern life also described by Charles Baudelaire, Edgar Allan Poe, Alfred Döblin, Franz Hessel among others – as the moment of a revelation, in which human dialogue beyond the communicated, or even beyond any communicable, contents, occurs factually and becomes evident. And he does not think of 'the erotic' as the allegedly pure 'compression and unfolding of dialogue', but rather 'as an inconspicuous, but significant nook of being ... as the glances that fly up in the bustle of the street between strangers, who pass each other without altering their step; among those glances, there are some that, swinging fatelessly, reveal two dialogical beings to one another.'[5] Steps and glances pass by, fly up in the bustle of the crowd, encounter one another, and fly away again. But it is not the singular human being who shows and reveals himself to another one; the glances that encounter one another in passing do not disclose lives and destinies that were unknown to, and unrecognised by, one another. Rather, the strangers leave each other at their unexplored distance. Two destinies touch each other lightly for a moment and then separate again; those who encounter one another quite fleetingly in these glances nevertheless enter into a proximity that is common to them and in which they reveal to one another, in the fleeting glances of their eyes, a particular relation, namely their dialogical being.

For Buber (unlike Kierkegaard: 'the lightest touch, a glance in passing etc suffices for that ... The revealing can occur in words ... it can occur in expressions, in glances; since there is a glancing of the eye, with which a human being reveals involuntarily what he conceals')[6] this *Augen-Blick* does not break a secret, something concealed that breaks forth from inside a human being. This *Augen-Blick* is not a revealing declaration, no deposition, no confession.

Dialogue relates addressing, attending and demanding and decisively calls for the entering into the specific, always unknown situation, into the entirely unknown of a not-yet, an always particular constellation, which cannot be assimilated by, or into, a (formal) generality. Every specific, thus always unique, indivisible, inseparable, not derivable situation, which is assigned to the human being and handed over in every moment, demands attending; as an address, therefore, it is at the same time insistence, demand and response. As Buber notes:

> Only thus, faithful to the moment, do we experience a life that is something other than a sum of moments. To the moment we respond, but we respond at the same time for it, we assume responsibility for it. A newly created concreteness of the world [*neuerschaffenes Weltkonkretum*] has been laid into our hands; we assume responsibility for it.[7]

Responsibility expects responding, responding to given situations, in which the individual exposes himself, enters into the situation, dares, offers and stands for himself. The *Augenblick* that leaps out of the steady series of insignificant moments and founds the concreteness of life, comes forth in, and through, the response. And it denotes responsibility not merely as the capability to respond, but also as an demand, an obligation. Who bears responsibility becomes, so to say, an author; an author, who responds to others, who commits himself to become an author in the face of a situation, of the given situation, for which we bear responsibility, which made us oblige and which constitutes existence. 'The internal dynamics of *Verantwortung* (responsibility; capacity to give a response) necessarily refers to the one of *vocatio*. It is not possible to be responsible without being called.'[8] Responsibility requires the response to a call, to an address that presents itself simultaneously as a demand and as a exigency. The moment turns into an *Augenblick* only in this – productive – entanglement of the glance that is offered and the glance that is returned.

Franz Hessel, who strolls the streets of the metropolis and its inglorious and inconspicuous corners without a compass, also knows this returned glance, the reply to the glance. 'We only see what looks at us.'[9] Seeing succeeds only as a response to being-looked-at; attending succeeds only in this returned glance of open eyes.[10] If everything fleetingly given is always already remembrance,[11] such attention also opens up towards the incalculable and, thus, to time.

'Not that I saw him, but that he looked at me was what made me tremble' – the glance that sometimes breaks forth from among human faces can hit in an unexpected and sudden way – 'rarely, always unthought of, never to be sworn to'.[12] For the one who is being looked at by this unhoped-for glance, pauses, tarries, reads and responds to it, the glance of the other will turn into an *Augenblick*, into the divine glance of the other that changes everything and alters time for ever; a glance that conceives of 'that moment as an epoch' and that changes the glance of the other into that rare occurrence of an accomplished, fulfilled moment;[13] and maybe this *Augenblick* entails also a quite extra-ordinary clarity of silence, an interruption, which gives rhythm to the lingering of the glances. As a rare and imperishable event, this glance pertains to singular human beings – but as a space of the interim, as an interstice, it also belongs to the city and the inconspicuous things and situations housed by it.

Interstices, transitions, which separate 'situations, hours, minutes and words'[14] – these are not merely the fugitive '*architectures of the moment*', billboards, neon lights, imperfect edifices that are ageing in the presence of the observer and turn into ruins, temporary buildings like demolition fences, wooden sheds or the untidy transitional spaces of the city. Things in decay, dusk, interstice and passage; that is also the reading of the city itself. This reading is a passage, though, for which the present hardly is a steady transformation of the past into the future, but one for which, like a short-circuit, that which is experienced connects to that which is to come and turns into an abrupt change. And, for the one who reads the street like a book and leafs in a self-forgetful mood through alien destinies, who reads the dissimultaneous and anachronistic layers of the city and its inhabitants, the city turns into a reverie. This unconscious, ungrounded, undiscriminating seeing, which stands face to face with the things and gives the onlooker the time to respond to their glance while leaving them in their state of difference, rejects any hierarchisation of things and discovers true history in the inconspicuous, in that which is left over by alleged progress, that which Ernst Bloch names *Ungleich-zeitigkeiten*, dissimultaneous times, and which Walter Benjamin will call the 'rags' of history. Such seeing does not require the calculated intervention of the eye, which keeps the fragile balance between 'too early' and 'too late'. Rather, it demands a glance that arises from the eyes. Such a glance refuses to participate in modern speed, in the quick event; it practises purposeless seeing, which, practised for its own sake, resembles the abundance and high spirits of poetics (*dichtender Übermut*, Goethe) and permits the moment of seeing to emerge. In this moment, which explodes chronological time, the moment of authentic seeing and the authentic present, in this still image, the 'monumental still life' of the inconspicuous, never separated from its frailty, the reality and the truth of the things, and of the human beings, is closer than in the judging, hierarchising, evaluating gaze of historians and philosophers of history.[15] Further, this glance does not transcend its own uncertainty and does not present itself as positive and definitive knowledge, but rather as an uncertainty saved from the onslaught of a seizing curiosity and its concepts, a lonely glance, thus, which never knows definitively, but always learns, a glance that alters things and necessarily remains incomplete and open. This is a seeing that neither sifts and sorts nor discloses and noisily announces things that step out of concealment, but one that answers the glance of the things.

To the one who is being looked at by the things and responds to their glance, things let their 'older times shimmer through the layer of the present'.[16] Once released from the indifference of the fleeting glance, the times assemble in this moment, that which is vanishing gets linked to the present, that which is past looks into the present, it gains duration and reality, and that which has been emerges to experience. True experience relies on the seeing of such shimmering of the times, which permits the remembrance of things once lived, of things once read. Such a glance demands not to fix things by secure concepts in one's judgement or in the law of firm convictions, but to speak to them, like a magician speaks to an ill person by incantation.[17] Hessel's images of remembrance, in which vanishing things, human destinies and his own life are preserved as in a *rêverie* and in which the glances of the things and of the human beings tell the one who sees who he is, are unexpected memories of *mémoire involontaire*, arising unexpectedly from an 'unapproachable layer in an area of the memory'.[18] They are stored in the archive of the script and enable a dialogue with those who are no longer, a dialogue in which reading becomes a dialogue with the script and in which the reader is read by the script.

The attention to the word, the script, the glance for that which they will en-counter, such dialogical seeing, the 'great-enduring glance of the eyes' (*großaus-haltenden Blick der Augen*),[19] the work of the held glance in the face of the other is not only linked to the remembrance of that which has long been, the inconspicu-ous nooks of life and the ruins of the city; it does not merely open towards time and experience; it also unfolds, through this interweaving, a particular relation between closeness and distance.

In his appraisal of the aura, in a silent dialogue with Franz Hessel, Walter Benjamin will point to this glance that gives itself, responds and opens the eyes, a glance that opens towards somebody other in its gift.

> The glance is inhabited by the expectation of being *responded to* by the one to whom it gives itself. Where such experience is reciprocated, ... the experience of the aura then falls to it in all its abundance. 'Perceptibility', Novalis argues, is 'giving attention'. The perceptibility of which he thus speaks is no other than the one of the aura ... The one who is looked at or believes himself to be looked at opens up the glance. To experience the aura of an appearance, means to en-dow it with the faculty to open up the glance.[20]

Glance and reply, expectation and experience, answer and response, face and reci-procity – again an ethical relation – are entangled with one another in this net of connections (in thinking, too, expectation goes towards, is indebted to, the – intentional – glance of attention). To expect, this is the insistent demand for a symmetric gesture and the hope that it will be redeemed. Gift and return, an al-ways singular equation of glances that give themselves to one another simultane-ously, present themselves in their reciprocity and allow the aura to be experienced.

Such glance, however, dissociates itself from a mere immediate closeness. The 'glance burdened with remoteness' has no means to shorten the distance, since the glance, opened up and lost, with which the poet endows the appearances and the human beings, draws him into the remote – 'the glance of the thus awakened nature dreams and draws the poet to follow his dream'.[21]

The *Augen-Blick*, and its happiness, resides in the relation between being-seen and seeing, between gift and the (expectation of a) return; and that is precisely why 'describing', as Benjamin says, is 'sensual pleasure, because in describing the object *returns* the glance of the onlooker, and the pleasure with which two glances that look for one another encounter each other, is captured in every good descrip-tion'.[22] But these reciprocated glances never fully merge into one another; the glance is also, as Benjamin notes elsewhere, 'the incline of the human being' (*die Neige des Menschen*).[23] *Neige*, in its multiple connotations, refers to something that inclines, is inclined towards somebody, thus giving liking attention to somebody, and reciprocates his glance. But in every glance there is a remainder (*Neige*), something left over, not fully exhausted, indeed inexhaustable, not at one's disposal, an unreachable remoteness. In the glance remains that which points to the rest as decay, as finitude, as the withering away and dilapidation, but which nevertheless, like the aura, never disappears entirely.[24] The inclined glance is then as much the one that responds to the other as the one that points to finitude but, despite that, remains – as the remainder. The glance demonstrates such transitoriness, finitude and at the same time that which, in this remainder, always stays and stays as something unavailable – because it has altered the time by turning, inclining towards somebody else. Such glances cannot be repeated, they are unique.

Augen-Blicke: *Das Eräugnis*

The glance of the eye expects to be responded to, it expects a response and the never-certain redemption of the *Augenblick*, which always ever unfolds only in its uniqueness. But when the eyes turn, does the glance not also respond to a – long past – encounter, to an irreducibly unique, sole moment, a moment that has come to be an event, a datum and thus a mark? Is the returned glance (*Wieder-Blick*) not always also a response to the unique datum of an event, of a moment? Does the returned glance not always also remind of another one, a long lost one, which it repeats, or rather aims to repeat? Can single, unique events enter into alliances with one another, move close to each other to thus mutually eradicate their singularity?

The *Augenblick*, even though it may be expected or, in contrast, feared, can neither be derived from experience nor predicted; it is unique and stubbornly resists every predictive forecasting. And it is only because of this that the encounter can come to be a sudden intervention, an event: 'thus, one can hold the one who towards all events [*Eräugnisse*] [of happiness] has hardened, for well happier than the one whose joy for life has languished because of gloomy outlooks',[25] as Kant writes in the context of expectation and forecast, using words that address highly various modes of knowledge and vision, brought together in the one word *Eräugnis* linking event (*Ereignis*) to the glance of the eye (*Auge*). An accomplished happy life, it appears, demands indifference against that which can happen suddenly and points to fate as the insight that becomes unavoidable. It rejects a prophetic-foreboding seeing that rememberingly looks backward to look forward (*vorhersehen* and *voraussehen*) and with this outlook holds life in check, a seeing that aims at taking that which is to come into the custody of the look-out and at arming itself against a not-yet of unforeseeable facts. The *Eräugnis* is posited against such foreseeing sight, such outlook as that which comes into sight quite suddenly, unpredictedly and unpredictably and has to be taken into view and be glanced and borne by the glance of the eye.

'The word *Ereignis* [event] is taken from living language. *Er-eignen* [to occur, to happen] means originally: *er-äugen*, that is, to view, to call towards oneself by viewing',[26] as Heidegger remarks, pointing to the untranslatability of this word as well, since 'that which it names, occurs [*ereignet*] only in the singular, no, not even in any number at all, but uniquely'.[27] The event of a glance brings beings into their own, into what is appropriate to them. As event it defies any amenability to chronological planning and the familiar measure of time. An event is that which, being called towards itself by glances, presents itself only once; it is that which is taken out of reckoning and calculation and decisively defies any number and any counting. The event occurs singly and alone. The event that bears this word cannot be doubled, reproduced or infinitely multiplied without being – peculiar correspondence to the aura and its decay in the course of (technical) reproduction – doomed to decay. As event, *Ereignis* and *Eräugnis*, it presents itself ever only once and yet subsists only through the response, the reply of the glance to its unique occurrence. The event here crosses views with the appropriating occurrence of presencing. And yet it also points to the untranslatability of that which is named, an impossibility that resides in the uniqueness of the event. Its translation can succeed only in the sudden leap, and that is in the leap of 'a single glance', in the leap of the glance (*Blick-Sprung*) of thought. Thinking, therefore, is renewed as the response to the momentary relation, to the momentary response to the unique event. It is not necessary to share the further linkage of the event to being in Heidegger to follow the connections of event and glance, of the *Eräugnis* in its uniqueness. The event, namely, is joined together in the encounter of sudden occurrence and reply, concentrated in a single site; such moment enters once and only once into its particular constellation and bundles its manifoldness.

In its singularity – and in the sudden break with the course of time and the steady repetition of its ever-same moments, the *Augenblick* always only leads towards itself; the event in its singularity can hardly stand for anything else, by exchange of words, and be thus represented. In such concentration of meanings and in its irreplaceable uniqueness, it is the event itself of the *Augenblick* that only permits its dating. As a datum, that is, as that which denotes itself as unique, as singular, the unrepeatable event eludes any return, and, if the word is to be taken seriously, it also defies any simple recourse or return to any other datum.

The event comes into being, as the *Augenblick*, in its unspeakability, in its namelessness – such is grounded its ungraspability – and depends nevertheless on language (and images). That which language calls 'event' and refers to in its singularity, shares thus the fate of all appearances that are named by means of words and concepts, since

> every word turns immediately into a concept by virtue of the fact that it is not to serve – as, for instance, a remembrance – for the unique and entirely individualized original experience to which it owes its emergence, but has to suit countless, more or less similar, that is, strictly speaking, downright dissimilar cases. Every concept emerges by setting equal that which is unequal.[28]

A concept obviously performs different operations: to become at all sayable, it not only includes the unique into a generality, but it thus also gathers different and paradoxical times. It marks a unique *Augenblick*, but simultaneously also the repetition. To remain readable, namely, the concept needs to wipe out the *Augenblick* and the datum, the noteworthy mark (*Merkmal*) of its irreducible uniqueness, needs to reconcile them with permanence and let singularity inevitably disappear in the continuity. To be able to persist, the concept, like the datum, needs to permanently eradicate any remembrance but yet repeat it; it needs to consign the event of the one and single time to oblivion and yet to recall it.[29] Just as the word is always already marked by that single time, the unrepeatable event is annihilated by the always already used-up word 'event'. Tied into the aporia of the datum and the concept, the event has been betrayed of its singularity.

The *Augenblick* as a unique event, like the word and like historical meaning, is locked into a particular relation in which 'remembrance' and forgetting mix. Being unique, it gives itself both as remembrance and as farewell, as that final farewell that refutes the normalisation of uniqueness.[30] But just as language only comes to be through the encounter with language, as the response to language, just as dialogue only comes to be in the encounter, in the rejoinder, into which forgetting is always also imprinted, precisely to give testimony to uniqueness, in the same way the event of the *Augenblick* demands something. It demands the labour of the glance, and it expects, no, it insists on a response, a response that responds specifically to the uniqueness. An event, to become event, does not only need to occur, it needs also, and precisely, to be held, to be kept. Such holding, keeping, through which the *Augenblick* can maintain itself, however, does not mean either remembrance or memory, either recollection or ritualistic repetition – a repetition that can never succeed – or even the representation of an irretrievably lost *Augenblick*. Rather, it demands a holding that responds to the singularity of the *Augenblick*. This is neither annihilation, nor repression, nor a shoving aside of that which is past in the attempt at its repetition; rather, it is the safeguarding of its uniqueness and of that which once occurred and will never occur again. Such insistence of the glance is possibly the nameless and unique happiness of the *Augenblick*.

Augen-Blicke: The Moment Held

A glance – from its very beginning it implicates somebody else and that which cannot be seen. 'The essential always happens suddenly. Lightning truly means in our language: glance. But the sudden, be it good or evil, requires a long time to be delivered', as Martin Heidegger writes to Hannah Arendt, a writing that does not make the glance and the *Augenblick* unreadable, but in contrast allows for its presence in writing – and a writing also, in which an *Augenblick* does not mean *the Augenblick* but the glance of *your* eyes, your singular glance, a singularity which turns the glance of eyes into an *Augenblick*.[31] With this letter, the glance returns after a twenty-year interruption, and with this 'returning glance',[32] a *Wieder-Blick*, a seeing-again, the correspondence starts anew, an exchange of letters in which glances are exchanged and in which writing, as the rhythm of the letters, becomes a held *Augenblick*. These are letters, like *Augen-Blicke*, which sustain themselves across the interruptions and at their long distance – an exchange of letters as response to the glance. Answer and the answering of letters – letters that persistently answer to the *Augenblick*. Letters whose rejoinders assume responsibility for the *Augenblick* and into which the *Augenblick* has been inscribed. A correspondence that does not remember a unique *Augenblick*, but delivers it, in which the unique glance does not simply last on, but is to be maintained in the *Augen-Blick* and to be 'saved' in a specific way.

What, then, are these lines to convey, lines in which time and moment, the conceptual pairs 'glance and lightning' and 'the essential and the sudden' are linked to one another in the *Augenblick*? Essential, that is to say that nothing other appears in its occurrence that lies outside of that which occurs. That is the essential, not as a supplement or as something that refers to something else. The essential *is* not, but it *occurs*, and it occurs immediately, without transition, unhoped-for, unexpectedly and uniquely. As the essential, it 'always' occurs in this very instance, 'always' at this one time. Just like glance and lightning 'truly' and without any dislocation stand together, so does the essential occur as the sudden. Thus, the sudden is not a *form* of appearance of the essential, not a temporal predicate, a temporal mode, in which something other than the sudden occurs, but the occurrence of the sudden itself. Nothing happens 'in' the sudden moment, since as the authentic present it only lets *encounter* that which can be in time.[33] Should one then say that the sudden is at first ethically indifferent, that the *Augenblick* is blind and requires a 'long time', before (when?) revealing the 'good' or the 'evil'? (Then, however, the event of the essential would be equally the origin of good and of evil, and as such it would – mediated by the 'temporal' mode of its appearance – carry in, or with, itself something other than the sudden. The sudden, though, is characterised as the immediate, as that which enables an encounter with the good or the evil to happen.) And how is the essential linked to time, even to the long time, which 'delivers' the good or the evil?

Such sudden event can hardly refer to a moment in the present, locked in between the past and the future. Instead, the essential occurs suddenly, precisely as this unexpected, unique There of the sudden. This moment is that which breaks the synchronism of time. With this *Augenblick*, though, it announces itself as already something different, since this *Augenblick* demands to be 'delivered'. Delivering is different from mere becoming or having effects, no irrefutable causality, no continuous, automatic process, delivery demands something. Delivering, that means also: to let something take place, to bring something to decision.

The sudden event does not simply come to be because it just happened, but it demands its holding, it needs to be long delivered, and can only thus be arriving. The essential does not unfold as causality, in its mere effects, not in the pure duration of time, or in a supplementary posterity (*Nachträglichkeit*), but it depends on something. The essential, which occurs suddenly – and the possibility of dating the *Augenblick* is grounded in such Now of significance – can unfold only if its possibility is *replied* to. Such response, which assumes responsibility for the delivery of the event, is thus neither a repetition of the unique *Augenblick* nor its return nor its duration, neither recovery of that which has been nor mere endurance, neither its realisation nor its effect. And, anew, lines in which philosophy tries to write poetry – 'in the sudden, the rare, being flashes for us' (*in Jähen, raren, blitzt uns Seyn*), and Hannah Arendt rewrites the lines that were thought and destined for her and restores them to philosophy:

> 'the truth' can be 'rare', 'sudden', like a 'lightning'. Here is the authentic connection between Nietzsche and Heidegger. If life is being, 'that which is most alive' is the 'most being' [*das Seiendste*]. If 'the living is merely a very rare species of the dead' [Nietzsche], then that which is most rare is most alive and the most being.[34]

Such 'There' of the *Augenblick*, which does not exclude anything, occurs in the sudden strike; it cannot be derived from either retention or protention. The sudden is unique, it breaks duration, tears apart the succession of the moments. The sudden is that which arrives unthought of. And thus lightning is linked to fear, to horror, to the gruesome. The sudden is not neutral – Heidegger to Arendt: 'The demonic has hit me ... Never before has anything similar happened to me.'[35]

Kierkegaard already, as is well known, had linked the sudden to fear and to the demonic (as the fear of the good). 'The demonic is the sudden. The sudden is the expression for that which is locked and closed' – the good, in contrast, is the revealing and coming into the open, a first expression of liberation.[36] Both poles are determined by their temporality, since communication, the imparting, is expression of the connection, that is, of duration, the negation of which is the sudden.[37] 'At one moment it is there, at the next one, it is gone ... It cannot be formed into any connection';[38] it is the 'complete abstraction from that which precedes and that which follows.'[39] What is decisive here is the lack of any connection between the sudden and mere duration. And: the demonic is the sudden in directed movement, in movement towards oneself, the diminution of distance. Kierkegaard wanted to consider such incalculable suddenness (of the demonic) only mimetically represented: as the silent *leap* namely.[40] Despite all divergence, Heidegger, too, determines the unexpected, unforeseen approach of the threatening as that which is decisive in fear. And precisely such possible strike of danger, 'sudden in each moment', creates the horrendous crescendo, since the sudden, in its encounter with it, turns the threat into *fright*, the sudden makes the unfamiliar threat a *horror*, the sudden increases the horror to turn it into *terror*.[41]

The sudden oversees truth and horror. 'The beautiful is the beginning of the horrible', Heidegger writes, quoting Rilke, and recalls Hölderlin, 'that the beautiful has the faculty of uniting towards warmth those who are utterly opposed to each other', and then continues, 'who else reaches into the depth of the beautiful other than lovers'.[42] The simultaneity of closeness and distance, the unexpected 'return' of the unique *Augen-Blick*, of the glance turned towards him, even of the 'same glance' that flashed towards him once, 'at the rostrum',[43] that glance that 'looks right into the middle of the heart', this 'gift' upsets thinking, it 'always again confounds' thinking. This event is fathomless, and, curiously, here appears what the thinking of the *Augenblick* banned and completely erased without any trace from *Sein und Zeit* – where it was cast merely with regard to the situation of action and to fear: the beautiful, and love. While there it was fear which releases the moment, here it is love that opens the *Augenblick*.[44]

The scenarios of the sudden let truth, the essential, being, horror appear. This event is not neutral. 'Closeness here is being at the greatest distance from the other – distance that lets nothing blur – but that places the "Thou" into the transparent – but ungraspable – only-there of a revelation. That the presence of an other may break into our life is something that no soul [*Gemüt*] can master',[45] as Martin Heidegger writes to Hannah Arendt. The other becomes revealed in this event, and what appears is *her* presence. This presence, at the same time the 'greatest distance', lets the other become clearly visible, a distant closeness, a present otherness, and the otherness of the present that can hardly be reconciled or tamed.

That which has been, the peculiar 'secret around time', which changes everything and gives everything anew,[46] is not remembered, the *Augenblick* not preserved in memory to reappear as a remembrance. 'The time seems long ago since the attempt at interpreting Plato's Sophist. But yet, I often feel as if everything past assembles on one single moment that shields, rescues, recovers and contains [*bergen*] that which remains.' And Hannah Arendt rewrites and responds, in a more than ambivalent way: 'My thoughts, too, were often in the lectures on the Sophist. That which remains, it seems to me, is where one can say – "Beginning and end are always ever the same".'[47] Where, namely – in contrast to the long stretching of time – that which has been once assembles *on* one single, unique *Augenblick*, where the *Augenblick* collects that which has been and shields it, thus preserves and rescues it, there beginning and end have been set equal, have been turned into one, and have been subjected to the infinite course of time as an unalterable unit.

> The unfathomable meaning of *heoraken hora*, of the held glance; all miracles of language, which is thinking more than we are; the French *regarder*. 'To rescue' does not merely mean to just tear away from a danger, but rather, from the start, to liberate it into essence (*freimachen ins Wesen*). Such *infinite intention* is the finitude of man.[48]

Such an *Augenblick* alters the glance of the eye. Time will be marked by this *Augenblick* of the responded glance, which transforms time. The holding of the glance, that is the held *Augenblick*, the glance that is returned, is given back, the response, the responsibility of the glance. To guard, to hold, is an act, a discontinuous positioning, a positioning of the site of that which never stays the same, but which always already changes in this very act and becomes another one. Not its repetition, its representation, its after-effects or its return, but its insistent holding in the response. This held glance is an infinite task, which gives testimony to finitude and considers its possible failing – as a held glance the returned glance is always also a glance that objects.[49] And the accomplished, happy *Augenblicke*, in which the multiple-digit equation is solved without using numbers, these *Augenblicke* are always rare, since these are two glances, 'and only two, because among four eyes only one can have that absolute momentariness [*Augenblicklichkeit*] of the glance-into-one-another, to which the evidence of simultaneity is assigned.'[50] A long story: for Hannah Arendt already, 'six eyes' meant strangeness.[51]

HEIDRUN FRIESE

Notes

1 R.M. Rilke, 'Duineser Elegien', in *Werke*, I, Frankfurt/M.: Insel, 1987, pp.693–726, 704.

2 The German term *Augenblick*, literally 'glance of the eye', will be used when a particular understanding of the 'moment' is referred to, as will be explained below.

3 F. Nietzsche, *Die fröhliche Wissenschaft*, in *Kritische Studienausgabe*, III, ed. G. Colli and M. Montinari, Munich/Berlin/New York: DTV/de Gruyter, 1988² [1882/1887²], pp.343–651, 5. Buch, 'Wir Furchtlosen', no. 355, pp.593–94.

4 An obvious reference in this context is to the attempts to grasp the glance phenomenologically, in discussion with Edmund Husserl; see J. P. Sartre, *L'être et le néant*, Paris: Gallimard, 1943; and M. Merleau-Ponty, *Le Visible et l'invisible*, Paris: Gallimard, 1964 (Engl. edn *The Visible and the Invisible*, Evanston: Northwestern University Press, 1968); M. Merleau-Ponty, *L'œil et l'esprit*, Paris: Gallimard, 1964 (Engl. edn *The Primacy of Perception*, Evanston: Northwestern University Press, 1964).

5 M. Buber, 'Zwiesprache', in *Das dialogische Prinzip*, Heidelberg: Lambert Schneider, 1997⁸, pp.139–96, 144.

6 S. Kierkegaard, *Der Begriff Angst*, in *Gesammelte Werke*, ed.E. Hirsch and H. Gerdes, XI, Gütersloh: Gütersloher Verlagshaus, 1995⁴ [1844], p.133.

7 Buber, 'Zwiesprache', p.163. For Buber, the authority in front of which human beings assume their responsibility is founded transcendentally, it is the face of God; the law and the dogmas of religion are nothing else than a shield against its revelation.

8 M. Cacciari, *Arcipelago*, Milan: Adelphi, 1997, p.113. The *vocatio*, however, is not to be founded in an transcendental instance, but is to be thought as strictly this-worldly.

9 F. Hessel, *Heimliches Berlin*, in *Sämtliche Werke*, I, ed. H. Vollmer and B. Witte, Oldenburg: Igel-Verlag, 1999 [1927], p.253–336 (in the following quoted as *SW*, vol., year, pp.). See F. Hessel, *Spazieren in Berlin*, in *SW*, V, 1999 [1929], pp.42–47; *idem* 'Von der schwierigen Kunst spazieren zu gehen', in *SW*, V, 1999 [1933], pp.68–73 (French trans. *Promenades dans Berlin, précédé du Flâneur de Berlin*, trans. J.-M. Beloeil and J.-M. Palmier, Grenoble: Presses Universitaires de Grenoble, 1989); *idem*, 'Die Kunst spazieren zu gehen', in *Ermunterungen zum Genuß*, in *SW*, II, 1999 [1933], p.435.

10 The root of the German word for attending, *aufmerken*, connotes at the same time also 'to take note of', and 'to keep in mind'.

11 'Billboards at the rear walls along the tracks of the elevated railway, in waiting-rooms and on the window-screens of the subway cars, titles, inscriptions, instructions for use, abbreviations, there you get the entire life of the present, you can read it in passing, you do not need to touch anything, it would only crumble in your hands and turn into the gray ash of the past' (Hessel, *Heimliches Berlin*, p.317). For the *flâneur*, the disappearance of the writings in the streets, thus a writing to which one cannot leaf back as in a book, turns into the 'all-visible symbol of transitoriness' (Hessel, 'Die Kunst spazieren zu gehen', p.435).

See especially Franz Hessel, 'Architekturen des Augenblicks', with photographs by G. Krull, in *SW*, III, 1999 [1927], pp. 340–41 (a text which was to be inserted into the book *Frauen und Städte*). 'Advertisements participate in the architecture of the moment, in the works that keep alive the transitional period, in which the old house is demolished and the new one erected. The ruin of the old and the building-shed of the new stay both, at least to the eye, inhabitable.' These architectures of the moment and their vertical writings have been – observations migrate across texts – described by W. Benjamin in *Einbahnstraße*, in *Gesammelte Schriften*, IV:1, ed. Rolf Tiedemann and Hermann Schweppenhäuser, Frankfurt/M.: Suhrkamp, 1991 [1928], pp.83–148, 103 (in the following quoted as *GS*, vol., year, pp.). In this context, see Hessel's review of Benjamin's *Einbahnstraße* (*SW*, V, 1999 [1928], pp.155–57) and Benjamin's review of Hessel's *Heimliches Berlin* (*GS*, III, 1927, pp.82–84) and *Spazieren in Berlin* ('Die Wiederkehr des Flaneurs', in *GS*, III, 1929, pp.194–99). Hessel does not only become Benjamin's city guide who introduces him to the art of strolling, of the *flâneur* (W. Benjamin, 'Berliner Chronik', in *GS*, VI, 1991 [1932], pp.465–519, 469); in a short text on the arcades, Benjamin's later project is also sketched ('Passagen', in *SW*, V, 1999 [1927], pp.33–35; see Benjamin, in *GS*, II, pp.1041–43). Surprisingly, the 'authors' couple' Hessel–Benjamin and the remarkable correspondences and mirrorings are hardly ever mentioned. On the obvious proximity, see also F. Hessel, 'Vorschule des Journalismus. Ein Pariser Tagebuch', in *SW*, II, 1999 [1929], pp.292–329.

12   F. Hessel, *Hermes*, in *SW*, II, 1999 [1929], p.330.

13   Hessel, *Hermes*, p.330. This is – peculiar vicinity to Martin Buber – the glance of a singular human bring (in this case, Karl Wolfskehl), a glance that looks towards him from 'some human faces' and which can only bear the name of a god. And this glance is liberated of all theological routine: 'For me, the divine is not omnipresent [as it is to pious people], and its power is conditioned by place and time, we have it, it has us only here and now. But to impart this, my knowledge lacks tenaciousness. And I have, as gloomily a wise man said about himself, in me thoughts without clothes, I am merely the "shadow of my flame, moved as it is, but dark".'

14   Benjamin's review of Hessel's *Heimliches Berlin*, in *GS*, III, 1927, p.82. See Hessel's text 'Paris', a city that is simultaneously past and remembrance, 'a city that [turns] the street into a dwelling' – a motif of the arcades project. F. Hessel, 'Paris', in *SW*, [n.d.], III, [n.d.], p.306. The street becomes a dwelling for the *flâneur*; he is as much at home among the façades of houses as a citizen is within his four walls. See Konvolut M ('Der Flaneur') of the *Arcades Project* (W. Benjamin, *Passagen-Werk*, in *GS*, V:1–2, 1991 [1927–], pp. 524–69).

15   'There is no other grip onto blessed eternity than the moment'; this sentence by Jean Paul was found a couple of times in Hessel's excerpts in his bequest; Bernhard Echte drew attention to this fact (*SW*, III, p.374).

16   Hessel,'Von der schwierigen Kunst', p.72.

17   Hessel, 'Die Kunst spazieren zu gehen', p.435. (The German term for 'to cure by incantation' means literally 'to speak to'.)

18   Hessel, *Hermes*, p.335.

19   Hessel, *Heimliches Berlin*, p.319.

20   W. Benjamin, 'Über einige Motive bei Baudelaire', *GS*, I:2, 1991 [1939], pp. 646–47, emphasis added. On the responded glance, see also W. Benjamin, 'Zentralpark', in *GS*, I:2., 1991 [1938/39], p.670. Different temporalities are unavoidably intertwined in the concept of the aura, which is inextricably both transcendentally and immanently grounded, linked to both cult and contemplation. Cf. K.H. Bohrer, *Das absolute Präsenz: Die Semantik ästhetischer Zeit*, Frankfurt/M.: Suhrkamp, 1994, p.182.

21   Benjamin, 'Über einige Motive', p.649 and p.647.

22   W. Benjamin, 'Gottfried Keller', *GS*, II:1, 1991 [1927], p.290 (emphasis added). Benjamin finds in Proust and Keller witnesses to the insatiable longing for happiness that feeds itself from the past and can be saved by being recalled.

23   Benjamin, *Einbahnstraße*, p.125.

24   S. Weber, 'Mass Mediauras, or, Art, Aura, and Media in the Work of Walter Benjamin', in D.S. Ferris (ed.), *Walter Benjamin: Theoretical Questions*, Stanford: Stanford University Press, 1996, pp.27–49, 35–36.

25   I. Kant, 'Anthropologie in pragmatischer Hinsicht', in *Werkausgabe*, XII, ed. W. Weischedel, Frankfurt/M.: Suhrkamp, 1977 [1798] pp.399–690, §32, p.491, §32.

26   M. Heidegger, *Identität und Differenz*, Pfullingen: Neske, 1990⁹ [1957], pp.24–25.

27   Heidegger, *Identität*, p.25. Cf. William McNeill, *The Glance of the Eye: Heidegger, Aristotle, and the Ends of Theory*, Albany: State University of New York Press, 1999, pp.216–18.

28 F. Nietzsche, *Über Wahrheit und Lüge im aussermoralischen Sinne*, in *Kritische Studienausgabe*, I, ed. Giorgio Colli and Mazzino Montinari, Munich/Berlin/New York: DTV/de Gruyter, 1988² [1873], pp.873–90, 879–80.

29 Derrida – drawing on Celan – pointed to this relation of uniqueness and repetition. J. Derrida, *Schibboleth. Pour Paul Celan*, Paris: Galilée, 1986.

30 Hölderlin already saw the moment as hardly providing any dialectical mediation between the old and the new. Transition does not belong both to the past and the future; the new, rather, emerges in leaving. Transition is not both becoming and passing away; the possible rather comes to be by remembering the old. Only remembrance as dissolution, as 'ideal dissolution' – in contrast to 'real dissolution' – opens up the unknown future. F. Hölderlin, 'Das untergehende Vaterland', in *Sämtliche Werke und Briefe*, II, ed. M. Knaupp, Munich/Vienna: Hanser, 1992, pp. 72–77.

31 M. Heidegger to H. Arendt, letter no. 47, 8.2.1950, in H. Arendt and M. Heidegger, *Briefe 1925–1975 und andere Zeugnisse*, ed. U. Ludz, Frankfurt/M.: Vittorio Klosterman, 1998, pp.74–75 (in the following quoted as *Briefe*, no., date, page number). In this writing, not directly addressed to the public (but nevertheless counting on publication) – which is always already, even though implicitly, signed by the (public) names of the two authors Arendt and Heidegger and encircled by their works – 'work' and 'intimacy', writing, friendship and love intersect in a peculiar way. Sentences move on the narrow ridge that is to separate the public from the private, the particular from the general, the objective from the subjective. In this writing, the glance of the other does not disappear in the philosophical text to allow the latter to constitute itself. Rather, the separation is shown here to be what it always has been: untenable. Such writing demonstrates the failure of the philosophical text in the face of the inherited separations and it refers to presences which always also co-write the philosophical text. It shows 'that you from now on live in and with my work' and makes 'your serving love in my work' recognisable – and it shows thus, too, that philosophical writing is always already contaminated by that which it tries to eradicate (Heidegger, *Briefe*, No. 12, 24.4.1925, p.26).

This is a writing, at the same time, which multiplies re-written published texts – as, for instance, *Being and Time*. It has to face the specific moment, has to respond to it, and such a moment shows itself to be different from the way it was before being philosophised. In the moment that does not belong to the vulgar understanding of time, but to 'authentic temporality', *Being and Time* argues, 'ecstatically understood future – the datable, significant "then" – does not coincide with the vulgar concept of the "future" in the sense of the pure nows that have not yet arrived and are only arriving. Nor does the ecstatic having-been, the datable, significant "on that former occasion", coincide with the concept of the past in the sense of the past pure nows. The now is *not pregnant* with the not-yet-now, but the present arises from the future in the primordial, ecstatic unity of the temporalizing of temporality' (*Sein und Zeit*, Tübingen: Max Niemeyer Verlag, 1984 [1927], §81, pp.426–27, emphasis added [Engl. edn *Being and Time*, trans. J. Macquarrie and E. Robinson, 1995¹², Oxford: Blackwell, 1995¹²]). In contrast to the lines of the letter quoted above, the moment is here not 'delivered' and requires a long time to show itself. The exchange of glances in the letters thus also develops a theory of the specific, particular moment, which comments upon *Being and Time*.

32 M. Heidegger, 'Der Wieder-Blick. Zum 6. Februar 1950', Fünf Gedichte, in *Briefe*, No. 63, p.108.

33 Heidegger, *Sein und Zeit*, §68a, p.338; and *idem*, 'Beiträge zur Philosophie', in *Gesamtausgabe*, LXV, Frankfurt/M.: Vittorio Klostermann, 1989, p.204.

34 Arendt, *Briefe*, September 1951, Abb. 16 and p.387; a comment on the poems dedicated to her, February 1950, *Briefe*, p.79.

35 Heidegger, *Briefe*, No. 3, 27.2.1925, p.14.

36 Kierkegaard, *Der Begriff Angst*, p.131.

37 Kierkegaard, *Der Begriff Angst*, p.134 [IV 396].

38 Kierkegaard, *Der Begriff Angst*, p.134 [IV 397].

39 Kierkegaard, *Der Begriff Angst*, p.137 [IV 399].

40 Kierkegaard, *Der Begriff Angst*, p.136 [IV 398].

41 Heidegger, *Sein und Zeit*, §30 p.142. Bohrer directed attention to the analogies to, and differences with, Ernst Jünger, who distinguished fright (*Schrecken*), the horrible (*das Entsetzliche*) as an increase of fright, from dread (*Grauen*), anxiety (*Angst*) and fear (*Furcht*). K.H. Bohrer, *Plötzlichkeit: Zum Augenblick des ästhetischen Scheins*, Frankfurt/M.: Suhrkamp, 1981, p.52 (Engl. edn. *Suddenness: On the Moment of Aesthetic Appearance*, New York: Columbia University Press, 1994).

42 Heidegger, *Briefe*, No. 55, 16.3.1950, p.90.

43 Heidegger, *Briefe*, No. 60, 4.5.1950, p.98.

44 'The moment has ultimately … to be cast as the glance of love.' G. Wohlfahrt, *Der Augenblick: Zeit und ästhetische Erfahrung bei Kant, Hegel, Nietzsche und Heidegger mit einem Exkurs zu Proust*, Freiburg/Munich: Karl Albert, 1982, p.144.

45 Heidegger, *Briefe*, No. 2, 21.2.1925, p.13.

46 Heidegger, *Briefe*, No. 55, 16.3.1950, p.89.

47 Heidegger, *Briefe*, No. 91, 6.10.66, p.153 and Arendt, *Briefe*, No. 92, 19.10.1966, p.155.

48 Heidegger, *Briefe*, No. 51, 15.2.1950, p.81.

49 'A counter-glance [*Gegenblick*] to the flash of being / that is thinking' (Heidegger, Vier Gedichte, in *Briefe*, No. 56, March 1950, p.92), and that is how poetry is written by a philosophy in which thinking becomes responding, responding to the event. 'Counter-glance', however, also means the 'reply' as well as the 'objection' in the encounter with the event. Heidegger, Vier Gedichte, in *Briefe*, No. 56, March 1950, p.92.

50 H. Blumenberg, 'Ich-bin und Urgleichzeitigkeit', in *Ein mögliches Selbstverständnis: Aus dem Nachlaß*, Stuttgart: Reclam, 1996, pp.213–19, 216. 'Among four eyes' (*unter vier Augen*) is the German expression for 'between ourselves'.

51 Letter from Hannah Arendt to Heinrich Blücher, 12.8.36, in H. Arendt and H. Blücher, *Briefe 1936–1968*, ed. Lotte Köhler, Munich/Zürich: Piper, 1996, p.45.

CHAPTER 5

On Alain Badiou

SIMON CRITCHLEY

It was her voice that made
The sky acutest at its vanishing.
She measured to the hour its solitude.
She was the single artificer of the world
In which she sang. And when she sang, the sea,
Whatever self it had, became the self
That was her song, for she was the maker. Then we,
As we beheld her striding there alone,
Knew that there never was a world for her
Except the one she sang and, singing, made.[1]

Wallace Stevens

I have two questions in this chapter: What is ethical experience for Badiou? What can be said of the subject who has this experience in his work? The hopefully significant consequences of these questions for our understanding of Badiou will emerge as we proceed. But first I need to explain what I mean by ethical experience and how such experience implies a conception of the subject. What, then, is ethical experience?

The Structure of Ethical Experience and the Ethical Subject (Kant, Heidegger)

Let me begin to answer this question by trying to pick out the formal structure of ethical experience or what, with Dieter Henrich, we can call the grammar of the concept of moral insight (*Einsicht*).[2] Ethical experience begins with the experience of a demand (*Anspruch, adresse*) to which I give my approval. Approval and demand: that is, there can be no sense of the good (however that is filled out at the level of content, and I am just understanding it formally and emptily) without an act of approval or affirmation. That is, my moral statement that '*x* is good' or '*x* is bad' is of a different order to the veridical, epistemological claim that 'I am now seated in a chair'. This is because the moral statement implies an approval of the fact that *x* is good, whereas I can be quite indifferent to the chair I am sitting on. If I say, for example, that it would be good for parrots to receive the right to vote in elections, then my saying this implies that I approve of this development. Practical reason is in this way distinct from theoretical reason, the order of the event is distinct from the order of being.

(A naïve initial question I have for Badiou is whether his dualism of *être* and *événement* risks repeating and reinstating some version of the Kantian distinction between theoretical and practical reason, more particularly the version of this distinction that one finds in Wittgenstein's *Tractatus*, where the order of being is explicable through logical form, but where that which is really important for Wittgenstein is the order of the event, about which nothing meaningful can be said, the domain of ethics, aesthetics and religion.)

To return to the argument: if the good only comes into view through approval, it is not good *by virtue* of approval. The approval is an approval *of* something, that is, of a demand that demands approval. Ethical *noesis* requires a *noema*. In my example, my approval of parrots receiving the right to vote is related to the fact that, at least in my imagination, parrots make a certain demand, namely the demand for political representation. Ethical experience is, first and foremost, the approval of a demand, a demand that demands approval. Ethical experience has to be circular, although hopefully only virtuously so.

Leaving parrots to one side, in the history of philosophy (and also in the history of what Badiou calls anti-philosophy), this formal demand is filled out with various contents: the Good beyond Being in Plato, faith in the resurrected Christ in Paul and Augustine and Kierkegaard, the fact of reason or the experience of respect for the moral law in Kant, the certitude of practical faith as the goal of subjective striving (*Streben*) in Fichte, the abyssal *intuition* of freedom in Schelling, the creature's feeling of absolute dependency on a creator in Schleiermacher, pity for the suffering of one's fellow human beings in Rousseau or for all creatures in Schopenhauer, eternal return in Nietzsche, the idea in the Kantian sense for Husserl, the call of conscience in Heidegger, the claim of the non-identical in Adorno, or whatever.[3] All questions of normativity and value, whether universalistic (as in Kant in the categorical imperative, and his latter-day heirs like Rawls and Habermas) or relativistic (as in Wittgenstein on rule following and his latter-day heirs like Rorty), follow from such an experience. That is, without some experience of a demand, that is, without some experience of a relation to the otherness of a demand of some sort, to which I am prepared to bind myself, to commit myself, the business of morality would not get started. There would be no *motivation* to the good, the good would not have the power to move the will to act. Kant calls that which would produce the power to act, the motivational power to be disposed to the good, 'the philosopher's stone'. So what is essential to ethical experience is that the subject of the demand assents to that demand, agrees to finding it good, binds itself to that good and shapes its *subjectivity* in relation to that good. A demand meets with an approval. The subject who approves shapes itself in accordance with that demand. All questions of value begin here.

Let me take this a little further. If we stay with the example of Kant, then this dimension of ethical experience or moral insight, that is, the capacity of being motivated to the good, resolves itself, in a rather complex fashion, in the seemingly contradictory notion of the fact of reason. That is, there is a *Faktum* which places a demand on the subject and to which the subject assents. There is a demand of the good to which the subject assents, and this demand has an immediate apodictic certainty that is *analogous* to the binding power of an empirical *Tatsache*. The difference between the apodicticity of a *Faktum der Vernunft* as distinct from an empirical *Tatsache* is that the demand of the fact of reason is only evident insofar as the subject approves it. It is, if you like (and Kant wouldn't), the *fiction* of a fact constituted through an act of approval. However things may stand with the doctrine of the fact of reason, Dieter Henrich argues, rightly I think, that the entire rational universality of the categorical imperative and Kantian moral theory follows from this experience of moral insight. The philosopher's stone would consist precisely in the link between the motivational power of the fact of reason and the rational universality of the categorical imperative. Now, because Kant's entire moral theory is based on the principle of autonomy, this *Faktum der Vernunft* has to correspond to the will of the subject. The fact of reason is a fact, it is the otherness of a demand, but it has to correspond to the subject's autonomy. Hence, for Kant, the ethical subject has to be a priori equal to the demand that is placed on it.

It is arguably this structure that Heidegger repeats in his analysis of *Gewissen* in *Sein und Zeit*, where conscience is constituted in the experience of a demand or appeal that *seems* to come from outside *Dasein*, but which is really only *Dasein* calling to itself. Heidegger writes, 'In conscience *Dasein* calls itself'. In this sense, the grammar of moral insight in Heidegger, at least in the analysis of authenticity, would be an existential deepening of Kantian autonomy. Heidegger recognises as a 'positive necessity' the *Faktum* that has to be presupposed in any analysis of

Dasein. The Kantian fact of reason here becomes the ontic-existentiell testimony, attestation or witnessing (*Zeugnis*) of conscience which is relativistically translated into the key notion of the 'situation'.

We can see already, from this little sketch of Kant and Heidegger, that the claim about ethical experience being constituted in a demand which I approve, is also a claim about the nature of the self or subject. The response to the question of ethical experience also entails a response to the question of the subject of that experience. An ethical subject can be defined as a self relating itself wilfully, binding itself approvingly, to the demand of the good. The self is something that shapes itself through its relation to whatever is determined as its good, whether that is the law of Moses, the resurrected Christ, the suffering other, the intuition of freedom, the call of conscience, the non-identical, or whatever. That is, if the demand of the good cannot be constituted without the approval of that demand, then that approval is given by a self. The good is good insofar as the self approves of it. For me, the ethical *subject* is the name for the way the self relates itself bindingly to the good.

This claim about the relation of ethical experience to the subject can be buttressed not by simply claiming, rather neutrally, that the demand of the good requires approval by a self in order to be experienced as a demand, but by claiming that this demand of the good *founds* the self, or is the fundamental organising principle of the subject's articulation. In other words, what we think of as a self is fundamentally an ethical subject, a self that is constituted in a certain relation to a good. This is perhaps best proved negatively through the experience of failure, betrayal, or evil: as Badiou notes, if I act in a way that I know to be evil then I am acting in a manner destructive of the self that I am, or that I have chosen to be. I have failed myself or betrayed myself. Once again, such a claim is quite formal and does not presuppose specific content for the good. For example, my good could be fucking little boys, or whatever (although that would be difficult to universalise). The point here is that the ethical subject is constituted through a certain relation to a demand that is determined as good and that this can be felt most acutely when I fail to act in accordance with that demand or when I deliberately transgress it and betray myself. This is why Plato is perfectly consequent when he claims that vice is destructive of self. Anyone who has tried – and failed – to cure themselves of some sort of addiction, whether cigarettes, alcohol, little boys or whatever, will understand what is meant here. The subject that I have chosen to be enters into conflict with the self that I am, producing a divided experience of self as self-failure and the concomitant overwhelming effect of guilt. Guilt is the effect that produces a certain splitting or division in the subject, which is something that St Paul understood rather well.

Three Applications of the Structure of Ethical Experience: Levinas, Lacan and Badiou

Leaving Kant and Heidegger to one side, my question is whether this formal structure of ethical experience can be used to illuminate other moral theories. I think it can. Before turning in detail to Badiou, let me make some remarks on Levinas and Lacan, and attempt a small rapprochement between them that might be shocking to some readers. For Levinas, the core of ethical experience is, indeed, the demand of a *Faktum*, but it is not a *Faktum der Vernunft* as much as a *Faktum des Anderen*, a fact of the other. In *Totality and Infinity*, at least, the name for this fact is the face of the other (*visage d'autrui*). Now Levinas's difference from Kant (or Heidegger for that matter) is that ethical experience turns around the alterity of a demand that does not correspond to the subject's autonomy, but which places that autonomy in question, at least at the ethical level (although autonomy can be said to come back at the level of justice, politics and *le tiers*). What Levinas tries to articulate in his work is the experience of a demand to which the subject assents ('tu ne tueras point'), but which constitutes the ethical subject in a certain founding heteronomy. The ethical subject in Levinas is constituted through a relation, an act of approval, to the demand of the good to which it is fundamentally inadequate. The Levinasian ethical subject chooses to relate itself to something which exceeds its relational capacity. This is what Levinas calls 'le rapport sans rapport', which is, as Blanchot rightly observes, the anti-dialectical kernel of Levinas's work.

This dimension of ethical experience can be explored in relation to the theme of trauma in Levinas's *Autrement qu'être*. What is a trauma? The source of trauma is a heteronomous event that comes from outside the self (for example, a terrorist explosion or an earthquake) but which lives on in the subject after the fact in, say, traumatic neurosis. Levinas constructs what he calls 'an ethical language', composed of several rather strange and hyperbolical terms: persecution, obsession, substitution, hostage and trauma. Focusing on the notion of trauma allows one to bring out the links between Levinas and the psychoanalytic dimensions of ethical experience, dimensions studiously refused by Levinas himself. But for Levinas, ethics is the dimension of a traumatic demand, something that comes from outside the subject, but which leaves its imprint, trace or mark within the subject. My completely heterodox but, I think, justified claim in relation to Levinas is that the condition of possibility for ethics, that is for the ethical relation to the other, is found in a certain picture of the subject, i.e. it is because of a disposition of the subject that relatedness to the other is possible. This is why I privilege Levinas's later work, *Autrement qu'être*, over his earlier work, *Totalité et infini*, for it is here that ethics is worked out as a theory of the subject, conceived as the other within the same, and not simply in terms of the relation to the other. So, the grammar of moral insight in Levinas is that ethical responsibility begins with a subject approving of an impossible demand, or a demand that it could never meet. This makes responsibility infinite and splits open the subject through a founding heteronomy. I, as it were, decide to be a subject that I know I cannot be, I give myself up to a demand that makes an imprint on *me* without my ever being fully able to understand *it* (you can see the psychoanalytic implications of such a claim). In other words, for Levinas, ethics is not ontology, which simply means that the ethical relation to the other that lives on as an imprint within the subject is not a relation of comprehension, of totality. So, the notion of ethical experience that I am trying to elicit produces a certain picture of the subject as constitutively split between itself and a demand that it cannot meet, but which is that by virtue of which it becomes a subject. To put this gnomically, the inside of the subject's inside is outside.

Once this psychoanalytically reconceived account of the Levinasian ethical subject is in place, it can be shown that there is a rather interesting homology between it and Lacan, i.e. that there is a common formal structure to ethical experience in both of them, although they obviously differ at the level of content, not to mention their rather different evaluations of the importance of Freud. But let us ask: what is the basic claim of Lacan's *L'éthique de la psychanalyse*? Lacan's thesis is that the ethical as such is articulated in relation to the order of the Real, which is variously and obscurely glossed as 'that which resists, the impossible, that which always comes back to the same place, the limit of all symbolisation, etc. etc.'. Indeed this thesis is finessed in the following, crucial way: the ethical, which affirms itself in opposition to pleasure, is articulated in relation to the real insofar as the latter can be the guarantor of what Lacan calls, following a certain idiosyncratic and radical reading of Freud, *das Ding, la Chose*. The main example of *das Ding* in the ethics seminar is the Freudian figure of the *Nebenmensch*, the fellow human being (*le prochain*), and I think what we might call 'a *Nebenmensch* complex' is at work in both Levinas and Lacan: that is, there is a Thing at the heart of the subject that defines the subject in terms of an 'interior exteriority', as it were, what Lacan calls something 'strange or foreign to me that is at the heart of me'.

However, what is interesting is how perfectly Lacanian ethics fits into the structure of ethical experience and the subject that I have tried to describe. For Lacan, ethical experience begins with recognition of the *demand* of the unconscious, the impingement of unconscious desire. In the analytic situation, i.e if the analysand has agreed to the interpretation of the symptom, the *Faktum* of this desire provokes an act of *approval* of the part of the subject. That is, the ethical subject decides henceforth to relates itself approvingly to the demand of its unconscious desire. This demand, which in this case would be the demand of the good, produces what I see as the categorical imperative of the ethics seminar, namely 'do not give way on its desire' (*ne pas céder sur son désir*). That is, do not cease to approve of the demand of the good that is unconscious desire. For Lacan, as much as for Kant, it is this act of approval that founds the subject, where he claims that 'tout le cheminement du sujet' articulates itself around the Thing that shadows the subject. This is why Lacan can claim that Freudian psychoanalysis, as much as Kant's critical philosophy, subscribes to the primacy of practical reason. I will come back to Lacan below, but one version of my question to Badiou is whether his ethical theory loses sight of this dimension of the Thing, that is whether his privileging of Love over Law risks reducing the traumatic demand to the Real, to the symbolic order.[4]

Turning to Badiou, the structure of ethical experience I have described can be applied rather effectively to his wonderful reading of St Paul.[5] What interests Badiou in Paul is the connection between the subject and the event. More precisely, Badiou's question is: what law can structure a subject deprived of all identity in relation to an event, 'dont la seule "preuve" est justement qu'un sujet le déclare'? This event is the resurrection of Christ, something that can only have the status of a fable for Badiou. Let me emphasise here, as I will come back to it below, that what interests Badiou is the notion of an event which is not empirically demonstrable in the order of being. The event demands an act of belief that Paul rightly compares to folly. That is, the event is a *Faktum* that is analogous but irreducible to an empirical *Tatsache*. Now, the structure of ethical experience in Badiou's reading of Paul can be formalised into the following four moments.

1   There is the universality of the demand of the good, or what Badiou calls the *adresse*, which is what Paul calls grace, *charis*.
2   *Charisma* of the subject consists in the declaration of this grace in an act of faith, or what Badiou prefers to call *la conviction*. Thus, faith is the *surgir du sujet*, its subjective certitude that approves of the demand that is placed on it.
3   If faith is *le surgir du sujet*, then love (*agape*) is the practical *labeur du sujet* that has bound itself to its good in faith. The practical maxim of love is 'love your neighbour as yourself'. That is, if the human being is justified by faith, then she or he is redeemed by love. Love is what gives consistency to an ethical subject, which allows it to persevere with what Badiou elsewhere calls 'un processus de vérité'.
4   Love binds itself to justice on the basis of hope (*espérance, elpis*). The hope is that justice will be done and the subjective maxim that this requirement of justice produces is, as elsewhere in Badiou, 'Continuez!' That is, continue to love your neighbour as yourself. We might, then, define hope as *political love*.

In terms of the account of ethical experience given above, it is the first two moments of this structure that are essential. Ethical experience begins with the experience of a demand or address, which is the event of grace, and the subject defines itself by approving of this event in a declaration of faith. Thus – and this is the essential thing – the Christian subject does not pre-exist the event that it declares. Subject and event come into being at the same time. As I have already shown, in ethical experience, the subject defines itself by binding itself approvingly to the demand that the good makes on it. For Badiou, it is this feature of Paulinian Christianity, its singular universality based on the *Faktum* of an event irreducible to an empirical *Tatsache*, that provides an exemplary figure for contemporary political militantism.

The Place of Ethics in Badiou's System

With this in mind, I would now like to turn to the more detailed account of ethical experience presented in *L'éthique. Essai sur la conscience du Mal.*[6] The 80 pages of *L'éthique* fall, very roughly, into two parts: (1) a refreshingly direct presentation and critique of the so-called 'return to ethics' in contemporary French philosophy; and (2) a more interesting exposition of Badiou's ethical theory in relation to the problem of evil. Consequent upon this division of the argument, the intention of *L'éthique* is twofold: (1) to show how the contemporary inflation of ethics in French philosophy is a symptom of a more general nihilism; and (2) to provide a quite other meaning to ethics, by relating it not to abstractions, like Man, God or the Other, but to concrete *situations*. That is, for Badiou, what is ethical is the production of durable maxims for singular and determinate processes, what he calls 'processes of truth'. Thus, what is at stake in ethical debate is not some generalised victimology, or the massaging of a conservative good conscience, but what Badiou calls 'le destin des verités' ('the destiny of truths'). This view leads Badiou to make a justified critique of the so-called 'return to ethics' in France, with its defence of human rights, individualism and democracy, which is essentially a reactionary response to the foundering of French revolutionary Marxism. It also leads Badiou to make, in my view, a rather less justified critique of Levinas, that the claim that ethics is first philosophy is dependent upon an axiom derived from religion and therefore that Levinas reduces philosophy to theology. This is not wrong, but I just think there are other ways of reading Levinas, for example *my* way, where I try to read Levinas through the categories of psychoanalysis. But let us suppose that Badiou is right, that 'l'éthique pour Levinas est une catégorie du discours pieux', then wouldn't Levinas simply be another in that long line of *anti-*

philosophes, like St Paul, Luther, Pascal, Rousseau, Kierkegaard and Nietzsche, some of whom he elsewhere praises? On this point, let me attempt a small criticism in terms of the four conditions of philosophy for Badiou (*art, science, politique et amour*).

For Badiou, quite simply, there is no God. This is also to say that *l'Un n'est pas*.[7] Hence, multiplicity is the general law of being, what Badiou means by *être*. Every situation is a multiplicity composed of an infinity of elements. Given this facticity of the multiple, there is a requirement when thinking about ethics for a return to the Same (*le Même*). For Badiou, the Same is not what is simply given – *être* – but rather *ce qui advient*, that which comes to itself in relation to the facticity and alterity of multiplicity. What Badiou sees as the *être immortel* of each singularity is its capacity for the true, that is, to become this Same that constructs itself, that advenes to itself, through the processual character of Sameness, *Mêmeté*. A subject is not something that I *am*, it is something that I *become*, that comes to itself in a process of becoming. Thus, for Badiou, there is only an ethics of truths, that is, an ethics of processes of truths, of the labour that allows truths to *advient au monde*, to ad-vene to the world. Thus, ethics in general does not have any validity, it is always an ethics in relation to a specific situation under particular conditions. Thus, although Badiou's ethical theory is highly formalistic, it only takes on flesh in relation to specific and by definition variable situational conditions. That which is ethical, then, corresponds to what Badiou adjudges as the four sole conditions for philosophy: politics, love, mathematics, poetry.

This brings me back to the question of religion. If it is granted that religion, at least for St Paul but perhaps also for Levinas, is anti-philosophical, then I do not see why it cannot be a condition for ethical action. Obviously for Paul, Pascal and others, such as Luther and Kierkegaard, religion plays *precisely* this role and it is privileged *because* it is anti-philosophical. In this sense, at the very least, one would have to admit that in addition to the four conditions of philosophy that can be conditions for ethical action, one needs to add a fifth, namely religion. Yet, one might want to go further and claim that precisely because of the exemplary way in which the logic of the event plays itself out in relation to Paul, namely that Paul's notion of grace shows most clearly the subjectivity of the event, religion is perhaps the paradigm of ethical action, a paradigm upon which the other four conditions should be modelled.[8]

In terms of my account of ethical experience, Badiou's ethics is an entirely formal theory, a grammar of ethical experience, and not a specific determination of the good. However, what is motivating this formalism is a theory of the subject that has strong normative connotations – located in Badiou's Beckettian formula: 'il faut continuer' – although the specific content given to the good is subject-relative. As I have shown, every account of ethical experience has at its base a demand on the self to which the self assents. The ethical subject is the name for this structure. Ethics, for Badiou, cannot be premised upon any pre-given account of the subject because the subject is not something that one is, it is something that one becomes. One can only speak of the subject as a subject in becoming or a becoming-subject. As Nietzsche, the shadowy twin to St Paul, would say: *werde was du bist!*

For Badiou, we are simply the sort of animals who are claimed by circumstances to become a subject. *What are those circumstances?* For Badiou, they are the circumstances of a truth. *What are they?* These circumstances cannot be what there is (*ce qu'il y a*). What there is for Badiou is the factical-being-multiple of the world, a plurality irreducible to any theological principle, henology or even post-ontotheological *singulare tantum*. Thus, the circumstances of the being-multiple of the world do not place a claim or demand on the subject. For example, our ordinary life in the world with others only places a claim upon us when the relation to the other becomes a relation of love, trust, hate or whatever. A subject – which is that which becomes – demands something more, it demands that something happens that supplements its ordinary insertion into that which is. As everyone knows, Badiou calls this supplement an *event*, hence the distinction between *l'être* and *l'événement*. Thus, the event is what calls a subject into being, into the creation of a truth, whereas being is that which simply is, which is the order of *episteme* in Plato, which is to be explained by mathematics. As Badiou states in the initial thesis of *L'être et l'événement*, 'l'ontologie s'accomplisse historiquement comme mathématique'.[9]

Let us just note *en passant* that this founding dualism of being and the event might raise certain philosophical worries: first, simply because it is a dualism and hence, in Heidegger's terms, splits the phenomenon of being-in-the-world; second, insofar as it does split the phenomenon, Badiou's theory might bear a certain family resemblance to other dualisms, for example that of the Sartrean dualism of *en soi* and *pour soi* to which, Badiou confesses at the beginning of his little book on Beckett, he was attracted in his youth: 'j'étais un parfait sartrian'.[10] Third, the dualism of being and event risks reproducing the Kantian or early Wittgensteinian distinction of pure and practical reason, between the ontological order of knowledge and the ethical order of truth, an ethical order which, like that of Kant and perhaps more particularly Fichte, is based on an infinite *Streben*: 'Continuez!'

The Logic of the Event in Badiou – Virtuously or Viciously Circular?

Thus, Badiou's theory of ethical experience and the subject of that experience turns entirely on his account of the event. I would now like to bring out the logic of this event, a circular logic, although hopefully only virtuously circular. On this basis, certain critical questions can be raised.

From the standpoint of being, the event is, one might say, *invisible* (I can't think of a better word, but this is not satisfactory). That is, there is only an event for the subject that assents to the event, declares it, and defines its subjectivity in terms of a fidelity to the event. The event is the event only *for* the subject that pledges itself to the event. But – and this is important – this is not to say that the event is the *act* of the subject, or that the event is the subject's *invention*. Rather, the event is an event *for* a subject who carries out the act that *binds* its subjectivity to that event, defines its subjectivity through a fidelity to the event.

Thus, the event is only visible to the subject that *decides* to pledge its subjectivity to that event. For example, the event of Christ's resurrection is just not visible as such to the non-believer, who sees only an empty tomb. This is not to say that Christ's resurrection did not take place – we have all read enough Pascal to keep a rather selfishly open mind on such matters – but that it only becomes an *event* for the subject that pledges itself to the event, for the subject with *pistis*, the conviction of faith. In a similar way, the event of the French Revolution or the October Revolution does not *appear* as a revolution to the opponent of the revolution, say the supporter of the *ancien régime*. For the latter, the revolution is only visible as chaos and disorder. The 'event' of the French Revolution is not the same event for Edmund Burke as for Thomas Paine. Analogously, multinational global capitalism looks like chaos to its insurrectionary opponent, whereas it looks like order to the capitalist. To put this into a formula: *the event is not the mere act of a subject, but it only becomes an event through a subjective act*.

On the question of the 'reality' of the event, thinking of St Paul's faith in the event of Christ's resurrection, Badiou emphasises that the only 'proof' of the event is the subject who declares it. What interests Badiou is a notion of an event which is not empirically demonstrable in the order of being. As Erasmus – another *anti-philosophe* – emphasises in his *Enconium Moriae*, if Christ's crucifixion and resurrection were an act of folly, then such madness is all the more true of the Christian who decides to make the leap of faith. The only 'evidence' for Paul's leap of faith is the presence of grace, which is hardly a strong empirical guarantee.

Of course, there are events and events, and Badiou's choice of Paul as a paradigm for the event is all the more compelling because his act of faith is so strange to the modern atheist. For example, I can imagine pledging myself more easily to the event 'French Revolution' than I can to the event 'Christ's resurrection'. But that, of course, is to miss the point. The choice of Paul is intended to show the extreme subject-dependency of the event, i.e. that the event is not reducible to the act of a subject, but that the event is only visible as such to the subject that acts in such a way as to pledge itself to the event. This is the purpose of my epigraph from Wallace Stevens, a poet whom I know Badiou greatly admires. An event is an idea of order, it is something that we impose on the world, the grid through which and in terms of which we see it. But the event is also what makes the world a world *for us*, that is to say, a *meaningful* world:

> She was the single artificer of the world
> In which she sang. And when she sang, the sea,
> Whatever self it had, became the self
> That was her song, for she was the maker. Then we,
> As we beheld her striding there alone,
> Knew that there never was a world for her
> Except the one she sang and, singing, made.

How to Distinguish a True from a False Event – the Question of Hegemony

Autrement dit, the eventhood, *événementalité* of the event is the consequence of a *decision*. For Badiou, a subject is the always local occurrence of a process of truth, and the subject binds itself to a process of truth, an event, on the basis of a decision. I have a couple of questions on this notion of decision, but let me try to formalise my argument in order to recapitulate what I have said so far and to make one further step.

1 First, the logic of the event, as I have tried to describe it, is very close to the description of ethical experience given above, i.e. that an event is a demand made *on* the subject, *of* which the subject approves, and *to* which it decides to bind itself. Thus, the logic of the event corresponds to the structure of ethical experience.

2 The consequence of this argument is that *every* event is an ethical event; that is, every exception to the order of being belongs to the domain of practical rather than theoretical reason.

3 In this sense, the circularity of the logic of the event is not a problem, it is just the way it is, the very nature of practical reason. The event, like ethical experience, is virtuously and not viciously circular.

4   But if that is the case, then my question is very simple: how can one speak of the event as an event of *truth*, a process of truth, or whatever? I shall try to explain myself.

If the event is the consequence of a decision, namely the decision to define one's subjectivity in terms of a fidelity to the event, then this event is *true* only in the sense that it is *true for* a subject that has taken this decision (true = true for a subject). Now, if that argument is valid, *then how and in virtue of what is one to distinguish a true event from a false event?* That is, I don't see how – on the basis of Badiou's criteria – we could ever distinguish a true event from a false event. The only realm of superior evidence to which such questions can be referred is the order of being, which is a priori excluded from discussions of the event. Now, if there is no way of distinguishing truth from falsity at the level of the event, then might we not be better advised to stop talking about truth in this domain?

One inference from this argumentation – let us call it the pragmatist inference – would be the following. We might imagine the pragmatist saying, 'Sure, we cannot distinguish between a true and a false event. True just means true for a subject who decides in favour of this event. False just means that the subject decides *not* to define itself in terms of such an event, and perhaps to define what is true *for it* in terms of explicit opposition to such a perceived falsehood.'

Now, if one accepts this pragmatist inference, that is, if true just means true for the subject, then why not go on to conclude that every event is the consequence of what Gramsci or my colleague Ernesto Laclau would call a *hegemonic articulation*? That is, why not conclude that every event is the consequence of a *decision* to relate oneself to the situation in a certain way, and that every decision is a hegemonic act? Therefore, otherwise stated, my question is how and in virtue of what is one to distinguish between truth and hegemonic articulation in Badiou's theory of the event? Isn't Badiou's talk of truth in ethical and political matters simply, as Wittgenstein would say, *a way of talking*, and doesn't it risk obscuring the real question in ethics and politics, which is that of *power*?

The Heroism of the Decision in Badiou

Allow me a final series of questions on the decision. If the eventhood of the event is the consequence of a decision, then how might that decision be characterised? Is a decision something taken by a subject? Badiou, it seems to me, would happily say 'Yes'. But if that is the case, then doesn't the notion of decision have to presuppose some conception of the subject defined in terms of an active, virile *will*, as it does, say, in Carl Schmitt? That is, doesn't Badiou's concept of the decision have to presuppose some notion of an autarchic will? Obviously, if this criticism is justified, then it would have significant political consequences, particularly as the very concept of the political (*le politique*) depends on how we understand the voluntaristic power of decision.

Against this, and I am thinking of Derrida's reading of Schmitt in *Politiques de l'amitié*,[11] can one, might one, should one, not try to rethink the concept of decision, and hence the concept of the political, in terms of a passive or unconscious decision, what we might call *the decision of the other in me*? That is, rather than thinking of the decision taken by the subject, might we not do better to think of *the subject taken by the decision*? In this sense, the decision is an event with regard to which I am passive, the decision taken by the other in me, a decision based not on a sheer autarchic act of will, or even a *Faktum der Vernunft*, as much as on what one might call a *Faktum des Anderen*, a fact of the other.[12]

Love and Law – Badiou and Psychoanalysis

Furthermore, to my mind, such a position on the decision would seem to be entailed by the very logic of Badiou's position; that is, I think there is the risk of a certain *heroism of the decision* in Badiou's work, a heroism enshrined in the central maxim of his ethics: 'Continuez!' Yet, I also think that this heroism can be avoided by another understanding of Badiou that can be seen by considering his relation to Lacanian psychoanalysis.

In *L'éthique*, Badiou provides a formal definition of an ethics of truths: *the ethical is defined as the free submission to a principle that decides to continue with a process of truth.* In relation to psychoanalysis, we might say that the ethics of the psychoanalytic situation consists in the decision to *continue* in the process of the transferential interpretative situation under the normative constraint of a desire which is not to be given way on. More generally, the ethical is that which gives consistency to the presence of someone (*un quelqu'un* – the specific, punctual individual that pledges itself to a process of subjectivisation) in the composition of the subject that effectuates the process of truth. This ethical consistency on the part of someone is a fidelity to a process of subjectivisation that is in excess of that someone. That is, it is a process of subjectivisation that passes through the specific, punctual individual, but which the latter cannot exhaust or fully know. Thus, the someone is ethically committed to a process of subjectivisation that exceeds its knowledge, that *existe à son insu*, and is, to this extent, *unconscious*.

But if this is the case, then the subject has to commit itself to a process of truth that is in part unconscious; that is, the subject has to commit itself to a decision that has already been taken within me, *à mon insu*, as it were. This takes us back to Lacan's ethics of psychoanalysis. Badiou reads Lacan's ethical imperative from Seminar VII, 'ne pas céder sur son désir' ('do not give way on its desire, i.e. unconscious desire'), as 'ne pas céder sur ce que de soi-même on ne sait pas' ('do not give way on that of oneself one does not know'). For Badiou, the someone who embarks upon a path of subjectivisation is seized by a process of truth that cannot be cognitively or reflectively exhausted. Thus, the someone has to be faithful to a fidelity that it cannot understand, which is one way of understanding the analytic pact of transference in psychoanalysis.

In this sense, the heroism of the decision in Badiou can be avoided by showing that ethical decisions are always about elements of the Real that are irreducible to the conscious will. Thus, the decision is taken with regard to the other within me, the *Faktum* of unconscious desire. However, there is also a problem in Badiou's understanding of Lacanian psychoanalysis that I alluded to above when I said that his ethical theory risks losing sight of the dimension of the Thing. Badiou claims that his theory is an ethics of the real insofar as the real is of the order of the *rencontre* for Lacan, it is what we cannot know, that which resists symbolisation, where *das Ding* addresses and claims the subject without the subject being able to address and claim it. This is the structure of *der Komplex der Nebenmenschen* installed at the heart of the Lacanian and Levinasian ethical subject as its Law.

Now, although Badiou describes his theory as an ethics of the real, my question is: *isn't this traumatic dimension of the Thing as the Law that divides the subject overcome in Badiou through his emphasis on love*, something which is revealed particularly clearly in his reading of St Paul? Badiou writes in his seventh theorem in *Saint Paul*, 'Le processus subjective d'une vérité est une seule et même chose que l'amour de cette vérité'.[13] That is, the way in which a subject relates itself to the event is through an act of love which overcomes the dimension of Law, which is always identified with death: 'le premier des noms de la mort, c'est: Loi'.[14] In this sense, perverse as it may sound, Badiou's moral theory would be structurally Christian, whereas Lacan and Levinas would be structurally Judaic insofar as their conception of ethics is based around a dimension of Law that cannot be overcome through the work of love.

Let me put the same criticism another way. On the one hand, Badiou would seem to grant that there has to be a dimension of *l'innomable* in all ethical action, 'le Bien n'est le Bien qu'autant qu'il ne prétend rendre le monde bon'.[15] In this sense, the subject always abuts elements of the real, aspects of the situation that remain inaccessible to it. Yet, on the other hand, how is this claim consistent with the emphasis on love, which would seem to entail the overcoming of the law of the

105

Real in an act of mystical identification with the *événement*? That is, in Lacanian terms, isn't there a risk of a reduction of the order to Real to the Symbolic through Badiou's emphasis on love? This is revealed most clearly perhaps in Badiou's seeming hostility to the death drive as the basic law of the unconscious in Freud and Lacan.[16] Two things are revealed here: (1) the *structural Judaism* of psychoanalysis is confirmed through its preoccupation with the unsurpassable character of the death drive, the Law and the Real, a fact that would simply confirm my attempted rapprochement between Levinas and Lacan; (2) the *structurally Christian* character of Badiou's work is revealed in what is perhaps its most attractive feature, namely its persistent and restless affirmation of life and its refusal of the tragic pathos of Lacanian psychoanalysis in the name of courage and energy. In this sense, Lacan would be closer to Levinas than to Badiou. But maybe for precisely this reason Lacan, Levinas, and everybody else should try to be closer to Badiou. This brings me to the question of comedy.

Beckett as Heroic Comic Anti-Hero of Badiou's Work: Against Tragedy

I would like to return to the question of heroism and wager a final series of questions on the figure whom I would choose to see as the real hero of Badiou's work, not St Paul but Samuel Beckett. Let me begin with a wonderful quotation from Badiou's *Thèses sur le théâtre*:

> Je ne crois pas que la principale question de notre époque soit l'horreur, la souffrance, le destin ou la déréliction. Nous en sommes saturés et, en outre, la fragmentation de tout celà en idées-théâtre est incessante. Nous ne voyons que du théâtre choral ou compassionel. Notre question est celle du courage affirmative, de l'énergie locale. Se saisir d'un point, et le tenir. Notre question est donc moins celle des conditions d'une tragédie moderne que celle des conditions d'une comédie moderne. Beckett le savait, dont le théâtre, correctement complété, est hilarant.[17]

It's true, Beckett understood this very well; but have we really understood Beckett? Let me take a small sideways step to try to explain myself. Ethics, for Badiou, is that which governs our lives as subjects, what gives them consistency, and its only maxim is 'Continuez!' Submission to this ethical principle involves a certain asceticism, a certain renunciation, but this is only at the service of our desire, which sometimes seems close to Spinoza's notion of *conatus essendi*. As is well known, and in fidelity to a largely German tradition that stretches back from Heidegger to Hegel and Hölderlin, Lacan's prime example of someone who acts in accordance with her desire and who *continues* is Antigone. She exemplifies the position of being *entre deux morts* which, for Lacan, best describes the situation of human finitude. Antigone is the heroine of Lacanian psychoanalysis; that is, she is possessed by that transgressive *atè* or madness that enables her to stand out against the conformism of the State, where all ethical action is reduced to *le service des biens*, and achieve an authentic relation to finitude.

Now, I have problems with Antigone, not so much with her *personnage*, but with its exemplarity. I have elsewhere attempted to criticise Lacan for employing tragedy as his paradigm of sublimation, arguing that the reading of *Antigone* in Seminar VII makes psychoanalysis the inheritor of a tragic paradigm that stretches back to Schelling's Identity Philosophy.[18] I criticise this paradigm for making finitude too heroic, where the tragic heroine achieves a certain purification of desire in the experience of being-towards-death. Inspired by Lacoue-Labarthe's anti-Heideggerian reading of Hölderlin's translation of the *Antigone*, I call this *the tragic-heroic paradigm*.[19] I argue simply that a quite different picture of finitude emerges if we focus on the phenomena of the comic and humour. The picture of finitude that I want to recommend is not accessible in the form of tragic affirmation, but rather in that of comic acknowledgement, the acknowledgement of the ubiquity of the finite, but also its ungraspability. My approval of the demand of finitude is not equal to that demand, but makes that demand even more demanding. To put this in a formula, I think that humour is a form of minimal sublimation that corresponds to the structure of depression in the Freudian sense, but which is not at all depressing. *Au contraire*, Freud concludes his essay on humour by claiming that humour – dark, sardonic, wicked humour – is 'liberating and elevating'. 'Look!', he concludes, 'Here is the world, which seems so dangerous! It is nothing but a game for children – just worth making a jest about.' Ethical subjectivity is comic rather than tragic.

To return to Badiou, what perhaps most interests me in his work is the link between affirmative ethical courage and comedy as the form of aesthetic sublimation that would best exemplify this ethical stance. This is what Beckett understood so well and it is why his tragi-comedy uses the strategy of humour, hilarity and *drôlerie* to attain an ethical stance of courage and love of humanity. As Badiou rightly writes,

> Il faut jouer Beckett dans la plus intense drôlerie ... et c'est alors seulement qu'on voit surgir ce qui de fait est la vraie destination du comique: non pas un symbole, non pas une métaphysique déguisée, encore moins une dérision, mais un amour puissant pour l'obstination humaine, pour l'incrévable désir.[20]

Thus, for Badiou, it is the strange cast of characters who populate Beckett's fiction and theatre that best exemplify the maxim 'Continuez!': 'il faut continuer, je ne peux pas continuer, je vais continuer'.

Pleinement d'accord. And yet, I have a question on this interpretation of Beckett. For Badiou, Beckett practises a form of *ascèse méthodique*, an asceticism that reduces all ethical considerations to the bare maxim: 'Continuez!'[21] The problem I have here is that this makes Beckett sound like a stoic. Now, although there are obviously strongly stoical elements of discipline, denial, rigour and exactitude in his work, I don't think that Beckett is *only* a stoic. That is, Beckett does not just say 'il faut continuer', but also 'je ne peux pas continuer', and what is perhaps the most characteristic feature of Beckett's writing is not just the decision to continue, but also the acknowledgement that I cannot continue. That is to say, *Beckett's prose is characterised by an aporetic rhythm of continuity and discontinuity*, of being able to go on and not being able to go on. This aporetic rhythm is the very movement of Beckett's writing, what he calls 'a syntax of weakness', a self-undoing language that cannot go on and cannot but go on, that continues *in* its failure, and continues *as* that failure. For example, 'Live and invent. I have tried. Invent. It is not the word. Neither is live. No matter. I have tried.'[22] Or a longer example:

> What am I to do, what shall I do, what should I do, in my situation, how proceed? By aporia pure and simple? Or by affirmations and negations invalidated as uttered, or sooner or later. Generally speaking. There must be other shifts. Otherwise it would be quite hopeless. But it is quite hopeless. I should mention without going any further that I say aporia without knowing what it means. Can one be ephectic otherwise than unawares? I don't know.[23]

But this syntax of weakness is at its most explosive when it becomes a *comic syntax*, as it does so powerfully in Beckett's work. For example, Clov to Hamm in *Endgame*, 'Do you believe in the life to come?'; Hamm to Clov, 'Mine was always that. Got him that time.'[24] Or again, as I began with mention of parrots, here is Molloy on Lousse's parrot:

> Fuck the son of a bitch, fuck the son of a bitch. He must have belonged to an American sailor, before he belonged to Lousse. Pets often change masters. He didn't say much else. No, I'm wrong, he also said, Putain de merde! He must have belonged to a French sailor before he belonged to the American sailor. Putain de merde! Unless he had hit on it alone, it wouldn't surprise me. Lousse tried to make him say, Pretty Polly! I think it was too late. He listened, his head on one side, pondered, then said, Fuck the son of a bitch. It was clear he was doing his best.[25]

Beckett's work is characterised by a syntax of weakness, a comic syntax that continues and then decides not to continue, simply to realise that it cannot not continue and that it must continue. It is this experience, like that of Vladimir and Estragon trying and failing to hang themselves in *Godot*, that is so comically tragic, or tragically comic. But if that is the case, then there are two conflicting norms in Beckett's work: on the one hand, there is 'Continuez!', and on the other hand, 'Ratage!' The logic of Beckett's work follows the aporetic rhythm of these two imperatives, between the demand to continue and the acknowledgement that all continuation is failure. The courage to continue does not simply derive from a stoical act of ascetic will, from some Spinozist *conatus essendi* or Fichtean *Streben*, but rather from the continual experience of failure: 'Try again, fail again, fail better.'

Let me try one last time. There seems to be a residual heroism at work in Badiou, the heroism of resistance and militant activism: St Paul, Jean Cavaillès, or Georges Canguilhem. But this doesn't seem to be Beckett's world, filled as it is with anti-heroic personnages, a gallery of moribunds who seem riveted to the spot, unable to move: Murphy, Molloy, Malone, Mahood, Watt and Worm. But is such blatant inactivity another form of resistance? Might not Beckett's heroes best exemplify what it would mean to be, in Badiou's allusion to Mallarmé, *les militants de l'action restreinte*?[26] Now, I would like to be a militant of restrained action, particularly as it doesn't sound too demanding, but what is it?

The question of heroism is urgent because the stakes are not just ethical, they are also political. As Badiou admits at the beginning and end of his *Abrégé de métapolitique*, true politics is rare, the last good example being 1968.[27] Now perhaps this is right, but nevertheless what I suspect in Badiou is *the seduction of a great politics*, the event that would, in Nietzsche's words, *casser en deux l'histoire*. Now, perhaps the epoch of great politics, like the epoch of great art for Heidegger and Hegel, is over. Perhaps. And perhaps that is a good thing. Perhaps we have had enough of the virile, Promethean politics of the will, the longing for total revolution. In my view, to be seduced by great politics is to risk nostalgically blinding oneself to the struggles of the present. As such, the seduction risks being politically disempowering. What we have to hope for, in Paul's sense of the word, is the knowledge that it *is*, in Beckett's words, all quite hopeless. But such hopelessness is not resignation and could provide a bridge to a smaller politics, what I would see as an micro-politics of continual interruption, interruptions both internal to civil society and at the international trans-State level. Such interruptions would be movements of dissensual emancipatory praxis that work against the consensual horizon of the State. Perhaps we just have to content ourselves with smaller actions and smaller victories, an everyday and heroically anti-heroic militantism. That is, we have to learn to expect much more from much less. To my mind, such a politics is not approached through the figure of the tragic hero – lofty, solitary, derelict and *unheimlich* – but rather through what Badiou calls 'le pragmatisme humoristique' of Beckett. As Malone quips in what I would like to imagine as an ironic response to St Paul, 'For why be discouraged, one of the thieves was saved, that is a generous percentage.'[28]

Notes

1 Wallace Stevens, 'The Idea of Order at Key West', in *Collected Poems*, London: Faber, 1956, pp.58–59.

2 D. Henrich, 'The Concept of Moral Insight and Kant's Doctrine of the Fact of Reason', in *The Unity of Reason*, Cambridge, MA: Harvard University Press, 1994, p.55–87.

3 The philosopher who doesn't really fit here is Hegel, who rejects the Kantian version of moral insight in the strongest terms as that 'cold duty, the last undigested log in our stomach, a revelation given to reason' (quoted in Henrich, *Moral Insight*, p.69). However, one might say that the notion of moral insight in Hegel is the awareness of freedom as the self-consciousness of Spirit in its historical development, something to be learned by consciousness by recapitulating the experiences described in the *Phenomenology of Spirit*. In other words, moral insight would be identical with the achievement of rational self-determination.

4 A very similar line of criticism of Badiou can be found in Slavoj •i•ek's fascinating book, *The Ticklish Subject*, London and New York: Verso, 1999; see ch. 3 'The Politics of Truth, or, Alain Badiou as a Reader of Saint Paul', pp.127–70.

5 A. Badiou, *Saint Paul. Le fondation de l'universalisme*, Paris: Presses Universitaires de France, 1997.

6 A. Badiou, *L'éthique. Essai sur la conscience du Mal*, Paris: Hatier, 1993.

7 Badiou, *L'éthique*, p.25.

8 For a useful critique of Badiou on this question of religion, see Jean-Jacques Lecercle, 'Cantor, Lacan, Mao, Beckett, *même combat*: The Philosophy of Alain Badiou', *Radical Philosophy*, 1999, 93, pp.6–13.

9 A. Badiou, *L'être et l'événement*, Paris: Seuil, 1988, pp.9–10. The same thought is expressed in the *Court traité de l'ontologie transitoire*, Paris: Seuil, 1998, p.189.

10 A. Badiou, *L' incrévable désir*, Paris: Hachette, 1995.

11 Jacques Derrida, *Politiques de l'amitié* (trans. G. Collins), Paris: Galilée, 1994 (Engl. edn *The Politics of Friendship*, London/New York: Verso, 1997).

12 I have argued for such a view in detail in the final chapter of my *Ethics–Politics–Subjectivity*, London and New York: Verso, 1999. See also my 'Remarks on Derrida and Habermas', forthcoming in *Constellations*, 7:4.

13 Badiou, *Saint Paul*, p.97.

14 Badiou, *Saint Paul*, p.78.

15 Badiou, *Saint Paul*, p.75.

16 A more detailed version of this line of criticism can be found in •i•ek, *The Ticklish Subject*, pp.145–67.

17 A. Badiou, *Petit manuel d'inesthétique*, Paris: Seuil, 1998, pp.117–18.

18 The most succinct version of this argument can be found in 'Comedy and Finitude: Displacing the Tragic-Heroic Paradigm in Philosophy and Psychoanalysis', *Constellations*, 1999, 6:1, pp. 108–22.

19 P. Lacoue-Labarthe, *Metaphrasis*, Paris: Presses Universitaires de France, 1997.

20 Badiou, *L'incrévable désir*, pp.74–75.

21 Badiou, *L'incrévable désir*, p.19.
22 S. Beckett, *The Trilogy*, London: Picador, 1979, p.179.
23 Beckett, *The Trilogy*, p.267.
24 S. Beckett, *Endgame*, London: Faber, 1958, p.35.
25 Beckett, *The Trilogy*, p.36
26 A. Badiou, *Abrégé de métapolitique*, Paris: Seuil, 1998, p.118.
27 Badiou, *Abrégé de métapolitique*, pp.17, 167.
28 Beckett, *The Trilogy*, p.233.

CHAPTER 6

Instants of Diminishing Representation: The Problem of Temporal Modalities

KARL HEINZ BOHRER

The exceptional moment has come to be recognised as a central theme of modern literature. The concept of 'instant' (*Augenblick*) has proven useful in this regard.[1] In order to explore it – as has become more and more clear – various works of classical and romantic modernity can be considered, so that beyond intellectual-historical or monographic insights, an understanding of its structure can be achieved.[2] A promising start can be made with a comparative analysis of representative instants, which helps provide an initial clarification of the semantic and symbolic complexity of this concept, for here the underlying problem of this theme, that is the intellectual reference of the emphasis peculiar to the exceptional temporal modality, will appear in all its clarity. Stated baldly in a formula: the instant with a claim to eternity must be distinguished from the instant as a moment without duration. The instant with a claim to eternity finds its paradigm in Goethe's negative Faustian sentence on the instant that should linger. Positively, one could reckon spiritual epiphanies to this category, as well. The Pentecost in Hölderlin's hymn 'Patmos' (1801),[3] and the emphatic concept of a 'now' as developed by Heidegger in his reading of Hölderlin, can serve as examples here.[4]

However, it is already clear that the status of such an instant, referring to an eternal time or a transcendentally invested point in time, is not actually the 'instant' that so characterises modern literature, and primarily classical modernism, and which is here considered. None the less, it can serve an important comparative function, for it allows us to investigate the extent to which the alternative conception, the instant as moment without duration, that is, the 'suddenness' of classical modernism, truly escapes metaphysical reference. For the particular sense of such a structure of 'suddenness' as we find in texts of James Joyce, Virginia Woolf, Marcel Proust, Robert Musil, Franz Kafka, Walter Benjamin and not least the French surrealists[5] consists precisely in the paired aspects of an emphasis and an unclear justification for that emphasis. One could speak as well of an absent reference. Here Wägenbaur's distinction between 'epiphanic', 'Romantic', and 'postmodern' instants is helpful,[6] since the criterion that establishes this sequence is the diminishing presence of a content for the instant (even though Wägenbaur understands this in a performance-theoretical manner, that is, as the presence of the instant of writing itself, and even despite the disadvantage of its presuppositions in terms of teleology and philosophy of history). Without placing too much weight on categories that are themselves conceptually not strictly analogous with one another, we can say roughly that the epiphanic instant appears in texts of Goethe and Hölderlin, as well as Heidegger, while the Romantic instant, the instant, that is, in which the presence of what appears is ambiguously at hand, can be discerned in the texts of classical modernism that we are here considering.

Before I examine these relations more closely it has to be stressed that determinations in terms of the history of literature or even the philosophy of history cannot help us here: the appearance of the temporally limited modality of the sudden instant in classical modernism – as opposed to the eternal instant of German Idealism – cannot be specified in an intellectual-historical way. Pre-modern literature exhibits forms analogous to the modern suddenness and its lack of reference, and it does so at points which are representative of the history of consciousness. Kleist's explanation of the French Revolution as an abrupt accident, or the language-philosophical justification of the decisive insight by discursive argument[7] amounts to the separation of the suddenly appearing event from any causal reference. Rousseau's report of his sudden fall at Ménilmontant, brought about by the sudden appearance of a great hound, stresses the unique instant, remarkable as being a pure present, without any reflectively constituted identity, while none the less being freighted with a high intensity of feeling.[8] And finally, Montaigne's depiction of a nearly fatal fall from a horse – an episode in the *Essais* that, if not the source of Rousseau's account in the 'Second Rêverie', most probably lent it its tone – contains a phenomenal awareness in which the discontinuous and contingent instant appears, all the more as Montaigne had already discovered, for himself so to speak, the temporal modality of the pure Now.[9]

These three examples, all of which, despite their sustained and significant historical differences, show instantaneousness without any ideal reference, are not explicable either by an intellectual-historically similar motivation or through literary intertextuality (even if the Rousseau–Montaigne relation is considered). To describe them as premonitory signs of a modernity in which they participate to different degrees would be, however tempting, a teleological argument that would respond to the problem of the instant exclusively historically just at the point where it represents an escape from history. The 'suddenness' character in the intended sense of weak reference cannot be explained in terms of an automatic progress towards modernity, since the cited and not less modern examples of Goethe, Hölderlin and Heidegger exhibit precisely a metaphysical reference.

The Avoidance of the Metaphysical Reference: Joyce, Woolf and Musil

We cannot therefore determine the metaphysical referent of suddenness through a more or less explicit conception of modernity, but only by means of its metaphoric-semantic signs. Thus the most obvious, the historical reference, is excluded. But then, how is the metaphysical reference, hidden as it may be, to be understood? In the authors with which we are here concerned, the answer varies. Most explicitly, the 'epiphanies' of James Joyce seem to indicate a metaphysical referent, if only in the choice of a paratheological category that appears to gesture towards a spiritual event of a higher order. Without discussing this again in detail here,[10] let it suffice to say that despite the lingering thomistic determination of beauty in its three qualities (as Joyce translates them in *Stephen Hero*: 'wholeness', 'harmony', 'radiance'), he stresses not the ideal content of beauty, but the aesthetic perception *vis-à-vis* the radiant phenomenon itself.[11] The rendering of time in *A Portrait of the Artist as a Young Man* is analogous: what arises is the pure immanence of the instant, not the revelation of a soul and therefore the mode of appearance of meaning.[12] As the classical categories of space and time disappear in favour of a phenomenological sensation, no ideal symbolism or archetypal metaphoric arises in their place. None the less, there is a deeper *causa*. It lies not in a substance correlated to the object of perception, but in the happiness of perception itself, in the reflexive 'blink of an eye' (*Augenblick*). When the content of this momentary happiness is examined more closely, none the less, a utopian fantasy of nature appears, one that remains, however, within the element of perception and does not come together as a mythology. What is important to note here is that a tension has been produced between, on the one hand, a substantial referent only just avoided, and, on the other hand, the metaphoric production of fascination.

This structure of the instant without duration is most closely approximated in the representation of 'moments of being' in Virginia Woolf's *A Sketch of the Past* (1939–40). Here, too, the instant of pure appearance is presented in the medium of the impressions of nature – the difference between Joyce's fiction and Woolf's autobiography not being essential to our problem. The remarks on the remembered phenomenality of natural objects in the landscape of her childhood (St Ives in Cornwall) do not recall any meanings, but call forth instead vague, hardly conscious impressions of form and colour. But – and here is the first analogy to the 'epiphanies' of Joyce's *Portrait* text – they provoke an 'ecstasy'.[13] Here, as well, a theological concept drawn from mystical experience of the divine is employed as emphatic expression for the conceptless perception of the things that happen. Likewise, the concept of 'intensity' appears,[14] a notion that has become quite important in the scientific discussion of self-referential phenomenality.[15] What is at stake here is the production of a past, extraordinary feeling by means of a feeling which is still present, whereby another concept we have already encountered, that of 'happiness', shows up.[16] Particularly at this point it is clear the extent to which the thematic of the 'instant' has to do entirely with internality, not externality: namely with literary modernity's fascination with the *mémoire involontaire* since Proust's *Recherche*. The decisive sentence in Woolf runs: 'That means, as I suppose, that my memory produces what I have forgotten'.[17] The condition of one who remembers is understood as a dissolution of personal identity.

The representation does not, however, remain at the level of the diffuse perceptions of a subject not sure of its own personality, but rather the perceived phenomena are differentiated according to the character of their ontological marking. A few special instants of 'being' ('moments of being') are distinguished from the myriad banal conditions, in that they transcend the moments of ordinary psychic reality ('moments of nonbeing').[18] Three elements are determinate for the inner constitution of these moments of being. They effect, in a way similar to Joyce, a tension between ideal reference and non-reference. These elements are suddenness, shock, and wholeness.[19] The suddenness of the shock in which the imaginary experience occurs is captured in the process of its linguistic rendering, whereby a 'wholeness' arises that is characterised as the 'reality behind the appearance'.[20] This is not the place to pursue the objective relation either to the two-phase structure of Proust's *mémoire involontaire* or to Benjamin's notion of *chock*. What is essential for our question of the metaphysical reference of the instantaneous appearance is rather the character of 'wholeness'. This category, in contrast to the temporally abbreviated categories of 'suddenness' and 'shock', is a category of 'duration', indeed, a concept that contradicts temporality as such, and in which something like the idea of a thing seems to be sublated (*aufgehoben*). Woolf speaks as well of a 'pattern' behind the 'cotton wool' of the banal moment that is expressed in the 'moment of being'. Is she therefore guided, intentionally or not, by a Platonic-mystical idea? After she mentions 'Shakespeare' and 'Beethoven' as further names bringing the material together, and identifies these as 'the true', there follows the autopoetic counter-explanation that dissolves the Platonic ontology: 'But there is no Shakespeare, there is no Beethoven; certainly and emphatically there is no God; we are the word; we are the music; we are the thing itself. And I see this when I have a shock.'[21]

Where James Joyce does not reject *expressis verbis* a substantial identification of his epiphanies, but rather subverts such an identification through his metaphoric representation, Virginia Woolf considers it necessary to deny explicitly a transcendent or idealist understanding of her moments of being. Against, so to speak, her own inclinations: these instants are not objective messages from heaven, but products of the language of an imaginative subject, freed from the laboratories of the unconscious – if one can take seriously the quasi-psychological context for the notion of shock in the above citation. Now the explanations of the author are one thing, the theoretical examination of an aesthetic another. One might very well read the 'moment of being', despite Woolf's admittedly *ex cathedra* resistance to Platonic Ideas, as a metaphysically referential sign. Still, it is significant that representative exponents of classical modernism feel compelled to defend themselves against any equating of their fantasies of an 'instant' with an absolute content. Interestingly, but not surprisingly, this holds as well for Marcel Proust's *Recherche*, where, in the context of phenomenological descriptions of moods of the landscape, assurances are constantly repeated that this is not an identity or identification with an absolute. Nowhere is this peculiar resistance to transcendence together with an insistence upon intensity so conceptually apparent as in Walter Benjamin's category of 'profane illumination'[22] or Robert Musil's image of 'daylight mysticism'.[23] Both of these conceptions exhibit a *contradictio in adjecto*: they address a spiritual condition or orientation that definitively transcends the profane everyday, while at the same time insisting that this remains immanent or without any element of darkness. For classical modernism, this is a quite promising polarisation: to understand itself transcendentally without transcendence. One might be tempted to see in this a radically intellectual, even quasi-mystical, posture that rejects reality while simultaneously finding itself forced to acknowledge a completely secularised, demystified world. This explanatory strategy is certainly promising in the specific cases of Walter Benjamin and Robert Musil, who attempt to maintain and assure materialistic or rational-scientific methods in the face of their utopian themes.

In order to decide between these alternative possibilities, Robert Musil's conception of the *anderer Zustand* (alternative condition) can serve as a third example for our enquiry. Musil is concerned with the mysterious immediacy of an ideal 'now' purified of all experience of reality and everything already known: psychic eventness, not yet devalued by *déja-vu*: the ego in a singular, unrepeatable condition, before it again becomes an 'Idea', the identity of a character.[24] Once again we find the familiar structure of an instantaneousness that is simultaneously significant. How can this structure be meaningful, without some sort of conventional representation intervening, without, that is, in the higher order we are here considering, an idea of the absolute? Musil insists here in a particularly original way, to which we will return in another context, upon the sheer facticity of things that happen: 'Important for the deed is that it be done; for the experience that it be experienced.'[25] Such a sentence emphasises its predicate by downplaying its subject. Virginia Woolf achieves something similar by downplaying the sense of self against the sensation.[26] The instant without duration, but none the less full of meaning, can be understood as an invention of the phenomenological consciousness that bursts all systems. It was prepared for by the Romantic category of the 'vague', developed by the Impressionists in their conception of reality, and is brought to an aporetic modality in the hardened, highly intellectually reflective representatives of a modernist consciousness that we have cited as examples.

André Breton: The Surrealist Event

One finds metaphoric forms that work through the possibility of an instantaneous pathos without transcendence in an even more radical way, by taking the category of facticity particularly seriously, without however adopting Musil's argumentative strategies. Paradoxically, this occurred in French Surrealism. We will restrict ourselves here to the work of André Breton. Let us start with his definition of beauty, the last sentence of *Nadja*: 'La beauté sera CONVULSIVE où ne sera pas.' ('Beauty will be *CONVULSIVE* or will not be at all').[27] One must recall that the concept of beauty plays a central role both in Joyce's 'epiphanies' and in Musil's *anderer Zustand*[28] – not only in the form of an emphasis upon nature, where idyllic or heroic nature shines forth, but as an abstract highest principle of the instantaneous event. In what way can Breton's definition be related to the instantaneous event? First, with the image of convulsiveness, which is more of a trembling or cramped twitching than a quaking, beauty is equated with a process of movement and not with a qualitative condition. Beauty is the course of a subjective impulse, for in a discussion preceding the definition, Breton links the beauty with which surrealism is concerned to passion (*fins passionelles*).[29] Beauty is thereby principally distinguished from the 'static' as well as the 'dynamic' forms in which it had traditionally been understood. This type of beauty is thus differentiated from classical beauty, whether it be 'the shadow of the Odalisk', the 'depths of tragedy' or the Romantic version as expressed in Breton's famous 'wild gallop'.[30] This convulsiveness is cast as an itself convulsive, that is, no longer mimetic, image of an event:

Beauty is like a train that ceaselessly roars out of the Gare de Lyon and which I know will never leave, which has not left. It consists of jolts and shocks, many of which do not have much importance, but which we know are destined to produce one Shock, which does. Which has all the importance I do not want to arrogate to myself.[31]

The analogy between this definition and Woolf's moment of being or Joyce's epiphany should not be overlooked. The comparison of Breton's image of 'convulsion' to Woolf's shock and Joyce's trembling is useful, even though the process Breton is describing is objective while the other two describe subjective processes. The fundamental proximity of the central concepts of these three authors gains support with the recognition of the structural similarity between Breton's and Woolf's notion of 'jolt' and 'moment of being'. First, the jolt or, more importantly, the instant in which it occurs, appears along with many other unimportant instants or jolts. Second, it is freighted with significance; although, in contrast to Woolf's category of 'wholeness', Breton does not say in what this significance consists. And herein lies precisely the important intensification of things which happen and which lack any unambiguous reference. So, too, the metaphoric staging of the train that never leaves the Gare de Lyon means that the event of beauty, as opposed to the occurrence of Woolf's moment of being or Joyce's epiphany, manifests an extreme advance in self-referentiality. By establishing things which happen as predicate, the determination of the subject has been powerfully suppressed. Only apparently is this a result of the technical-industrial scenery that is, after all, surreally alienated. This scenery may itself, when compared to Woolf or Joyce, hinder a transcendental reading – though the pathos of the train motif at this historical point ought not to be underestimated. But the displacement of the meaning of the event results from the presentation of the process of movement itself, which achieves here something simultaneously bizarre and sublime.

Where the concept of beauty is thematised in the context of an instant without a referent, *one* subterranean reference is implied as emphatically as can be. Let us return briefly to the category as it appears in Joyce and Musil. For both writers, the ultimate identification of the unique moment culminates in the word 'beauty'. As we have already seen, this does not mean that beauty is understood as an ideal, metaphysical quantum, a substance ordered alongside truth and goodness. In the *Phaedrus*, Plato famously distinguished beauty from 'justice' and *sophrosyne* or even-temperedness through its 'spectacularity' or sensuous appearance.[32] Thus Joyce stresses the isolated moment of appearance in beauty, not its ideal content. He emphatically insists upon the act of perception, and designates his aesthetic as an aesthetic of perception. Musil as well: to the touch of a vague and sudden condition he adds the word 'beauty', as a word to which he assigns validity only before it solidifies into the status of a firm concept.

Does the word 'beauty' thus give the notion of an instant greater reference? Or is it rather – and this would be the new perspective – the expectation of a referent that has finally disappeared and with the word 'beauty' submitted to a most radical substitution of determinate content by indefinite form? An aesthetic criterion dominates Joyce's, Musil's and Woolf's 'instants' in their identification of the instant with beauty or, more exactly, the subjective instant with the perception of the beautiful, and this criterion resists metaphysical principles. At the same time – this holds for all three of these classical modernist authors – a spiritual atmosphere remains that serves a medial function and continues to point expectations of significance in a strongly referential direction.

In the case of Breton's convulsive beauty this is different, initially because the conceptual relation has been inverted here: the 'instant' is not explained by means of 'beauty' but rather 'beauty' by means of the 'instant'. The defining category is thereby transformed into one less definite. Breton is the first to posit the peculiar analogising of instant and beauty in its ultimate incommensurability but also in its necessity: beauty as the instant, the instant as the Beautiful. Moreover, the fact that twentieth-century art and literature as a whole have set themselves under the law of beauty – and not, say, of ugliness[33] – in a singularly emphatic way lends the surrealistic formula something approaching the force of law. That it is beauty that gives the instant its instantaneous quality is not a self-evident explanation that would necessarily follow from the emphatic structure alone. Literary examples from the early twentieth century would provoke rather a contrary expectation – ugliness, the terrible, qualities, that is, that could only be understood as variants of the sublime. But, in the tradition exemplified by Joyce and Musil, it is precisely the beautiful – as Rilke's Beauty as *Anfang des Schrecklichen*, the 'beginning of terror'[34] – that is hypostatised into sublime dimensions, and Breton's application of this can be understood as the concomitant methodical avoidance of rhetoric in order to achieve a new immediacy. What is incommensurable and mysterious in Breton's instant of beauty becomes even clearer when he presents it directly in an imagined scenario:

I have always, beyond belief, hoped to meet, at night and in a wood, a beautiful naked woman or rather, since such a wish once expressed means nothing, I regret, beyond belief, not having met her. Imagining such an encounter is not, after all, so fantastic: it might happen. It seems to me that everything would have stopped short – I would not even be writing what I am writing. I adore this situation which of all situations is the one where I am most likely to have lacked presence of mind. I would probably not even have thought of running away. (Anyone who laughs at this last sentence is a pig.) At the end of one afternoon, last year, in the side aisles of the 'Electric-Palace', a naked woman, who must have come in wearing only her coat, strolled, dead white, from one row to the next. This in itself was upsetting. Far, unfortunately, from being extraordinary enough, since this section of the 'Electric' was the most commonplace sort of illicit sexual rendezvous.[35]

The surrealistic event in the form of a naked beauty in the woods – what distinguishes this from the collective eroticism of a fairy-tale? First, such a hidden affinity between the two can indeed be observed, since the surrealistic *objet trouvé* – and the 'beautiful naked woman' appears thus as well – exerts the fascination of a trans-subjective symbol or sign no longer encompassed by quotidian psychology. To this is added the particular quality of Breton's event, those 'facts which may belong to the order of pure observation, but which on each occasion present all the appearances of a signal, without our being able to say precisely which signal, and of what'.[36] This status as a signal, not any message content that might be provided, distinguishes the surrealistic event: it even encompasses the rhetorical aspects of the pseudo-Longinic sublime, that is, 'a sudden manner of appearing', the form of 'lightning'.[37] An event, that is, an instant with a signalling effect, proceeds from a 'particular, undefinable movement', stimulated within us by 'extremely rare objects' or the 'arrival at this or that place'. Breton's exclusive emphasis on things that happen (*Vorgängigkeit*) is more clear than the relatively more determinate Joycean epiphany or Musil's *anderer Zustand*, both of which remain, none the less, as we have seen, pure perceptual events. The surreal event has no other referent than 'the distinct sensation that something momentous, something essential depends upon [it]'.[38]

The 'beautiful naked woman' is such a signifying event, cast in the form of possibility. Were the image of her appearance to be realised, 'everything would have stopped short'.[39] And the one perceiving the appearance would have lost his 'presence of mind'. The explanation says nothing about the content of the appearance that initiates this effect, but only about the allusions of the perceiving awareness. The theoretical construction closest to this is Nietzsche's description of the Dionysian instant: suddenness and a loss of self-consciousness. But this proximity is in turn distanced by the Dionysian–Romantic pathos: Breton's presentation of the event by contrast concludes by relativising the event 'naked beautiful woman', by placing a vulgar duplicate beside it – as an actual experience in a real scenery of amusement. What is being relativised here? Apparently the notion of the event's realisability. In other words, it is constitutive of the surreal experience that, unlike Joyce's and Woolf's 'epiphany' and 'instant', it indicates more than a mere exceptional state of the psyche, but remains in principle a perceptual category of the unreal, with which the surrealist engages in semiotically reflective play. If this is true, then every surreal event depends upon itself alone for its significance, and necessarily lacks a substantial relevance. Walter Benjamin, despite his criticism of *Nadja*'s 'very disturbing symptoms of deficiency' with regard to the 'profanity' of its illumination,[40] none the less saw its concept of love as supporting the unity of his own famous formula of 'profane illumination'.[41] He justified this view through Breton's annihilation of sensuality, comparable to erotic mysticism.[42] Without going into this analogy between surrealism and mysticism, we can merely note that Benjamin, in linking profanity and illumination, is not addressing the problem we are here discussing. He by no means denies, that is, that there is a determinate cause of the illumination, but he stresses that this cause is not spiritual, but quasi-political, 'preparing the decisive moment'.[43] However, even if this view produces wonderful thought-images, it is a narrowing of Breton's and surrealism's concept of the event, which – quite independently of any fitness for revolutionary purposes – represents, of all the ways modernist poets have conceptualised the instant, the one that dispenses with reference most consequentially.

This declaration of renunciation, as our glance at the signal character without significant content has already suggested, was theoretically formulated in the *First Manifesto of Surrealism (Manifeste du surréalisme)*: the 'mind' in a 'state of wakefulness', so the manifesto claims, has such a relative equilibrium that Breton must restrict himself to the saying 'that that idea, that woman makes an impression upon him', while being 'in no way ready' to specify 'which impression'.[44] The explanation follows:

> That idea, that woman touches him, makes him less rigid. For an instant she makes it so that he, separated from his dissolution, is dropped into the heavens as beautiful precipitation, that he can be, that he is. Because he knows no explanation, he conjures an accident, a darker godhead than any other, and attributes all his confusion to him. Who can claim that the perspective from which this idea moves him, that what he loves in the eyes of that woman, is not what connects him to his dream, chains him to given things, that have fallen away from him through his own fault?[45]

The genesis of the insight of the instant here developed can be understood as a metaphorically alienated, surreal reading of impulses from the unconscious; just as the surrealistic variant of the exceptional moment without reference can itself be largely explained with reference to the influence on the surrealists of a genuinely original reading of Freud's *Interpretation of Dreams*. The 'that' of the appearance results then from 'what' has been dreamed. Though there be a cause of the particular perception, its content remains peculiarly puzzling: the temporality of the 'instant' of perception is emphasised, as well as the absence of an explanation. The perceptual theoretical emphasis on the instant means as well a total sublation of a metaphysical reference-point in the surrealistic event; all the more since where Breton's language becomes immediately imaginative, as in the passage on the 'beautiful naked woman' from *Nadja*, it can accommodate no concepts that would have referents. It remains a pictured event that is restricted exclusively to subjective factors. The fact *that* something occurs absorbs all the emphasis that would actually be appropriate to the 'what'. The 'what', that is, the naked beauty in the woods, remains complete appearance. The aspect of beauty, which was equally important for both Joyce and Musil, and which contained an echo of utopian ideality, has disappeared from the surreal image. Here we encounter merely the visual appearance of the erotically beautiful itself in the sense of a surrealist allusion or diversion with signs, which does not proceed to any ultimate identity.

The surrealist radicalism that plays a contingent 'that' against a substantial 'what' is clarified by a formal-aesthetic argument of Lyotard's. In linking the sublime to the avant-garde through a consideration of the picture series *Here I, II, III* by the American painter Barnett Newman, as well as Newman's essay 'The Sublime is Now' (1948), Lyotard distinguishes between on the one hand the traditional ecstasy of a 'now' in the sense of an instant of consciousness, and a different 'now', that is not controlled by consciousness, on the other.[46] And he elucidates this distinction by means of the same argument as Breton, without in fact mentioning him. 'That it happens "precedes", so to speak, the question pertaining to what happens. Or rather, the question precedes itself, because "that it happens" is the question relevant as event, and it "then" pertains to the event that has just happened.'[47] Event means the pure facticity of the taking-place, not the expression of something hidden, not yet determined. This would make Newman, and following him Lyotard, the theoreticians with the most advanced formulation so far of the 'instant' without reference – all the more in that Newman discovers in Burke's presentation of the sublime a 'surrealistic' moment that, according to Lyotard, means that he criticises surrealism for its pre-Romantic/Romantic understanding of the indefinite. Lyotard extends Barnett Newman's remarks as if he were unable to see in this question a difference between Romantic and surrealistic understandings of art: to which he opposes his non-referential 'here and now'.[48]

Still, we have seen that Breton identifies this here-and-now-effect both imaginatively and theoretically, so that Lyotard's objection to Newman's critique of surrealism appears to construct something of a straw man, particularly as Newman uses the word 'surrealistic' quite metaphorically, without really examining the relationship between a surreal instant and its hidden reference. But even had Newman wanted to distance himself in principle from a surrealistic rendition of the 'indefinite', that is, the Romantic rendering of vagueness (Delacroix), he could not have based this on Breton. Walter Benjamin, in discussing surrealism's appearance of deficiency *vis-à-vis* the 'profane illumination', seems to have found such reasons, as we have seen. And it was with *Nadja* in particular in mind that he spoke of 'pernicious romantic prejudices' in an art that is the reaction of one who is surprised.[49] None the less he is, we remember, quite far away from our problematic: Benjamin counts not at all on the here and now, but works from the concept of a 'mystery' in the 'everyday world'.[50] From Benjamin's perspective surrealism as a whole, and not least Breton's *Nadja*, corresponded to this mystery in the everyday world. The absence of reference in Breton's instant escaped Benjamin, despite his knowledge of the text; Barnett Newman, on the other hand, probably did not have the relevant texts before him. This is certainly also true for Lyotard, his interpreter in these matters. Finally, therefore, the question arises: what formulation of the 'that'-argument is most advanced, where has the instant without reference been presented most plausibly? Lyotard's debate with Newman's 'now' suggests itself as a criterion. 'Advanced' means: furthest removed from the relation to a concept of substance. 'Most plausibly' means: despite this insubstantiality, unfolding the appearance of intensive meaning. André Breton's 'instant' seems more plausibly advanced than Lyotard's reading of Barnett Newman's 'now', because Breton's imaginative texts dispense philosophical explanations while being at the same time always theoretically reflected. This is no methodological objection to Lyotard, who, as a philosopher, has no other choice but to argue with substantial concepts, even where, as in his understanding of the sublime, he intends something else entirely. But with the application of philosophical categories – Heidegger's concept of 'event' or the speculation upon 'nothing happens'[51] – Lyotard freights the 'instant' with discursive meaning, in which even a teleological aspect is discernible that is at odds with all the conceptions of the instant here discussed. For the fact that 'something happens' is translated into the categories of ontology: such turns of phrase as 'pleasure in receiving the unknown', or 'joy in the intensification of being', that Lyotard uses for the 'that' contain an objective claim, one, that is, that establishes an identity, while Breton's comparable sentences always stress the subjective dimension. That should be emphasised all the more, since recent research has evinced a tendency to emphasise the mystical elements in classical modernism at the expense of its modernist–atheistic dimension,[52] granting the essential Western European texts only peripheral consideration.

The Negative Moment: Baudelaire and Leopardi

The more the momentary character of the instant is stressed, and the emphasis of the event drawn from this momentariness itself, the more insistently does a thought appear that makes this emphasis disappear forever and replaces it with a contrary motif, that of utter disappearance: the negative 'instant' or the 'instant' that is already extinguished in its appearance. This modality can be understood structurally as the reversal of the emphatic moment as it is manifested in Joyce's epiphanies, Woolf's moments of being, the *anderer Zustand* of Musil and Breton's surrealistic appearance. It is no peripheral figure of the literary imagination, but rather occupies the centre of the work of several of the greatest poets of the nineteenth and twentieth centuries.[53] Baudelaire's poem 'A une Passante'[54] can be taken as a significant paradigm of such a reversal of the emphatic instant into a negative or disappearing instant. At first the sudden appearance of the attractive woman dressed in mourning is represented as a flash of lightning (*un éclair*) to the one who perceives her and loses himself in this sight. Then, however, in the disappearance of the lightning, the 'night' arrives. The sentence in which the disappearance of the singular moment is thematised is: 'Fugitive beauté / Dont le regard m'a fait soudainement renaître, / Ne te verrai-je plus que dans l'éternité?' ('Lovely fugitive / whose sudden glance has brought me back to life! / Where is that life – not this side of eternity?').[55] Without dwelling upon the specific symbolism in the context of Baudelaire's metaphoric practice,[56] we merely observe the precipitous way the poem moves from appearance to non-appearance: the instant of perception is also the instant in which perception is no longer possible. The word 'eternity' imparts a particular force to the temporality of the reflective figure of an instant that has already slipped away. For the sudden instant of appearance, as emphatic, would demand precisely temporal permanence. This would be the eternity of the instant, here expressly denied. The instant of appearance is thereby relativised as well. Confronted with the criterion of eternity, and rejected by it, the sudden instant loses, if not its value, then at least its real content: it becomes something imagined. The closing stanza attempts to determine more exactly the reason for this loss: 'Ailleurs, bien loin d'ici! trop tard! jamais peut-être! / Car j'ignore où tu fuis, tu ne sais ou je vais, / O toi que j'eusse aimée, O toi qui le savais!' ('Elsewhere! Too far, too late, or never at all! / Of me you know nothing, I nothing of you – you / whom I might have loved and who knew that too!').[57] The suddenness of a repetition in eternity is, despite a hypothetical undecidability, in fact answered negatively and renders the instant's collapse out of existence instead of its eternal preservation all the more powerful: the *jamais* ('never') moves into the place of the *soudain* ('sudden'). That the *soudain* is only available on the condition of the *jamais* is the sublime-tragic point of the poem: there is no eternity on this side of death, whatever the other side, in transcendental eternity, may contain. Naturally Baudelaire is connecting here with the traditional motif of the 'little death',[58] brought in by the second stanza, about *le plaisir qui tue* ('joy that kills') and also the image of 'drinking' from her 'eyes' (*je buvais ... dans son œil*).[59] What follows from this is that the instant of love in the negativity of its temporal modality first awakens to itself only here. This instant is thus no less emphatic than the positive instant, or rather here the emphasis is even greater. In the fact that something 'absent' in the moment of its appearance already disappears, and as something disappearing becomes something desired, a reflective trope of the instant arises, one that anticipates what Breton was seeking: the event character of the pure 'that'. This is so regardless of the complex symbolic character, which we have not discussed, of the fleeting figure in mourning, which indeed indicates a massive representation or referent.

Is it merely coincidence that Breton presents as his 'that' example the appearance of an unknown 'woman', or 'idea'? Breton, who knew this literary tradition, must have seen in Baudelaire's poem to the passing pedestrian on the boulevard at least a premonition of his own Parisian mythology. From this perspective, the symbolic content of Baudelaire's appearance can be brought into accord with the priority of appearing in itself. The fleetingness of the appearance is part of the fascination it exerts, but requires as if by law that every instant of such imaginative weight be necessarily a negative one. Baudelaire did not invent the reflective figure of the negative 'instant' – as that instant which has always already been. It can be found many times in Goethe's later lyrics, 'Alexis and Dora', or 'Pandora' for example.[60] I mention this in order to forestall any hasty conclusions drawn from a theory of modernity that would make the notion of a negative 'instant' first possible in the late nineteenth century. A terminus dating in terms of historiography of literature cannot and ought not to be ventured here. One finds hints of temporal events understood as temporal loss as early as the lyric of Petrarch, or even in medieval French 'Lais'. None the less, one can say that Goethe's late classical lyric concentrates exclusively on the motif of the vanished instant of love, while with Baudelaire's enigmatic appearance on the boulevard, one would not be mistaken to see in addition to the disappearing instant of the lover's glance a reflection on the character of imagination itself;[61] a reflection that would indeed open onto a truly 'modern' reflection on the instant.

Though Baudelaire mentions him only once, if entirely respectfully, as one of a paradigmatic series of foreign melancholics, his immediate precursor in thinking the negative 'instant' is Giacomo Leopardi, the Italian lyricist and author of philosophical fragments.[62] Leopardi was read by merely a few important authors, such as Nietzsche, only in the 1860s, after Schopenhauer had called him as a witness on behalf of his own philosophy.[63] A larger German readership, not least because of Heyse's translation of *Operette morali* (1889), developed more concrete understandings of him only in the 1890s. This reaction, whether affirmative or critical, was none the less limited to a vague identification of Leopardi with a late-Romantic sentimental pessimism and was not aware of the stringency of his temporal analyses. Even Schopenhauer does not go beyond the general claim that Leopardi was the most important author of pessimistic existence.[64] And one must conclude from his own discussion of time as transitoriness[65] that the specificity of Leopardi's reflective figure of the negative instant not only did not occupy Schopenhauer, but also did not even appear relevant to him, although he came close to thematising the temporality of time.

One finds the temporalising of the instant, that is, the precipitousness of the now into now-no-longer, both in the *Canti e frammenti* (*Songs and Fragments*) and the *Zibaldone di pensieri* (*Book of Thoughts*). For the sake of clear structure, without letting ourselves become distracted by the broad spectrum of motifs and their various ways of thematising the disappearing moment, we can begin by considering the close of fragment XXXIX. This invites an immediate structural, and not thematic, analogy with Baudelaire's 'A une Passante'. The tercettes of Leopardi concern the abrupt reversal of an unrepresented hour of love in idyllic nature into the demonic atmosphere of a tempest that surprises and kills the young woman. The final lines run as follows:

Yet before her eyes the gliding lightning stayed,
So bright and flaming, she paused at last dismayed
And strength and courage left her.

She turned round. And in that moment
the lightning was extinguished, the heavens grew dark,
and thunder, storm both ceased.
All was still. She petrified, and dead.[66]

Precisely because no intertextual correspondence holds between Leopardi's and Baudelaire's poems, we must attend to the fact that the ontological difference between being and non-being (and that is what is at stake for both Baudelaire's male pedestrian, who loses eternity, and Leopardi's female wanderer, who loses her life) is presented in the momentariness of two natural signs, lightning and night. In the instantaneousness of a perception and a bodily movement everything is decided, and Leopardi's mythological allusion (to Lot's wife, who was petrified for glancing back) is merely an additional thematic justification, the motifs of which do not themselves justify the thought of a sudden negative moment. Naturally the negative 'instant' in Baudelaire gains, through the shortness of the sonnet, a structurally greater impact, while Leopardi's quasi-epic rendering of the development of a fatal destiny in the form of 25 tercettes give the closing turn a ballad-like aspect. In spite of the narrative languorousness peculiar to this genre, however,

Leopardi gives the close all the inevitability of the *factum brutum* of the shortest temporal extension, which would seem to be a law of human experience. In that Leopardi chooses as metaphor for this insight the sudden transformation of a heroic idyll into a tempestuous landscape, to which Baudelaire's poem offers an analogy,[67] the closing moment achieves, above and beyond its dramaturgical effect, a touch of the tragic consciousness of shortened temporality, here simply slowly unfolded.

This is not, one notes, formulated as a thought *à la* 'nothing lasts'; that belongs to an older tradition of rhetorical lament over time. Rather, the formulation of the line runs 'nothing of what pleases and delights lasts here below and remains to us, except hope'.[68] What is essential is that it does not become a philosophical statement of principle, but presents temporality here and in other poems always as the temporality of a subjective perception. In this, Leopardi was quite different from, for example, his pessimistic admirer Schopenhauer.

This conclusion solidifies in the philosophical discussions of the *Zibaldone di pensieri*, the *Book of Thoughts*. There is the acclamation on the foundation of 'nothing'; there is the plumbing of the abysmal mood of hopelessness; there is the reflection upon the possibility of suicide and the analysis of antique and contemporary pain as discursive form. This must be distinguished from the reflection upon the negative instant as a quite similar, even corresponding, figure of thought, but one not necessarily bound to these other manifestations. This is apparent in two differing reflections that attempt to establish the negative 'instant'. First, let us reflect on Leopardi's impression of the past as actual transitoriness:

> the pain that I feel, when, late in the night before a holiday, I hear the nocturnal song of passing countrymen. The infinite past that this recollects within me, the Romans, who have fallen after so great a commotion, and all the intricate occurrences that I in my sadness held up against the silence of the night, in order to hear how the rural call or song freed itself from it.[69]

The medium within which the past determines what is present is, characteristically, the nocturnal hour, that renders the prior day irrevocably yesterday. Leopardi's pain is the bare mentioning that there is a pain at all, that one is confronted with a new sort of perception of the past. For it is not a matter here of the Roman past as a historical past, but rather of the disappearance of the past, the erasure of occurrences, the 'deep silence of the night' as the idea of a loss. The dispersal of the actual holiday in the succeeding night becomes the visualisation of vanished history. This is not, as one might be misled into thinking, the traditional form, inherited from late Latin lyric, of complaints about transitoriness. Leopardi knew these quite well, and we will not consider the difference between them and his own topos of transitoriness. It is sufficient to recognise the extent to which mourning the disappearing past results from the contemporary temporal transition from today to tomorrow.

A vanished instant that is categorically even sharper can be found in the following entry:

It is a sweet deception that issues from anniversaries. Such a day has, of course, nothing more to do with the past than any other day, and yet we say: on this day this took place, on this I was so happy, so despairing; and really it is as if all those things that have irretrievably gone for ever did return to life, and were present as shadows are; but this gives us endless consolation, it banishes the thought of destruction, of extinction, that is so contrary to us, and mirrors the present of those things that we wish really were present, or which we like to think of for one reason or another.[70]

The possibility of remembering a given day through its calendar repetition is recognised as an illusion. True, the memory takes place, and provides 'endless consolation'. And that is a great deal, compared with the rejection of the possibility of memory in Baudelaire's *Fleurs du Mal*. Leopardi already reflected upon the unconscious and unintended form of memory of particular perceptions, what Proust would call *mémoire involontaire*.[71] This constitutes the specific difference between him and Baudelaire, who deconstructs the possibility of unconscious memory as a revelation of happiness. Leopardi's negativity with reference to the experienced 'instant' shows itself, because of the philosophical prose form, not in apodictic images, but in considerate reflection. That is, in a form of discourse that excludes the one-sided emphasis on the shortest moment of time. But that the presence of the past, the achievement of memory, is recognised as illusion, means that consciousness knows that the 'present' of past 'things' is extinguished. Above all, though, it means that this pastness has something existentially destructive, and that our consciousness lives continually in a state of this destructive process, that is, in the knowledge that there is in fact no presence of the past. The perception of life is then characterised by the thought '... this is the last time; that will never occur again; I shall never see that again; or: this has disappeared forever'.[72] The actual thematisation of the temporality of our experienced time takes place as more of a logical demonstration than a melancholy sentence. Leopardi justifies his 'sense of the nothingness of everything' in the predictable dissatisfaction of our 'inclination towards the eternal'.[73] Structurally, this consideration is analogous to the notion of the instant that is consumed by the next one, formulated this way only in Leopardi's lyric. Every experienced joy contributes, since it is necessarily not limitless and never receives the extension demanded by the heart, the kernel of destruction within it: every joy is 'vain'.[74] It is here that the decisive and, for us, most interesting figure of negative instantism occurs in the argument: man suffers even in joy, 'because he instantaneously recognises the limits of its extent'.[75] It is the predictability of the coming end of something, whereby the duration, even if longer, is not positively experienced, but rather reduced to the instant of recognition of its end.

It is in fact philosophy to whose competence a discussion of the negativity of the 'instant' should have fallen. Leopardi makes the contemplative spirit a precondition of this negative sense of life, a spirit that observes how the high points of its own life sink and also how the today of the day surrenders to evening, while simple people merely celebrate this transition.[76] And yet, despite a philosophy of death within which the contemplation of temporal phases plays a necessary role, negative instantaneousness did not become a philosophical theme.[77] One can go so far as to say that only literary contemplation was able to entertain this motif, because the assumption of continuity is a presupposition of philosophical notions of truth. Important examples of literary contemplation of the negative instant in twentieth-century literature are Kafka, Cioran, Sarraute or Bassani. One finds the impulse in the quasi-literary prose of Adorno's *Minima moralia*, while he banishes these approaches from explicit philosophical consideration in his genuinely philosophical works (*Negative Dialectics*). Finally, with regard to the negative 'instant', the question arises whether this is a matter of a radicalisation of the emphatic or mixed 'instant' without representation, or an autonomous poetic notion. From a purely logical point of view, the first possibility seems more pressing; for if the 'instant' in its suddenness ultimately insists upon its suddenness but does not name the content of that suddenness, one is quite close to the thought that the temporal moment, the single index of the event, might be negatively thematised as well. On the other hand, and this is the second possibility, the emphasis on the 'instant' in the classical modernist texts examined here is so great that it represents an exclusively positive *qualitas* of sensation, a quality that, in spite of the deficient content, can never, as 'feeling', become negative, however easily thought can append a negation to it. If we understand the emphatic 'instant' as a rhetorical figure within the literature of classical modernism, then we must subjoin the negative 'instant' and say: structurally this is only the reversal of a figure of reflection that gains its value precisely out of its suddenness. For suddenness is the common presupposition of both literary forms of the instant; not merely the representation of a determinate temporal modality, but above all a representation of an imaginative dimension.

Translated by James McFarland

Notes

1 See Susanne Ledanff, *Die Augenblicksmetapher: Über Bildlichkeit und Spontaneität in der Lyrik*, Munich: Hanser, 1981; Karl Heinz Bohrer, *Suddenness: On the Moment of Aesthetic Appearance*, New York: Columbia University Press, 1994 (orig. *Plötzlichkeit: Zum Augenblick des ästhetischen Scheins*, Frankfurt/M.: Suhrkamp, 1981). For later publications in which the instant is thematised from perspectives of the history of literature, hermeneutics or philosophy, see Christian W. Thomsen and Hans Hollander (eds), *Augenblick und Zeitpunkt: Studien zur Zeitstruktur und Zeitmetaphysik in Kunst und Wissenschaften*, Darmstadt: Wissenschaftliche Buchgesellschaft, 1984; Manfred Sommer, *Evidenz im Augenblick: Eine Phänomenologie der reinen Empfindung*, Frankfurt/M.: Suhrkamp, 1987. The structural analysis of the phenomenological instant in this latter work, even though it touches only marginally on literary examples, is particularly elucidating for the modern topic of the instant. Even more important for our theme of appearance (*Schein*) and appearing (*Erscheinung*) is Thomas Wägenbaur, *The Moment: A History, Typology and Theory of the Moment in Philosophy and Literature*, Berlin: Lang, 1993. Western European authors of classical modernity whom I discuss are not addressed in Wägenbaur's book, but the differentiating feature of diminishing substantiality in the concept of the instant is of immediate relevance to my formulation of the question. Herbert Grieshop, in *Rhetorik des Augenblicks: Studien zu Thomas Bernhard, Heiner Müller, Peter Handke und Botho Strauß*, Würzburg: Koenigshausen und Neumann, 1998, links his analysis partly to Wägenbaur's. See further, Theodor Wolpers, 'Der Kult des Augenblicks. Ein Kunstprinzip bei Wilde, Conrad und Joyce', in U. Molk (ed.), *Europäische Jahrhundertwende: Wissenschaften, Literatur und Kunst um 1900*, Göttingen: Vandenhoeck & Ruprecht, I, 1999. A similar topic is addressed by W. Erzgraber, 'The Moment of Vision', in Thomsen and Hollander (eds), *Augenblick und Zeitpunkt*, pp.361–87.

2 Thus it seems to be a flaw in Thomsen's and Hollander's volume *Augenblick und Zeitpunkt* that the individual contributions seem to have been brought together willy-nilly, and fail to suggest any co-ordinating question, however stimulating the individual efforts. Although it proceeds comparatively, Wolpers's study does not get beyond the recounting of what is partially known already, since he fails to address the extant discussion on the structure of instantaneousness, but contents himself with a thematic overview of the motif in his three Anglo-Saxon authors. This type of literary–historical motif–report leaves the connection to philosophical phenomenology entirely in the dark.

3 'Drum sandte er ihnen / Den Geist, und freilich bebte / Das Haus und die Wetter Gottes rollten / Ferndonnernd über / Die ahnenden Häupter' (Friedrich Hölderlin, *Sämtliche Werke und Briefe*, ed. Günter Mieth, Munich: Hanser, 1970, I, p.382). 'Therefore he sent them / The spirit and the house / Shook and God's turbulence rolled / Thundering into the distance over / Their guessing heads' (Friedrich Hölderlin, *Selected Poems* [trans. D. Constantine], Newcastle upon Tyne: Bloodaxe Books, 1990).

4 M. Heidegger, 'Hölderlins Hymne "Der Isther"', in *Gesamtausgabe*, LIII, Frankfurt/M.: Vittorio Klostermann, 1984, p.9.

5 Bohrer, *Suddenness*, pp.197–245.

6 Wägenbaur, *The Moment*, p.325.

7 H. von Kleist, 'Über die allmähliche Verfertigung der Gedanken beim Reden', in *Sämtliche Werke und Briefe*, ed. Helmut Sembdner, Munich: Hanser, 1972, II, pp.320–21.

8 Jean-Jacques Rousseau, 'Les rêveries du promeneur solitaire. Deuxième promenade', in *Œuvres complètes. Les confessiones. Autres textes autobiographiques* (Edition publiée sous la direction de B. Gagnebin et M. Raymond), Paris: Gallimard, 1959, pp.1004–05. (Jean-Jacques Rousseau, *Reveries of the Solitary Walker*, trans. Peter France, Harmondsworth: Penguin, 1979, pp.35–36.)

9 Michel de Montaigne, *Œuvres complètes* (Textes établies par Albert Thibaudet et Maurice Rat), Paris: Gallimard, 1962, pp.352–53.

10 See Bohrer, *Suddenness*, pp.211–13.

11 Bohrer, *Suddenness*, pp.212–13.

12 Bohrer, *Suddenness*, p.216.

13 Virginia Woolf, 'A Sketch of the Past', in *Moments of Being*, ed. Jeanne Schulkind, San Diego: Harvest, 1985, p.65.

14 Woolf, 'A Sketch', p.65.

15 On the concept of intensity, see Karl Heinz Bohrer, 'Intensität ist kein Gefühl', in *Nach der Natur: Über Ästhetik und Politik*, Munich: Hanser, 1988, pp.86–87.

16 Woolf, 'A Sketch', p.66.

17 Woolf, 'A Sketch', p.67.

18 Woolf, 'A Sketch', p.70.

19 Woolf, 'A Sketch', pp.71–72.

20 Woolf, 'A Sketch', p.72.

21 Woolf, 'A Sketch', p.72.

22 Walter Benjamin, 'Der Sürrealismus', in *Angelus Novus, Ausgewählte Schriften*, Frankfurt/M.: Suhrkamp, 1966, II, p.202. (Walter Benjamin, 'Surrealism', in *Reflections: Essays, Aphorisms, Autobiographical Writings*, trans. Edmund Jephcott, New York: HBJ, 1978, p. p.189).

23 Robert Musil, *Der Mann ohne Eigenschaften. Roman aus dem Nachlaß*, ed. Adolf Frise, Reinbek bei Hamburg: Rowohlt, 1984, p.1091.

24 See Bohrer, *Suddenness*, p.222.

25 Bohrer, *Suddenness*, p.223.

26 Woolf, 'A Sketch', p.72.

27 André Breton, *Nadja* (trans. Richard Howard), New York: Grove Press, 1960, p.160. (orig. Paris: Gallimard, 1928, p.215).

28 Quoted in Bohrer, *Suddenness*, pp.213, 222.

29 Breton, *Nadja*, p.213.

30 Breton, *Nadja*, pp.159–60.

31 Breton, *Nadja*, p.124. 'Elle est comme un train qui bondit sans cesse dans la gare de Lyon et dont je sais qu'il ne va jamais partir, qu'il n'est pas parti. Elle est faite de saccades, dont beaucoup n'ont guère d'importance, mas que nous savons destinées à amener une Saccade, qui en a. Qui a toute l'importance que je ne voudrais me donner' [p.214].

32 See Bohrer, *Suddenness*, pp.11–12.

33 See K.H. Bohrer, 'Bilder und Zeiten', in *Frankfurter Allgemeine Zeitung*, 27.11.1999.

34 Rainer Maria Rilke, 'Duineser Elegien', in *Sämtliche Werke*, I, Frankfurt/M.: Insel, 1955, p.685.

35 Breton, *Nadja*, p.39. 'J'ai toujours incroyablement souhaité de rencontrer la nuit, dans un bois, une femme belle et nue, ou plutôt, un tel souhaite une fois exprimé ne signifiant plus rien, je regrette incroyablement de ne pas l'avoir rencontrée. Supposer une tel rencontre n'est pas sí délirant, somme toute: il se pourrait. Il me semble que tout se fût arrêté net, ah! je n'en serais pas à écrire ce que j'écris. J'adore cette situation qui est, entre toutes, celle où il est probable que j'eusse le plus manqué de présence d'esprit. Je n'aurais même pas eu, je crois, celle de fuir. (Ceux qui rient de cette dernière phrase sont des porcs). A la fin d'une après-midi, l'année dernière, aux galeries de côté de l'"Electric Palace", une femme nue, qui ne devait avoir eu à se défaire que d'un manteau, allait bien d'un rang à l'autre, très blanche. Cétait déjà bouleversant. Loin, malheureusement, d'être assez extraordinaire, ce loin de l'"Electric" étant un lieu de débauche sans intérêt' [pp.46–47].

36 Breton, *Nadja*, p.19. 'Il s'agit de faits qui peuvent être de l'ordre de la constatation pure mais qui présentent chaque fois toutes les apparences d'un signal, sans qu'on puisse dire au juste de quel signal' [p.23].

37 Breton, *Nadja*, pp.14–15.

38 Breton, *Nadja*, p.20; 'la sensation très nette que pour nous quelque chose de grave, d'essentiel, en dépend' [p.23].

39 Breton, *Nadja*, p.39.

40 Benjamin, 'Sürrealismus', p.202 [Eng. p.179].

41 Benjamin, 'Sürrealismus', pp.203–04 [180].

42 Benjamin, 'Sürrealismus', p.204 [181].

43 Benjamin, 'Sürrealismus', pp.204–05 [182–83].

44 'que telle idée, telle femme lui fait de l'effet' ... 'Quel effet, il serait bien incapable de le dire.' André Breton, *Manifeste du surrealisme*, in *Œuvres complètes*, Edition établiee par Marguerite Bonnet, Paris: Gallimard, 1988, p.318.

45 'Cette idéé, cette femme le trouble, elle l'incline à moins de sévérité. Elle a pour action de l'isoler une seconde de son dissolvant et de le déposer au ciel, en beau précipité qu'il peut être, qu'il est. En désespoir de cause, il invoque alors le hasard, divinité plus obscure que les autres, à qui il attribue tous ses égarements. Qui me dit l'angle sous lequel se présente cette idée qui le touche, ce qui le rattache à son rêve, l'enchaîne à des données que par sa faute il a perdues?' (Breton, *Manifeste*, p.318).

46 Jean-François Lyotard, 'The Sublime and the Avant-Garde', in *The Lyotard Reader*, ed. Andrew Benjamin, Oxford: Blackwell, pp.196–211.

47 Lyotard, 'The Sublime', p.197.

48 Lyotard, 'The Sublime', pp.197–98.

49 Benjamin, 'Sürrealismus', p.212 [189].

50 Benjamin, 'Sürrealismus', p.213 [190].

51 Lyotard, 'The Sublime', pp.197–98.

52 Martina Wagner-Egelhaaf, *Mystik der Moderne: Die visionäre Ästhetik der deutschen Literatur im 20. Jahrhundert*, Stuttgart: Metzler, 1989. Boris Groys has demonstrated more convincingly the spiritualist tendency among certain twentieth-century artists. See Boris Groys, *Gesamtkunstwerk Stalin: Die gespaltene Kultur in der Sowjetunion*, Munich/Vienna: Hanser, 1988. (Engl. edn *The Total Art of Stalin: Avantgarde, Aesthetic, Dictatorship and Beyond*, Princeton: Princeton University Press, 1992).

53 See Karl Heinz Bohrer, 'Möglichkeiten einer nihilistischen Ethik', *Merkur*, 51:1, January 1997, pp. 2–19.

54 Charles Baudelaire, *Les fleurs du mal*, in *Œuvres complètes*, Texte établie, présenté et annoté par Claude Pichois, Paris: Gallimard, 1973, pp.92–93. (Charles Baudelaire, *Flowers of Evil and Other Poems* [trans. Francis Duke], New York: Vantage, 1982, p.141).

55 Baudelaire, *Les fleurs*, p.93. [Eng. p.141]

56 See Karl Heinz Bohrer, *Der Abschied: Theorie der Trauer*, Frankfurt/M.: Suhrkamp, 1996, pp.164ff.

57 Baudelaire, *Les fleurs*, p.9 [141].

58 See Georges Bataille, *Die Tränen des Eros*, Munich: Matthes & Seitz, 1981, p.42 (orig. *Les larmes de l'Eros*, Paris: Pauvert, 1971).

59 Baudelaire, *Les fleurs*, p.92 [140].

60 Johann Wolfgang von Goethe, in *Werke*, Hamburger Ausgabe in 14 volumes, Munich: DTV, 1977, I, pp.185–90 and V, pp.332–65.

61 See Bohrer, *Der Abschied*, pp.178–79.

62 Charles Baudelaire, 'Lettre à Jules Janin', in *Œuvres complètes*, II, p.238.

63 Arthur Schopenhauer, *Die Welt als Wille und Vorstellung, Ergänzungen zum Vierten Buch*, in *Sämtliche Werke in 12 Bänden*, Stuttgart and Berlin, VI, pp.149–50.

64 Schopenhauer, *Die Welt*, pp.149–50.

65 Schopenhauer, *Die Welt*, p.133.

66 Giacomo Leopardi, *Canti e frammenti. Gesänge und Fragmente, Italienisch/Deutsch* (trans. Helmut Endrulat), ed. Helmut Endrulat and Gero A. Schwalb, Stuttgart: Reclam,

1990, p.267.

67 The eye of the passerby dressed in mourning is compared to a 'livid sky, pregnant with storm' (*ciel livide où germe l'ouragan*). See Baudelaire, *Les fleurs*, p.92 [141].

68 Leopardi, *Canti e frammenti*, p.263.

69 Giacomo Leopardi, *Das Gedankenbuch* (Auswahl, Übersetzung und Nachwort von Hanno Helbling), Munich: Winkler, 1985, p.20.

70 Leopardi, *Das Gedankenbuch*, p.21.

71 Leopardi, *Das Gedankenbuch*, pp.86–87.

72 Leopardi, *Das Gedankenbuch*, p.559.

73 Leopardi, *Das Gedankenbuch*, p.68.

74 Leopardi, *Das Gedankenbuch*, p.70.

75 Leopardi, *Das Gedankenbuch*, p.73.

76 Leopardi, *Canti e frammenti*, p.89.

77 Karl Heinz Bohrer, 'Poetischer Nihilismus und Philosophie', *Merkur*, 51:5, 1997, pp. 406–21.

CHAPTER 7

Poetry and the Returns of Time: Goethe's 'Wachstum' and 'Immer und Überall'

ANDREW BENJAMIN

Within poetry time cannot be given the slip. Not just because time is not one but endures as an array of differing possibilities and modalities, but also because time has the unceasing built into the continuity of its returns. (Return, here, has to be in the plural – *returns* – in order to mark the openings and ineliminable movements comprising time.) How is the plurality and the insistent nature of time to be signalled? Rather than signal it as though there could have been an act of differentiation in which the required distance from the object was envisaged as a possibility, the work of time has to be noted. In addition, time can be taken as comprising the work, and thus as being at work; work figuring as both place and activity. What, then, of any one work? How is that work to escape the trap of exemplarity in which it is proffered as no more than the instance of a universal; a universal which, in the end, would crush whatever particularity the instance may ever have had?

Any answer has to begin with a twofold recognition. The first is that time will have already been inscribed into the work of poetry; poems are timed.[1] The second is that any attention to the detail of that work would have to take time into consideration. Here, what is of concern is the work of time within – and as – poetry. Time works by slipping the hold of fixity and the naturalisation of continuity, while simultaneously allowing for the intrusion of measure; the latter being that form of measure maintaining the borders of poetry. What this complex set-up entails is that the structure of signification at work within the distinction between signifier and signified is checked by the operation of the language of time and thus timed language; one is already the other. The former – the language of time – may be those references to time that poetry may make, while the later – timed language – may be the work of time in poetry. The language of time may only ever refer to the work of time in passing. Moreover, within poetry, while present in words, time also sounds. Sounds – their absence and presence – are time at work. Silence becomes more than mere negation.[2] There will, however, be a specific occurrence in which time worked within the poem not simply as a register of its own concerns but as an interruption and thus as an opening. The interruption within poetry cannot be merely semantic and thus announced within, and as, content. The interruption also has to be understood as the work of time since it may appear as a literal pause or, more generally, as that which works to stem continuity by grounding continuity in the discontinuous. The productive co-presence of continuity and discontinuity is the emphatic moment within poetry. This moment is to be understood both as an interruption and as an allowing. Taken together they are central to the work of time within poetry and to the recognition of that work.[3]

The moment emerges therefore as that which occasions. Staging this occasioning is the other element constituting the presence of the poetic moment; namely interruption. The moment, as the interruption that occasions, becomes both a specific register of language and a form of internal causality. While precluding any automatic identification with an exclusive, even if singular, conception of form, the moment works to account for the internal particularity of the poetic. Moreover, it is a conception of poetic practice that takes the complex activities of time as yielding origins.

What follows from these general considerations is more than the simple conclusion that time figures within poetry. More is involved since consistent with the general argument that objects are timed is the claim that poetry is the opening up of time. And yet how is this position to be understood? Moreover, within this formulation, what is it that is wanted of poetry? Does poetry – poeticising understood as the work of poetry – afford access to that which is proper to language or to time? All of these questions concern the address of poetry. What is opened up by questions of this type is the possibility that poetry may take as its address that which is always in excess of the activity of poetry itself. What may have been wanted of poetry is its capacity to stage a concern with that which is proper either to language or to time. And here there will be no attempt to refuse that expectation. There is a sense of propriety. However, the propriety in question is not in excess of poetry – where poetry is understood as the activity of words and sounds operating in relation to the repetition of the poetic – nor does it refer to that which is other than poetry. What poetry stages is both its own particularity – the effective presence of poetry as poetry – as well as evidencing whatever is entailed by that particularity.[4] In other words, there is a twofold movement. In the first instance there is the insistent presence of the activity of poetry – its work – and in the second there is that which occurs with that work. Both these elements take place at the same time. Here, it will be suggested that what this means is that the practice of poetry works through the anoriginal presence of temporal complexity. As such, though this is a position to be shown, poetry refuses the possibility of the question – 'What is time?' – precisely because poetry, in its activity as poetry, will have already demonstrated that there are only differing and irreducible temporal formulations combining to comprise poetry as work. Indeed, the belonging together of these different temporal moments comprises the possibility of poetry itself. What occurs with the work of poetry and which cannot be separated from poetry's possibility is a reworking of the question of time such that it addresses the plurality of times and in so doing reinscribes the address of poetry by its making the work of poetic time internal to poetry itself. Poetry becomes the address of the plurality of times. What this sets in play is the need for the recognition that particularity is already the address of poetry. And yet there is an inevitable opening. To the extent that the work of poetry precludes the question – what is time? – as allowing for either a single response or as opening up a unique domain of investigation, then while this demonstrates the need to return to what would now be a reworked conception of particularity, it would also be the case that the very plurality of the return of time within poetry would have staged that which was proper to time itself. (It would be, of course, an 'itself' that was only ever offered in the plurality of its returns.)

As a preamble this may have opened the way to a consideration of two poems by Goethe: 'Immer und Überall' and 'Wachstum'.[5] How is the relationship between time as a named presence and the temporal nature of poetry to be understood? Part of the force of this question lies in the inevitability that the named presence of time is not the only way time figures within poetry's work, nor moreover does it follow that the naming of time is automatically the naming of a specific form of temporality. The first of these poems runs as follows:

Immer und Überall

Dringe tief zu Bergesgrüften,	Explore deep mountain chasms,
Wolken folge hoch zu Lüften;	soar high in the air in the wake of clouds;
Muse ruft zu Bach und Tale	to brook and valley the Muse calls
Tausend, abertausend Male.	a thousand and a thousand times.
Sobald ein frisches Kelchlein blüht,	When a fresh calyx newly blooms,
Es fordert neue Lieder;	it calls for new songs;
Und wenn die Zeit verrauschend flieht,	and though streaming time flees from us,
Jahreszeiten kommen wieder.	the seasons come again.

At the outset time figures. It is named in the first word of the title – *Immer* ('For ever') – and then, whatever conception of temporality has been opened by that word is immediately qualified by the conjunction *und* ('and') and the addition of the *Überall* ('Everywhere'). The addition not only qualifies the temporality inherent in the *Immer*, it places it. At the end of the first quatrain time is announced by the repetition of the word *Tausend* ('thousand'). More is necessary, however, since the repetition of *Tausend* within the formulation *abertausend Male* ('and a thousand times') demands, in the first place, that the question of repetition be addressed and thus the temporality proper to the repetition in question be noted; and in the second, that repetition allow for the possibility that the primary instance may come to be reworked in the context of its repetition. The original usage therefore would bear the effect of its own repetition. Whether this is the case depends on how repetition is this context is to be understood. (As with time, repetition must eschew generality.)

At least two senses of time are present within the poem. In the first instance there is the use of the temporalising term *Immer* and whatever temporality is set in play by the use of *Tausend* and *abertausend Male*. In the second it is the temporality inherent within the qualification of *Immer* in the title and enacted by the repetition of *Tausend*. A similar set-up is evident in the final two lines of the second stanza. Time (*Zeit*) is named in the first of these lines. It returns in the next held within the word *Jahreszeiten* ('seasons'). Again, therefore, it is essential that the question of repetition be taken up. Equally, there are the temporal considerations staged by the word *wieder* ('again'). A range of different temporal registers can be noted at work within (and as) the poem even in a preliminary reading.

Prior to pursuing the detail of that poem it is essential to work towards it. It is important to note that its title recalls a number of poems of this period – e.g. 'Dauer im Wechsel'[6] which mark a preoccupation with the relationship between change, separation and the enduring (where the latter also includes that which endures in the wake of change). As an opening, however, and in order to note a poem's own treatment of development and thus to begin to account for the work of poetic time, a start will be made with another poem from the same period, 'Wachstum'. An analysis of this poem will open the way towards the complex interplay between different possibilities of time and repetition and their relation to the philosophical problem of the Absolute that, it will be argued, is already staged by that poem's relation to nature. (Here Nature takes the place of the Absolute.) 'Wachstum' initiates some of the issues central to the returns of time. The poem runs as follows:

Wachstum

Als kleines art'ges Kind nach Feld und Auen	As a dear little child, to the field and meadows
Sprangst du mit mir so manchen Frühlingsmorgen.	you would jump along with me on many spring mornings.

'Für solch ein Töchterchen, mit holden
  Sorgen
Möcht ich als Vater segnend Häuser bauen!'

Und als du anfingst in die Welt zu
  schauen,
War deine Freude häusliches Besorgen.
'Solch eine Schwester! und ich wär
  geborgen:
Wie könnt ich ihr, ach! wie sie mir
  vertrauen!'

Nun kann den schönen Wachstum nichts
  beschränken;
Ich fühl' im Herzen heißes Liebetoben.
Umfass' ich sie, die Schmerzen zu
  beschwicht'gen?
Doch ach! nun muß ich dich als
  Fürstin denken:
Du stehst so schroff vor mir emporgehoben;
Ich beuge mich vor deinem Blick, dem
  flücht'gen.

'For such a little daughter I would suffer
  a father's sweet cares
I would build, with blessings, many a house!'

And when you began to open your eyes
  to the world,
You took delight in household duties.
'Such a sister! and I was provided for
Oh, how much could I entrust to her
  and she to me!'

Now nothing can stay her beautiful
  growth
I feel in my heart the hot madness of love
Shall I embrace you, to lessen my pain?
Ah, now must I think of you as a princess:
You stand towering above me so high
I bow before your glance, so fleeting.

In this instance the measure of the poem stages what initially appears to be a child's growth. Through differing moments the observing eye holds the growth and allows for its transformation. This observing eye has the quality of an outsider and thus has a position which while unchanged in terms of place, none the less experiences change in terms of differing responses to what changes before it. The poem charts a separation. The question, however, is: how is that separation to be understood? In pursuing that question – the question arising from the poem itself – it becomes possible to trace its inseparability from the complex work of time. It becomes the complex work of time.

In the first instance, as has been intimated, 'Wachstum' seems to recount the movement of a child growing beyond the hold of the observing eye. The return of the look, the exchanged laugh and the reciprocity of mutual trust and care, is in the end broken. Within such an interpretation the last line could be interpreted as sundering what connection there had been. The last line would have announced the sundering of that relation thus: 'Ich beuge mich vor deinem Blick, dem flücht'gen.' ('I bow before your glance, so fleeting.') The pause, reinforced by the hold of the comma after *Blick* ('glance'), holds and positions the fixed gaze of the 'I' in the face of the fleeting moment that is the 'glance'. And yet, as a description both in general and in regard to the final line – in relationship to which it will be necessary to return to this comma – it fails to note the other form of interruption within the poem – an interruption signalled neither by metre nor by sound, but by the place of the inverted commas around the last two lines of the first and second quatrains. They bring a complicating factor into consideration. What is complicated is the question of how the possessed glance – *deinem Blick* – is to be understood. What type of interruption does it stage, given that the occurrence that introduces spacing, and thus activity, is a glance which is fleeting? Answering this question and thus paying attention to the effect of this fleeting glance has to work with the recognition of its presentation having been mediated by the place and thus by the function of the inverted commas. In this instance, interruption forms part of a process. In allowing and thus in opening up the poem's work the occurrence – the staging of interruption – becomes the moment; i.e. it becomes the interruption that allows.

The poem opens by invoking the child who in all innocence accompanies the walker. There is no question that this is done other than with innocence and abandon. The child's presence and mood in accompanying the walker are joyful and immediate: 'sprangst du mit mir' ('you would jump along with me'). What occurs after these opening lines is staged in a specific way. A shift in register is introduced by the inverted commas. The poem begins with the direct evocation of the child and yet it is precisely this evocation that is distanced in the opening of line 3: 'Für solch ein Töchterchen …' ('For such a little daughter …'). While the inverted commas yield no sound, or at least not the standard relationship between graphic mark and sound, they alter what comes after. There are two questions which cannot be ignored: Who is speaking? To whom? These questions are introduced by the division – the interruption – staged by the inverted commas and as such condition the poem's tone. When it is no longer the child but *solch ein Töchterchen* ('such a little daughter') another voice will need to be speaking. The other voice may be that found in a distinction between outer and inner worlds. Moreover, there could be the staging of description and reflection. Neither of these possibilities can be straightforwardly refused. Even without clarifying what is going on it is none the less still clear that there are two registers at work. The possibility of either of these two distinctions – outer/inner, description/reflection – being in play is reinforced by the second quatrain. The growing child of the first two lines becomes *Solch eine Schwester* ('Such a sister') at the beginning of the third. The expression *solch eine* ('such a …') introduces a sense of detachment that is quickly turned into a personal utterance by the introduction of *ich* ('I'). There is therefore the opening up for a type of objectivity that is quickly rendered personal by the incorporation of an identified subject – the 'I' – for whom 'such a little daughter' or 'such a sister' exists and thus belongs, or would belong. The 'such a' has an additional function. It introduces an abstracting quality by allowing for the move from particularity to the generalised form of its presence. It introduces the possibility of a twisting free of the twofold determination given to the growing child by the operation of the two quatrains. Breaking the hold of the particular via abstracting is of course the possibility of gaining a self-determined particularity. From being a particular, where that designation comes from the other, there opens the realm where such a designation and thus such a naming could be self-imposed. Were it to be, then the particular will flee to be herself. Abstracting allows for the other form of particularity because *solch eine Schwester* ('such a sister') could always be named and thus become herself; neither daughter nor sister but individualised other.

The two tercets work without the division staged by the inverted commas. The first line of the first tercet announces the time of the poem. The line begins *Nun* ('Now'), and then goes on to state that the beautiful growth that is hers 'cannot be stayed' (*nichts beschränken*); it is blossoming. Specific questions emerge at this precise point in the poem. How is this *Nun* to be understood? If there is a division of register in the first two tercets, does it belong to both? Or does it interrupt the oscillation between them by generating a type of unity? The importance of this last question is considerable. If the *Nun* establishes a type of unity such that in the lines that follow not only are the inverted commas absent but the 'I' can be written as though their presence would not have been necessary, then the 'now' stages a division between past and present that, while announced by the 'now', is equally held in play by the presence and absence of inverted commas. The inverted commas would work insofar as they time by precluding the naturalisation of sequential continuity. In light of this possibility – poetic time held within marks which only minimally count as graphic – not only is there a further complication of the work of poetic time, but it also demands that the above questions be given answers. Responding to them would begin to link differing temporal registers.

Each of the questions concerns the place and work of the *Nun*. While obvious, it none the less needs to be noted that it begins the first tercet. The preceding line is held within the inverted commas. Consequently, it is not just a beginning, it heralds what will have become the disappearance of the divide marking the earlier quatrains. The first point in understanding the *Nun* stems from this 'earlier' division. The divide marking the quatrains does not present a simple perspectivism. On the contrary, within it presence is divided between different responses to that which is itself the subject of change. Rather than differing perspectives of the same object there is the discontinuous continuity of development marking the different sites and contexts in which it is registered. Introduced into those domains and thus as, in part, constituting the effects of change is the loosening hold of the *solch eine*. What slips away is the possibility that the positions of subject/

object or even self/other are permanent and fixed and do no more than unfold through natural time. The 'such a ...' loosens that hold precisely because it abstracts her presence and thus intrudes interruption into growth – and thereby allows discontinuity to be integral to continuity.

What has emerged thus far are not just different temporal registers, but also the way in which their presence cannot be divorced from the work of poetry. They bring the poem about. Having noted a number of such registers the temptation would be to redescribe the poem from the beginning in light of what has already been noted. Such a redescription would be committed to reading the poem as a sequence and thus as involving the temporality of sequential continuity. In fact the differing temporal registers that are operative within – and as – the poem preclude precisely this possibility. Any reading of the poem – the literal act that moves from beginning to end – stages, of necessity, the demand for a further reading. The subsequent reading, in holding to, while differentiating itself from, the demands of sequence – and it has to be both – opens up the poem's complex temporality. This aspect must be shown. The point of departure will be the *Nun* since it introduces a break by staging the position that from this 'now' what is will be different. (It is thus that *Nun*, in this context, should be translated as 'henceforth' – i.e. from 'now' on). It should be noted that the word *nun* occurs again in the first line of the second tercet. While it announces another break precluding any return, its effect is less emphatic than the first occurrence of the word. This is, first, because the initial usage begins the first tercet and, second, because the first occurrence takes place after the last set of inverted commas, thereby opening up the problem of the relationship between two moments of interruption.

Prior to the interruptive *Nun* there are two quatrains. Each one is divided between two lines without, and then two lines with, inverted commas. The movement unfolding within both is checked by what has been described as a shift in register. Between the two sets of two lines there is a gradual breaking and repositioning of self–other relations and thus the necessity that such activity occur through a time allowing for complexity. This is made possible by the way the lines work. In the first quatrain the innocence of the child is met by the introduction of the 'I' who cares. In caring, this 'I' has a certain mastery. The innocence of the child of the first two lines become the cared-for 'daughter' of the second two. In the second quatrain the child is open to the world and is placed within it. This is met by a posited relation of care; care marked by what from the position of the 'I' is necessarily reciprocal. Place would emphasise the I–thou (*ich–du*) relation. However, the question is, how are these moves and relations established by the poetry? The question therefore addresses the work of poetry – poetry's address – and not simply its narrative content.

142

Once the first line of the first tercet is met, the complex set-up of relations and movement – a set-up generating a certain fraying – opened up, the work of the inverted commas is reinforced. The first line is clear; 'Nun kann den schönen Wachstum nichts beschränken' ('Nothing can stay/limit/restrict the beautiful growth'). From the moment it is read the distinction carried by the inverted commas is reworked. (Here there is a productive repetition and thus the presence, as part of poetry, of a repetition involving a retroactive reworking; i.e. an 'iterative reworking'.)[7] What the inverted commas make possible is an interruption that allows the growth to be staged. While it may be continuous in a chronological sense, it is only able to be present because of the unvoiced interruption. The ruse inherent in the idea of continual development is that the one developing – growing – plus the context in which it occurs, and including the observations of that growth, are themselves continuous in development. The relations between child and adult from within the purview of that position would themselves be smooth and continuous. That such a formulation fails to grasp the complexity of development is not the point. Rather, the point is, how is that discontinuous continuity – i.e. the truth of growth and thus the truth of self–other relations – to be staged? The first significant element is the inverted commas, the second is the effect of the *Nun* on what preceded it, and also in how what preceded affects that which follows. An unvoiced interruption presents the discontinuous continuity. The *Nun* dramatises the interruption. It is as though what is unvoiced has become voiced. Interruption has been stated, and with it the 'I' retreats from the site of relation. It retreats into the self of feeling and thus the self without relation; or at least without a pre-given or already present relation. The self of feeling just has its self and its responses. Relations, henceforth, are purely projective. While the 'I' may be pained, the other – the growing girl – who may ease it, is indifferent to, or at least ignorant of, its existence. The severing of relations positions the other – the girl, daughter, sister, etc. and thus no simple other – outside and hence there is no need to maintain the work of the inverted commas. This is the effective presence of the *Nun* as the site of interruption and equally as site of continuity. The *Nun* takes on the quality of a moment within the poem's work. Its effect – the effect of the moment – is reinforced by the repetition of '*nun*' in the first line of the final tercet. It is repeated, thereby compounding the work that its first instance occasioned.

The final tercet announces the break of relations. Any possible reciprocity has now gone. The fraying of continuity occurring within the opening quatrains is now reinscribed within the last three lines in terms of a complete division. In part this is reinforced by the shift occurring within the work of the word *als* ('as'). As the line's opening word it announces a particular set-up. Rather than the *als* of seeming, it states a particular and identifiable point in time. The child is located at the point at which it was a 'dear little child'. The sense of an identifiable point in time is reinforced by the reiteration of *als* as the second word of the second quatrain. Indeed, it is possible to argue that it is the particularity of this point that is captured and then released within the lines appearing in inverted commas. The repetition of *als* in the first line of the last tercet introduces a different state of affairs. The line is as follows: 'Doch ach! nun muß ich dich als Fürstin denken' ('Ah, now must I think of you as a princess'). Here, the *als* announces a point in time while introducing the complexity of seeming. She can only be seen *als Fürstin* ('as a princess'). Semblance is not deception; rather it is the consequence – effected through the poetry's work – of the self–other relation; here it works as the final fraying of that relation. Whether she is a 'princess' or can only be seen as one is not the central question. What matters is that the repetition of *als*, the same word which located an identity that was given within relations – albeit the eventual fraying of relations – now posits the grown child beyond any relation. She can only be seen 'as'. In fact the rush of assonance in the second, third and fourth words within the second line leading to the elevation 'Du stehst so schroff vor mir emporgehoben' ('You stand towering over me so high') positions her as physically out of reach. (A point that could be further demonstrated by a phonetic analysis of the word *emporgehoben* which would indicate that its syllabic structure literally voices elevation.) The line works to realise this positioning. And yet what is immediately removed is the lingering gaze that such a position might invite. Rather than being able to dwell on the now ungraspable object, she is out of reach and her own response allows for the possibility of contact that is then withdrawn within the instant that it is given.[8] The giving and the withdrawing, while there in the line in terms of the 'fleeting glance', are staged by the pause announced by the comma. The glance is allowed to endure. The metric scheme is contained by the comma. Even though the 'I' bows, the comma allows for a pause. It only becomes an empty moment – a moment emptied of all possibility – by the emphatic phonic and semantic force of the words announcing the fleeting nature of the glance.

Before proceeding, in terms of a conclusion, with a more critical engagement with this poem it is essential to trace the work of time – its returns – in 'Immer und Überall'. However, what needs to be noted in passing is what would constitute a critical engagement. If the object of critique cannot be read from the poem's narrative content, but the content has to be read as the effect of the poem's work, then a critical engagement becomes one which addresses the way a work maintains itself as poetry.[9] And yet this formulation appears either as a simple tautology or one which demands an answer to the question, 'What is poetry?' The reason why both of these possibilities miss the mark is found in the attempt to answer the question, 'What is it to maintain poetry?' The first part of the answer involves attention to the work of the particular. Hence what is central is the non-generalisable particular. The second is not the abstracting move that construes the particular as part of the universal but the one that takes the poem's address as part of the repetition of poetry. What this second answer means is that the question 'What is it to maintain poetry?' is already addressed in the presence and practice of poetry understood as a repetition of the genre of poetry. The history of poetry becomes a history of its – poetry's – complex repetition. The claims made by a single work are to be identified in relation to the repetition of the site of its address. That site is poetry.

Within this allusion to poetry always being the poetry of poetry there reside two additional claims. The first is the above-mentioned one that links poetry to repetition and thus to the inevitability of poetry's grounding in its own history. The second has already been mentioned, though here it is essential to link it to the activity of critique. Poetry, in having as its condition of possibility the instantiation of temporal complexity, is constrained to stage that which is proper to the work of time. Time brings with it an anoriginal plurality that allows poetry to work as poetry. This is clear from what has been shown thus far concerning the way time returns in 'Wachstum'. What this indicates is that the identification of the work of complexity, and moreover its most insistent form, is the moment – where the moment is understood as that which interrupts while allowing for development and with it continuity. It not only shows poetry's work, it does at the same time indicate that poetry is the presentation of temporal complexity. Once again, it should be added immediately that this position can only be generalised to the extent that it is understood as claiming that time is already an integral part of the existence of objects and therefore all that can be addressed is the field of particularity. Positing a philosophy of time independently of its already being at work within the particular becomes a reiteration of Platonic Idealism insofar as it retains the causality of the 'Idea' as central. For critique generality is constrained by particularity. This recognition yields the object of critique. Critique works with that which poetry makes possible while also working with what makes poetry possible. Critique has to be attentive to the interplay of these two senses of possibility. In so doing it is not just concerned with the particular but also with the constitution of particularity as the object of critique and thus as itself.

'Immer und Überall'

While this is a poem that can be read as staging the enduring force of nature, there are more disquieting elements at work within it. Tracing the presence of these elements has a twofold effect. In the first instance, it opens up the relationship between nature and muse as being more complex than had been initially understood. In the second, it demands that a more detailed consideration be given to that conception of time as fleeing yet returning, even though in that return time has moved from the one – having a unified presence – to a form of original plurality. Given this twofold effect, a question arises. Is the poem working through the possibility that what flees is that conception of time allowing for its own *reductio ad unam*? If that is the case – if this reduction is impossible – then poetic time will always have been poetic times. This possibility has to be pursued within the detail of the poem. What has to be sought is the way this complex set-up actually comprises the poem's work.

In general terms 'Immer und Überall' is concerned with repetition. However, its concern is that which moves repetition away from its insertion into the realm of the Same, where repetition becomes the mere repetition of the Same, to a conception of repetition allowing for innovation and the New. The New will no longer be that which is recalled through a form of anamnesis, nor on the other hand is the New that which occurs without relation. Within the structure of repetition – the structure working through this poem though staged with sustained concision in the second quatrain – the New is always coming into relation. In fact, the movement from the first to the second quatrain can be read as staging the movement between these two different senses of repetition. As will be seen, however, they cannot be separated from the philosophical problem of the presence of the Absolute.

The poem consists of two quatrains. The first invokes the world of nature operating within heights and depths. With nature – more accurately; to nature – the muse calls: 'Muse ruft zu Bach und Tale' ('to brook and valley the Muse calls'). It calls not once; it calls *Tausend, abertausend Male* ('a thousand and a thousand times'). How is the call of the Muse to be understood? What is the relationship between the call of the Muse and the repetition of *Tausend* ('thousand') in the quatrain's last line? With these questions a start can be made with the first quatrain. Regardless of the content that could be given to the actions stipulated in the opening two lines, they are intended to cover the world of nature. Height and depth designate the totality of what there is; the All. Within this All the Muse calls. An important consequence – and it is a consequence envisaged by the poem's work – is that if chasms and clouds open the totality, then 'brook' and 'valley' are not specific places within the All, rather they name the generality of placing within it. Calling *zu Bach und Tale* ('to brook and valley') is the unending play of the Muse's activity within this setting. This opening concern with place allows for an interpretation of the poem's title; 'Immer und Überall'.

The word *immer* ('for ever') enjoins a form of continuity that resists any straightforward reduction to the language of eternity.[10] There is therefore a sense of permanence that marks the here and now. Eternity, the eternal and even the eternal as future (*das ewige Leben*) are not pertinent. What sense there is of endurance is given within and as nature. The force of the opening word of the title, *Immer*, only comes to the fore once the concern with place that is named in the *Überall* of the title is given a form. Place is not abstracted. Place is everywhere and yet it is an everywhere that is always devolving into particularity. This move to the particular is there in the evocation of *Bach und Tale* as naming the locations – places – to which the muse calls. There is no general evocation of the All other than through the continuity of its presentation with(in) the particular. This is the context within which the repetition in the final line – *Tausend, abertausend Male* ('a thousand and a thousand times') – needs to be understood.

Repetition here means continuity. It refers to the Muse. None the less, the question that has to be addressed concerns how this continuity is to be understood. On one level the answer is straightforward: it is the continuity of the call. However, once it is recognised that *Bach und Tale* ('brook and valley') designate particularity rather than a specific 'brook' or 'valley', then the call is always to be located within the potential infinite of the particular. Particularity only allows for generality to the extent that it is a generality that always devolves back to the particular. Each 'call' is a 'call', yet there is difference of place involved every time. Universality is always dispersed in terms of the place of the call. It is thus that the continuity established by the repetition in the final lines is one where particularity, and thus the demand to attend to the particular and with it to a version of difference, is itself always given *ab initio*. And yet, there is a difficulty. To the extent that these differences stem from the Muse, then they are potentially trapped within the Same. This possibility cannot be overlooked. While there may have been a number of muses, in the poem there is one. There are therefore two problems that arise. The first is the relationship between particularity and the universal – here the Muse is univocal and therefore universal – and the second is the inescapable problem of causality – the Muse's work – operative in these lines.[11]

On one level what is going on within them could be interpreted within a Spinozistic framework within which each attribute is the expression – expression rather than representation – of God. There is a possible pantheistic impulse that would allow for such a response insofar as the particularity of nature could be the only way the All can be made present. And yet it is more likely that what is being staged here is not explicable in Spinoza's terms but in relation to the problem of the Absolute within Romanticism. While there is an overlap between Spinoza and the Romantics, in this instance there is something else involved. The most productive way of staging what is at work here is to see it as given in the relation between the individual poem and *die romantische Dichtart* as presented by Schlegel, especially in *Athenäums-Fragment* 116, and Goethe's own formulation of the relation between Art and the particular, including the important analogy with science, as given, for example, in his *Geschichte der Farbenlehre*: 'art always [*immer*] establishes itself completely in every work of art, science, should also manifest itself completely in each application'.[12]

The project set in play by Goethe needs to be read in relation – what will emerge as a relation of content – to *Athenäums-Fragmente* 116 and 238. The latter fragment introduces the complex temporalising move that allows an initial point of comparison to be drawn with Goethe. When Schlegel argues that modern poetry is both the particular and the 'poesy of poesy', his formulation is that both occur *zugleich* ('at the same time').[13] The point of initial connection, though eventual differentiation, between Goethe and Schlegel hinges on the temporal and in this instance also on the ontological determinations at work in the staging of this sense of simultaneity.

It can be argued that central to the position presented by Goethe in the *Geschichte der Farbenlehre* is the impossibility of withdrawing the question of Art as a single question and thus as one that can be posed independently of its presentation in the artwork. However, there is a presentation. As such, what would have to be pursued is how that presentation was to be understood and thus what type of causality could be identified between Art and artwork. In other words, the question that would have to be taken up would concern the extent to which presence (understood as either presentation or participation) functioned as part of a teleological movement yielding the artwork as its end. The temporal dimensions of participation and thus presence – even allowing the question of causality to remain open – are necessarily absent from the formulation of an apparently similar position in Schlegel. The basis of any similarity would be the impossibility of effecting a radical separation of Art from artwork and therefore of the difficulty of there being a question of Art that could be posed independently of the work. And yet for Goethe, as has been intimated, that inseparability had to be thought in terms of an effective presence. The presence of Art is inseparable from the effectuation of artwork as the work of art. This connection is absent from Schlegel's position.

The distinction between Goethe and Schlegel is captured in the interpretive demands made by the word *zugleich* ('at the same time'). Before noting, if only in passing, the nature of these demands, what will emerge in their wake is the presentation of an intriguing tension within the poem under consideration. The first quatrain, while gesturing towards the Goethean conception of the Absolute (explicable in terms of the presence of Art in the particular work), can be contrasted to the second in which there is a more Schlegelian conception. Moreover, this contrast is effected by the poetry; in the first by the nature of the repetition in the last line of the first quatrain, and in the second in the conception of repetition in the final two lines of the second quatrain. This presentation of the relationship between the particular and the general, here understood as the Absolute, is formulated in detail by Schlegel in *Athenäums-Fragment* 238. Despite its length, it is vital to note the entirety of the fragment's formulation:

> There is a poesy, whose one and all is the relationship between the ideal and the real, and which following an analogy with philosophy must be called transcendental poesy [*Transzendentalpoesie*]. It begins as satire but with the absolute difference [*absoluten Verschiedenheit*] between the ideal and the real, hovers as elegy in the middle, and ends as idyll with absolute identity between them. This is why little value would be placed on transcendental philosophy that was not critical, that did not represent the producer [*Produzierende*] as much as it did the product [*Produkt*], and in the system of transcendental thought at the same time had the characteristics of transcendental thinking. In the same way, the poesy that unites the transcendental materials and the preliminary exercises of a poetic theory of writing common to modern poets with the artistic reflection and beautiful self-mirroring that is found in Pindar, in the lyric fragments of the Greeks, in the ancient elegy, and among the moderns in Goethe – this poesy should represent itself as part of each of its representations and should always be at the same time poesy and the poesy of poesy [*und in jeder ihrer Darstellungen sich selbst mit darstellen, und überall zugleich Poesie und Poesie der Poesie sein*].[14]

The necessity to quote the detail of this passage is twofold. In the first instance, it is essential to see how the position establishing the overall simultaneity of the work and the poesy of poesy emerges at the end of the fragment. And second, it is important to note that this simultaneity is reflected throughout the fragment in terms of the relationship between the producer and the produced. (In regard to this latter position what is central is the way simultaneity is also introduced.) In the fragment Schlegel is identifying a particular poetic practice which warrants the name *Transzendentalpoesie* ('Transcendental poesy'). What allows this name to be deployed is the inscribed co-presence of 'producer' (*Produzierende*) and 'product' (*Produkt*). Not only is a causal relation to an outside precluded, the distinction between inside and outside cannot be posed. Poetry becomes pure internality, where the internal is the temporal and ontological co-presence of the particular and the particular being the 'poesy of poesy'. It is in these terms that, when constrained to give an ontological description of 'the Romantic genre' (*die romantische Dichtart*), Schlegel describes it as 'still becoming' (*noch im Werden*).

That 'becoming' is its 'essential being' (*eigentliches Wesen*); moreover it is a be-coming without end. Poetry continually becomes itself.[15] In Schlegel's sense of the term, 'system' is always internal to the object. This conception of poesy is the practice of poeticising. Poesy cannot be withdrawn. It is only ever the practice of poetry itself. This further delineates the activity of critique to the extent that a critical engagement with poetry necessitates working through this simultaneity.

In general terms, therefore, Schlegel's use of the word *zugleich* ('at the same time') establishes the philosophical problem of accounting for the co-presence of the particular and the Absolute and the critical problem of tracing the work of that which occurs 'at the same time' within, and as, the activity of poetry. What is the time of this 'at the same time'? There are two answers. The first is that it presents a form of identity and difference as marking this type of poetry. Identity resides in the temporal and ontological simultaneity of the particular and the 'poesy of poesy', while difference inheres in the necessity to distinguish between particu-lar poems. Difference has to do with the way this simultaneity is present. The second answer concerns the identification within Schlegel of one of the elements identified earlier as constituting the address of poetry. (The absence of the second is, of course, the inevitable limit of Schlegel's conception of poetry.) As has been suggested, there are two elements which constitute that address. The first is par-ticularity. The second is the insertion of the particular within a structure of repeti-tion where particularity is to be understood, in part, in terms of the particular repeating its conditions of possibility and thus the genre of which it forms a part. Absent from Schlegel, despite the use of 'becoming' (*Werden*) to define the ontol-ogy of this form of poeticising, is a sustained engagement with repetition; evi-dence for this can be identified in the conflating of generic differences in the argumentation present in fragment 238. And yet, central to the position devel-oped in the *Athenäums-Fragmente* is the insistence on a conception of particularity in which the address of poetry is the particular's work. Here the limit of Schlegel's position – the refusal of repetition – is not the issue. The importance is twofold. In the first instance it lies in the relevance of the retention of particularity; in the second, it is the securing of particularity in relation to the necessary non-actuali-sation of the Absolute. These two elements are held by the temporal simultaneity announced in the use of the term *zugleich*.

The contrast between Goethe and Schlegel in this context is therefore between, in the first place, the presence of art within the artwork and, in the second place, the work already being the presencing of art. When in 'Immer und Überall' the Muse calls and that call is then repeated, what is significant is not the singularity of the call – the call could always be different and thus differently placed – but the singularity of the caller. To the extent that the Muse can be understood as taking the place of art, then not only does this inscribe causality back into the structure, it also positions the Muse as implicated in, though always other than, the work. The Muse stays the same. In the fourth line, the repetition of *Tausend* ('thousand') within *abertausend Male* ('and a thousand times') becomes a repetition in which what is generated may be different but it is a repetition conditioned by the retained causal centrality of the same. As the Muse endures as always the same, it follows that she is located beyond the hold of the ontology and temporality of the *zugleich* of Schlegel. However, it is this possibility – the retained effective presence of this 'at the same time' – that is opened up by the second quatrain.

The opening two lines of the second quatrain also involve a calling, though now it is a calling forth. (The contrast is between *rufen* and *fordern*.) The demand of the latter allows it to be linked to the 'new'. The first line opens with the particularising term *Sobald* ('When'). In its beginning the quatrain acts disjunctively. It interrupts. What it introduces is the moment of creation; the emergence of the new. Here it is *ein frisches Kelchlein* ('a fresh calyx') which blooms. Its instantiation can also be taken as an interruption. The work of the opening word – *Sobald* – works through the line. Not only does the effect of the interruption continue – continue by allowing – that continuity is also maintained by the internal rhyme of *ein* and the *ein* of *Kelchlein*. The interruption opens the way towards the 'new'. What figures here is the moment. The presence of the flower understood as the instance of interruption is that which demands *neue Lieder* ('new songs'). Any interpretation of the 'new' has to situate such an occurrence within the work of the poem. As such it is essential to note the effect of the last two lines on this formulation of the new. What cannot be ignored, for example, is the rhyme of *Lieder* and *wieder* and therefore the presence of an ineliminable link between that which is new and the work of repetition. Once again, the significance and the insistence of the link stem from its having been established by the poem's own activity.

Here there is a significant opening. The poem's own staging of the link between the new and repetition refuses any posited conception of the new as that which would have been the consequence of the work of genius. This occurs because the phonic link between the new and repetition – the rhyme of *Lieder* and *wieder* – wrests a conception of production away from the Kantian restriction of creation to that which falls either within or outside the confines of imitation. Here, new songs, and it must be remembered that they arise because they are called for by the new within nature, are ineliminably tied up with a structure of repetition that allows for the new. In other words, it will be a structure that distances the dominance of the same and thus takes place other than in response to the call of the Muse. It will be essential to return to this point.

The interpretation of the last two lines has to begin with the opening words *Und wenn* ('And though'). They mark neither a punctum nor conditionality, but a concession. What is being suggested is that even though time may flee the seasons return. The two lines are linked by the opening two words of the third line. They are also linked in other ways. In the third line 'time' is qualified as fading and then fleeing: 'die Zeit verrauschend flieht' ('fading time flees'). Even before the concession is taken up the nature of this 'time' must be addressed. What here is *die Zeit*? In the first place time is not at hand; it flees and fades. And yet time is stated, thereby raising the question of its status. In other words, what has to be addressed is the question of what is named by *die Zeit*. There is always the possibility that the use of the word does not name time. For example, in 'Germanien' Hölderlin used the formulation *in der Mitte der Zeit* ('at the centre of time') in the context of an engagement with the new.[16] Hölderlin was trying to allow for the difficult co-presence of an irrecoverable past that is still present within the now. The recognition of it as irrecoverable and yet as in some sense still present signals, within the poem, the recognition of myth as myth. For Hölderlin it is precisely that recognition that would mark the advent of the modern. In 'Germanien' 'time' is named. The question, however, concerns whether in that naming – thus in the line 'at the centre of time' (*in der Mitte der Zeit*) – time figures. The paradox is that when it is named Hölderlin seems constrained to maintain time as place. (This is reinforced by a formulation a few lines earlier where there is ringing 'from older times' [*aus alter Zeit*]. In being a place, 'time', as named in these lines from 'Germanien', is not timed; or at least not straightforwardly, since place predominates over time. Time therefore has become a setting. While it may be the case that the setting involves a certain temporality, that temporality is not named by *die Zeit*. Time has therefore been evacuated from its named presence. In the context of 'Germanien', *die Zeit* is not timed. In contradistinction to this form of evacuation, in the final two lines of 'Immer und Überall' time is not place. In not being a place *die Zeit* therefore demands to be given another description. Part of that description would necessitate the recognition that, in the context of 'Immer und Überall', *die Zeit* has a unifying force and thus presents the unity of time. For the work of the poem what is no longer possible is the presentation of time, if time is thought to be a unity demanding both its own philosophical investigation and poetic presentation. Of equal significance is that the vanishing of time does not give rise to a state of mourning for that which has been lost or is being lost. In part, this is realised through the concession introduced by the opening words *Und wenn* ('And though') and in part by the return occasioned by the last line.

The third line announces the flight of time. As unity, it is fleeing. It returns as the first word of the fourth line. Now, however, rather than time itself, the word

Zeit is incorporated into that which will always divide and pluralise it, namely the seasons. Within this move *die Zeit* returns within, and as, *Jahreszeiten* ('seasons'). The potential for loss is stemmed precisely because all that is lost is a specific conception of time and that which returns in its place is time as anoriginally plural. The question of time fades, to be replaced by the returns of time. The next two words – *kommen wieder* ('come again') – reinforce these returns. This occurs in at least two ways. Both are linked to the conception of repetition at work within the last line. In the first instance *kommen wieder* can be interpreted as the continuity of repetition. What is will continue to return. The second depends upon this initial usage, though now linked to the rhyme to which reference has already been made between *Lieder* and *wieder*. The force of this liaison is that continuity and the new – and here it is *neue Lieder* ('new songs') and thus new human creations and not mere nature – are articulated. In the poem they sound together, one calling and recalling the other. In contrast to the structure of repetition in the first quatrain in which the unity of the muse is maintained as a precondition for repetition, here it is the very impossibility of the retention of unity that sanctions repetition. Moreover, it is a repetition that in the continuity of its returns is constrained by the sound of the new.

The Schlegelian conception of the Absolute is at work in these lines. What they stage is the inscription of time within the continuity of time's returns. Each new song is to that extent both itself and the condition of its own instantiation. In contradistinction to the creative force of the muse the second quatrain develops a conception of creation that allows the force of production to form part of what is produced. This set-up is, as has been argued, the consequence of the entire work of the quatrain. From the interruption staged by the *Sobald* to the reworking of repetition, the Absolute is already incorporated and dispersed. It can only be staged in terms of the continuity of particularity. Creation therefore is always occurring again and anew. Even if the emergence of 'new songs' takes place as the result of the call of a new flower (and here it is vital to recognise that it is the new in each case) there is an unending continuity in the song's presence without that presence necessarily dictating the form of the song. What comes to be repeated is Schlegel's description of the ontology of 'the Romantic genre' (*die romantische Dichtart*) as 'still becoming' (*noch im Werden*). The continuity of becoming thought in relation to the new allows for continuity precisely because it does not identify a specific form as proper to 'the Romantic genre' (*die romantische Dichtart*). Contrary to the theory of genius, creation arises from the interplay of repetition and the new. At this point it becomes possible to see elements of early Romanticism as moving away from Kant. The object's internal causality takes the place of nature and thus of genius. Within the departure from Kant the force of the early Romantic concern with the object begins to appear. It is essential to note, if only in outline, how the object emerges.

In the *Critique of Judgement* Kant identifies the genius as the one through whom nature works; nature rather than the intending subject. The final line of §46 states this position clearly: 'Nature, through genius [*durch das Genie*] prescribes the rule not to science but to art, and this only insofar as the art is to be fine art [*schöne Kunst*].'[17] The important element here is the movement through the subject. Not only does this produce the subject as an effect of this movement, it also yields an implicit causality. Nature causes 'fine art'. It is not the consequence of an intentional action. Genius therefore cannot 'describe' (*beschreiben*) how a product comes to be present. Thus, when Kant famously argues that genius is necessarily opposed to 'the spirit of imitation' (*dem Nachahmungsgeiste*), it is not just that there will be another 'spirit' animating the work. More significantly, in this context, the refusal of imitation reinforces the work's immediacy and in so doing reinforces the causality of nature. The new, therefore, to the extent that it functions as a term within Kantian aesthetics, is always the particular instance of nature having been produced through the intermediary of the subject. Kant's conception of the object, therefore – where object is an instance of 'beautiful art' – is that which is given immediately within a causal relation between nature and product. Imitation is necessarily incompatible with immediacy and with the causality proper to the object's production. What is significant in the move from Kant to Schlegel and Goethe is the emergence of a concern with the object and the role of the Absolute in its construction and thus in its presence as an object. No longer external – Absolute as nature – it is internal to the particular. Moreover, it occurs with the particular and as such defines the mode of being proper to particularity.

Within Kant's conception of genius, understood as a theory of the production of 'fine art', the Absolute figures as either 'nature' or the 'aesthetic idea' insofar as neither can be presented in their totality and yet each conditions particularity. Regardless of the specific form taken by the relationship between the Absolute and the particular, the former – the Absolute – is always external to the latter. When in *Athenäums-Fragment* 238 Schlegel draws on Kant to establish the possibility of 'transcendental poesy' (*Transzendentalpoesie*) he is deploying Kant's critical method and not the implicit Kantian conception of the Absolute. Kant's formulation of the critical as that which grounds the possibility of philosophy within philosophy, such that critical philosophy is always the self-effectuation of the philosophical, is reiterated by Schlegel in regard to *die romantische Dichtart* ('the Romantic genre'). For Kant, any consideration of the object's presence has to account for that presence in terms of a causal relationship to an outside. The opposite is not that the object is self-caused but rather that the ground of the object is itself internal to, and thus forms an integral part of, the object. Once this state of affairs is considered in relation to poetry, then fundamental to that consideration is the centrality of time. Time is not merely within poetry. Poetry is the staging of the returns of time. In other words, the identification of the work of the poem's effectuation and thus its being a poem is the work of time.

'Wachstum' and 'Immer und Überall' do not allow this general hypothesis to be demonstrated. Rather, in tracing their persistence as poems, reference is invariably made to the different ways in which time returns within the poems. In addition, what has emerged is that central to the work of time is the presence of interruption. More than a simple hiatus or ending, the interruption within poetry's work is that which allows. Interrupting and allowing combine, discontinuity and continuity are at work together and at the same time. Their simultaneity, that occurrence in which the interruption opens, is the emphatic moment. The ground of expression is not the expressionless; it is the pause, or interruption, that is reinvested with the quality of an opening out; the reinvestment and thus the iterative reworking being integral to the operation of the moment. To be trapped within the opposition of expression/expressionless is to remain wed to the semantic quality of words and to the simple content of the poem. What is then overlooked is the force and in the end the meaning of sound, rhythm and time. In other words, what is overlooked is poetry.

Once poetry figures then to the extent that its address is maintained, what continues to be worked through is the object of critique. This occurs for the straightforward reason that what is detailed is the particularity of the poem: particularity freed both from its possible lapse into empiricism and its collapse within the constraint of the universal. Allowing for critique is to allow for poetry.[18]

Notes

1 This point has to be linked to a larger argument concerning the work of time within objects. Time would not just be an incidental predicate. On the contrary, time would be integral to the object's activity as an object. Rather than assuming that time can be generalised there will need to be distinctions between the operation of time – the plurality of time – within poetry as opposed, for example, to its operation within art and architecture. Here, as will be suggested, the contention is that the differing ways in which time is present do not point to a deeper concern with time, or being, that would allow itself to be addressed in terms of the singular question, 'What is time?' While it is not argued for in detail, this position demands that a distinction be drawn between Heidegger's concern with the question of Being, on the one hand, and an ontology of difference on the other. The latter is presupposed while also being worked out here.

2 Much as in music there needs to be a differentiation between literal silence and that which oscillates between a pause and an interruption. Continuity, after all, reinvests a certain spacing with the quality of having been – and thus of having become – a pause. One of the most important discussions of silence in literature is George Steiner's 'Silence and the Poet' in his *Language and Silence*, London: Faber & Faber, 1985, pp.55–75. In addition to a

concern with silence any reference to sound opens up the importance of the problem of rhythm. There is a significant distinction to be drawn between rhythm as the object of metric analysis and another rhythm at work in the poem which shows itself in terms of silences, interruptions and thus in terms of the staging and the appearing of the poetic. The attempt to wrest rhythm from its complete identification with the results of metric analysis can be traced in a range of different sources. An important location is the notes accompanying the poetry of Gerard Manley Hopkins. For example, the notes to 'The Wreck of the Deutschland' can be read as evincing such concerns. See *The Poems of Gerard Manley Hopkins*, ed. W.H. Gardener and N.H. MacKenzie, Oxford: Oxford University Press, 1970, pp.254–64. Indeed, there is an important project that endures with Hopkins. While it is always possible to see his work as involving variants of Romanticism, what remains is the link between, for example, Hölderlin's concern with what could be described as the complexity of rhythm in the opening to his 'Über die Verfahrungsweise des poetischen Geistes' (Friedrich Hölderlin, *Werke*, Munich: Carl Hanser Verlag, 1996, pp.617–19), where that concern is present in both form and content, and Hopkins' own preoccupations with rhythm and its articulations in terms of what he described as 'inscape' and 'instress'. One of the most significant philosophical treatments of rhythm – and again it is the complexity of rhythm – is David Farrell Krell's remarkable study of this 'topic' (perhaps *topos*) in Friedrich Hölderlin, Martin Heidegger and Georg Trakl in Part II of his *Lunar Voices*, Chicago: University of Chicago Press, 1995. The detail and dexterity of Krell's analysis opens up too many paths to be followed here. Important discussions on rhythm also appear throughout Giorgio Agamben, *The End of the Poem* (trans. Daniel Heller-Roazen), Stanford: Stanford University Press, 1999. See in particular pp.32–41.

3 Clearly part of what is intended by an interruption is explicable in relation to the caesura. The difficulty with this identification is that it leaves unexamined how the caesura itself is to be understood. Its initial formulation in Hölderlin gives rise to an interpretation in terms of an allowing. However, the Hölderlinian conception is itself traversed by the problem of what he identifies as *das reine Wort* ('the pure word'). The passage in which this occurs – from the *Anmerkungen zum Ödipus* – links this 'pure word' to that which interrupts the work of specific representations (*Vorstellungen*). What emerges is no longer the 'exchange of representations' but rather *die Vorstellung [die] selber erscheint* ('the representation [which] itself appears') (Hölderlin, *Werke*, p.661). For a generalised discussion of the role of the caesura within Greek literature, even though it is a treatment that links such concepts strictly to measure, see M.L. West, *Greek Metre*, Oxford: Oxford University Press, 1982. In regard to tragedy see pp.82–88. While Hölderlin's approach does not abandon measure there is an equal concern within the 'Remarks' (and this is also the case in other writings concerned with poetics) with that which resists the completing hold of measure. Within Hölderlin's text the argument concerning the caesura is linked to the particularity of tragedy. And yet, his position has become generalised in order to account for interruption itself. Whether there is that sense of generality in the term 'caesura' as stemming from the writings of Hölderlin remains an open question. For a more detailed investigation of the relationship between the caesura and tragedy see Philippe Lacoue-Labarthe, 'La césure du spéculatif', in his *L'imitation des modernes*, Paris: Galilée, 1986, pp.39–71. Central to any investigation of the caesura is Walter Benjamin's reworking of it in terms of *das Ausdruckslose* in his *Goethes Wahlverwandtschaften*. The 'caesura' reappears later in *Das Passagen-Werk* (Konvolut N, 10a, 3) in terms of what could be described as temporal montage (see Walter Benjamin, *Gesammelte Schriften*, I:1, ed. Rolf Tiedemann and Hermann Schweppenhäuser, Frankfurt/M.: Suhrkamp, 1991, pp.123–203; and V:1, p.595, respectively). Part of what is being questioned here, though it indicates a further project, is the viability, perhaps even the possibility of the 'expressionless' if the latter is understood as pure interruption. Fundamental to a retained conception of the Absolute is that it remains beyond the hold of

ANDREW BENJAMIN

expression. None the less, interruption itself – a generalised sense of the caesura – has to involve both interrupting and allowing; only to that extent is there a form of the expressionless. For an important discussion of Heidegger's interpretation of Hölderlin that touches on questions pertaining both to tragedy and the caesura see Christopher Fynsk, *Language and Relation*, Stanford: Stanford University Press, 1996; in particular pp.112–31.

4 See my discussion of the poetry of Celan and Jabès in *Present Hope*, London: Routledge, 1997, ch. 6, for a development of some of these points. What I tried to stage in that chapter was a brief – inevitably too brief – encounter with Heidegger. The assumption behind this chapter is that the real counter to Heidegger's writings on poetry stems from a reworking of the early Romantic tradition. It needs to be emphasised that it is a reworking and not a mere reapplication. There is little point trying to find affinities between Romanticism and contemporary work in philosophy or literary theory. Such an undertaking is constrained to neglect giving an account of the very act of establishing an affinity in the first place. Andrew Bowie's *From Romanticism to Critical Theory*, London: Routledge, 1997 is the most recent attempt to establish affinities rather than attempt to rework Romanticism. (There is not even the recognition that what he is attempting is, in fact, a form of reworking.) His approach becomes therefore a contemporary form of historicism. In contradistinction to Bowie's project – one which fails to think through the possibility of its own undertaking – it is possible to situate the critical writings of Paul de Man. In the opening chapter of *The Rhetoric of Romanticism* (New York: Columbia University Press, 1984, p.6), he argues, in the context of a discussion of Hölderlin, that, 'Poetic language can do nothing but originate anew over and over again'. This position will emerge as one that is to an extent compatible with the conception of poetic practice arising from Schlegel's work. There is no simple identity between Romanticism and a great deal of contemporary critical writing. It is rather that a concern with writing and thus with the activity of poetic practice – practice as that which is proper to poetry – stands counter to the Heideggerian tradition in which poetry is given a privileged status in responding to the question of Being. For a detailed discussion that explores the limits of Heidegger's engagement with poetry see Véronique Foti, *Heidegger and the Poets*, New Jersey: Humanities Press, 1992. For work on poetry that attempts to develop the Romantic project where that development is not a simple repetition see Timothy Clark, *The Theory of Inspiration*, Manchester: Manchester University Press, 1997.

5 Reference is to Johann Wolfgang von Goethe, *Werke*, Hamburger Ausgabe, I, Munich: DTV, 1998, pp.373, 296 respectively. Translations are from *Goethe: Selected Verse*, ed. David Luke, London: Penguin, 1986. The German text in the Penguin edition differs slightly from the Hamburger Ausgabe. Preference has been given to the latter. While, for the most part, I have followed the translation in the Penguin edition, slight changes have been introduced as demanded by the argument being presented. Where it is not essential or where the translation is self-evident I have left the German text to stand on its own.

6 Goethe, *Werke*, I, pp.247–48.

7 Fundamental to the argument developed in this chapter and part of that which would serve to differentiate it from any straightforward acceptance of Romanticism is the centrality accorded to repetition. Part of that project involves reworking aspects of the differing conceptions of repetition developed by Freud and then taken up by later psychoanalytic writers, notably Jean Laplanche. In regard to Freud, one of the central moments is the formulation of the concept of *Nachträglichkeit* in 'Entwurf einer Psychologie', in *Aus den Anfängen der Psychoanalyse*, London: Imago Publishing, 1950. The reference to this term in this paper is via the formulation 'iterative reworking'. I have taken this to be the most useful translation of *Nachträglichkeit* because what needs to be captured is the productive aspect proper to it. Of the many texts by Jean Laplanche, two which are of central importance are J. Laplanche, *Fantasme originaire, Fantasmes des*

origines, Origines du fantasme, Paris: Hachette, 1985; and 'Notes sur l'après-coup', in *Entre séduction et inspiration: l'homme*, Paris: Presses Universitaires de France, 1999, p.66. The best introduction to Laplanche's work is John Fletcher, 'Psychoanalysis and the Question of the Other', in J. Laplanche, *Essays on Otherness*, London: Routledge, 1999, pp.57–67.

8 As such the instant comes to be constituted as the moment of interruption and opening. The moment as the site of their irreducibility – the moment cannot be reduced to either but is maintained as both – takes on the quality of a plural event. The plural event is the form of anoriginal difference.

9 The point of departure for a more detailed explication of this position is the distinction drawn by Walter Benjamin in his text *Goethes Wahlverwandtschaften* between the *Wahrheitsgehalt* ('truth content') of the work of art and its *Sachgehalt* ('material content'). See Walter Benjamin, *Goethes Wahlverwandtschaften*, in *Gesammelte Schriften*, I:1, ed. Rolf Tiedemann and Hermann Schweppenhäuser, Frankfurt/M., Suhrkamp, 1991, pp.123–203. For Benjamin the 'truth content' is that which is sought by critique. While this distinction is central and while it does not lead to an abandoning of content but its reinscription into the activity of critique, it remains the case that Benjamin's position fails to take up the problem of the relationship between the particular and the genre of which it forms a part. As such not only is there a sustained refusal to account for particularity; what is also written out is the necessity to construe the relationship between particular and genre in terms of repetition.

10 It would, of course, be equally possible to translate *immer* more straightforwardly as 'always'. The important point is that it suggests a sense of continuity and permanence that fall outside the theologically charged language of eternity.

11 It should not be thought that this is the only way in which the Muse can be approached. The argument here is that the singularity of the Muse is fundamental to the quatrain's work. For an analysis that starts with the problems set by the already plural presence of muses, see Jean-Luc Nancy, *Les Muses*, Paris: Galilée, 1994. For a discussion of the Greek origin of the muses and their place within poetic inspiration and thus within poetry see the extensive treatment of this topic in Simon Goldhill, *The Poet's Voice*, Cambridge: Cambridge University Press, 1991; and Penelope Murray, *Plato on Poetry*, Cambridge: Cambridge University Press, 1996.

12 Johann Wolfgang von Goethe, *Geschichte der Farbenlehre*, in *Werke*, Hamburger Ausgabe, XIV, Munich: DTV, 1998, pp.7–269. It should be noted immediately that Benjamin also quotes this passage (*Gesammelte Schriften*, VI, p.47, fragment 26). Here it is not possible to pursue the detail of Benjamin's relationship to Romanticism. None the less, it should be noted that the staging of the contrast between Schlegel and Goethe taking place in this chapter can be additionally read as a commentary on Benjamin's own work in this area. Absent from both Benjamin and Schlegel is any real encounter with the work of repetition. This absence is of great importance here because the retained presence of the relationship between the Absolute and particularity – as it figures in Schlegel and as it will be developed by Benjamin – necessitates an engagement with repetition. I hope to be able to take up the problem of the absent presence of repetition within their work in a more sustained account of the task of criticism. I have taken up this problem in my *Present Hope*, ch. 2. For important work done on this topic see Winfried Menninghaus, 'Das Ausdrucklose: Walter Benjamins Metamorphosen der Bilderlosigkeit', in Ingrid and Konrad Scheurmann (eds), *Für Walter Benjamin*, Frankfurt/M.: Suhrkamp, 1992, pp.170–83; and Rodolphe Gasché, 'The Sober Absolute: On Benjamin and the Early Romantics', in David Ferris (ed.) *Walter Benjamin. Theoretical Questions*, Stanford: Stanford University Press, 1996, pp.50–75.

13 F. Schlegel, *Athenäums-Fragmente*, in *Kritische Schriften und Fragmente 1794–1828*, Studienausgabe, II, ed. Ernst Behler and Hans Eichner, Paderborn/Munich: Ferdinand Schöningh, 1988 [1798], pp.105–56, 127.

14 The English translation, slightly modified here, is in Jochen Schult-Sausse et al. (eds), *Theory as Practice: A Critical Anthology of Early German Romantic Writings*, Minneapolis: Minnesota University Press, 1997, pp.322–23.

15 The almost canonical status of the fragment (116) should not be overlooked (Schlegel, *Athenäums-Fragmente*, pp.114–15). It is another fragment that plays a central role in Benjamin's work on early Romanticism.

16 Friedrich Hölderlin, 'Germanien', in *Werke*.

17 Immanuel Kant, *Kritik der Urteilskraft*, in *Werkausgabe*, X, ed. Wilhelm Weischedel, Frankfurt/M.: Suhrkamp, 1994, p.243 (Engl. edn *Critique of Judgement* [trans. Walter Pluhar], Indianapolis: Hacking, 1987).

18 A slightly longer version of this chapter appears in my book *Philosophy's Literature*, London: Clinamen Press, 2001.

CHAPTER 8

'NOW':
Walter Benjamin on Historical Time

WERNER HAMACHER

(. . . . .)

(. . . . .)

What Walter Benjamin uncovers in his theses 'On the Concept of History' is the temporal structure of the political affect.[1] Historical time is founded upon political time directed towards happiness. Any theory of history – of historical cognition and of historical action – therefore will have to take this time of the affect as its starting point. The fact that *pathemata*, affects, passions were already to a large extent discredited within political theory during Benjamin's times must have been attributed by him to the disappearance of their genuine political dimension. Within prevailing historiography the political impulse was replaced by the rational calculation of an abstract cognition of the object. Thus, in order to clarify the force of political affects, it had to be shown that such affects are also decisive for objective cognition. This occurs in Benjamin's second thesis 'On the Concept of History'. The thesis demonstrates that cognitive acts, determined by the micro-structure of the affective time, are political operations. The cognition at stake here, however, is the cognition of happiness. Happiness never is experienced in a present without this present relating to that which has been (*Gewesenes*). It is not, however, experienced on a past reality, but on the *irrealis* of its non-actualised possibility. 'The kind of happiness that could arouse envy in us' – this is how Benjamin begins his argument, making envy the seal of authenticity in which happiness manifests itself – 'the kind of happiness that could arouse envy in us is only in the air we have breathed, among people we could have talked to, women who could have given themselves to us'.[2] The kind of happiness that alone can prove itself – and according to Benjamin's portrayal can only prove itself through envy – is not past happiness, it is the happiness that was possible in the past but was missed. Happiness is the *festum post festum amissum*. It does not reside in an event that could become the subject of objective cognition, but rather in a possibility, which proves to be a possibility only in the miss and which only by virtue of this miss preserves itself as a possibility for the future. Happiness is the possible in its miss: it is the possible that could impossibly have been realised at the time, it is the possible that springs from an im-possible. This kind of happiness only, im-possible happiness, provokes envy. For envy is an affect that is directed not towards anything real, but rather towards something possible that is disguised, not realised and therefore still open. For Benjamin, envy is not kindled by the happiness of someone else, but rather by one's own happiness that was possible and not seized. Envy is therefore without object like the intention of Lucifer's knowledge, an intention which aims towards the good. This good, happiness, maintains itself as if according to the platonic formula *epékeina tes ousías*, beyond the recognisable essences in the realm of their mere possibility. It is the other that could have been, and it preserves in what became actuality the possibility of its otherness.

Happiness is a contingent possibility of that which has been (*des Gewesenen*), a possibility that preserves itself for another time; that is, first of all for that future that is now present. In this present, however, it becomes understandable only to envy, for only envy is the organon of cognition of that which cannot be held, what cannot be grasped as given reality and cannot be registered as possession. Cognition is essentially a manifestation of this envy, an irreducible *vitium*, and it is just as essentially object-less, for the happiness towards which it is directed is not the actual and not the possible, but the possible that has become impossible. If happiness existed as possession or property, its cognition would be neither necessary nor possible any longer. Happiness is only cognisable in its pure – that is, missed, deferred and unseized – possibility. And only as such a possibility does it offer itself to a future cognition. Each such cognition, however, does not only have an ethical dimension, directed towards happiness, it is furthermore structurally historical, insofar as it concerns past possibilities; in these past possibilities, however, it concerns the possibility of a different future. Thus it must be said of the temporality of the cognition of possible happiness that it jumps out of traditional categories of time and history. Unlike those categories, which concern temporal and historical realities, rather this cognition addresses possibilities and first of all possibilities that are not actualised, that have not entered the series of historical events and have not become components of historical tradition. In one of the notes on Baudelaire, Benjamin says: 'The further the mind goes back into the past, the more the mass of that increases which has not yet become history at all'.[3] Historical cognition is cognition of that 'which has not yet become history, that which yet can become history', because its possibilities, and that is, possibilities of happiness, have not yet been actualised. History is only possible because of the possibilities that were missed.

The true historicity of historical objects lies in their *irrealis*. Their un-reality is the store-place of the historically possible. For their *irrealis* indicates a direction through which that which could have been is referred to those *for whom* it could have been and for whom it is preserved as a – missed – possibility. 'The kind of happiness', Benjamin writes, 'that could arouse envy in *us* is only in the air *we* have breathed, among people *we* could have talked to, women who could have given themselves to us'.[4] The possible stored in un-reality is not an abstract or ideal possible in general and for all times, but a possible always for a particular future, that is, for precisely the one singular future that recognises itself in it as missed. It is *we* who could have talked to people but didn't; it is *we* who did not seize an opportunity – and now have to enviously admit that we missed a possibility to speak that only *we* could have taken, for it was only *our* possibility, which already now is no more. It is *we*, again and again, who leave language in its possibility unused, although it was a possibility of our happiness, of ourselves, which was therefore an absolutely singular, unreplaceable and unrepeatable possibility. And it is only us, for and in whom this missed possibility lives on as missed and demands fulfilment in every moment.

If possibilities are only ever possibilities *for* someone, then they are intentions. We have been meant by our life's possibilities, be they conscious or unconscious, seized or missed. Possibilities are not abstractly categorical, relating to objects, conditions and actions in general, but are always possibilities only *for* those who could seize them, and belong to the existential structure of their existence. Therefore, the second thesis remarks: 'the image of happiness that we cherish is thoroughly coloured by the time to which the course of our own existence has assigned us'.[5] Benjamin is only drawing the conclusion from the intentional structure of possibilities and of the temporal space they open up, when he continues:

> The past carries with it a hidden index by which it is referred to redemption. Are we not ourselves touched by a breeze of the air that was around those who were there earlier? is there not in voices to whom we lend an ear an echo of those now silenced? do the women whom we woo not have sisters whom they have never met? If that is the case, then there is a secret agreement between the generations that have been and the present one. Then, our coming was expected

163

on earth. Then, like every generation that preceded us, we have been endowed with a *weak* messianic force, a force on which the past has a claim.[6]

Redemption, as Benjamin here talks about it, is meant most prosaically: a redeeming (*Einlösung*) of possibilities, which are opened with every life and are missed in every life. If the concept of redemption points towards a theology – and it does so without doubt and *a fortiori* in the context of the first thesis, which mentions the 'little hunchback' of theology – then this is not straightforwardly Judeo-Christian theology, but rather a theology of the missed, or the distorted – hunchbacked – possibilities, a theology of missed, distorted or hunchbacked time. Each possibility that was missed in the past remains a possibility for the future, precisely because it has not found fulfilment. For the past to have a future merely means that the past's possibilities have not yet found their fulfilment, that they continue to have an effect as intentions and demand their realisation from those who feel addressed by them. When past things survive, then it is not lived-out (*abgelebte*) facts that survive, facts that could be recorded as positive objects of knowledge; rather what survives are the unactualised possibilities of that which is past. There is historical time only insofar as there is an excess of the unactualised, the unfinished, failed, thwarted, which leaps beyond its particular Now and demands from another Now its settlement, correction and fulfilment.

The possible is a surplus over the factual. As such, the possible is time: excess over anything that can become a positive given; excess over that which is; remainder that itself *is* not. Every possibility, and *a fortiori* every missed possibility, survives as the time to fulfil this possibility. Time – historical time – is nothing but the capability of the possible to find its satisfaction in an actual. As a standing-out (*Ausstand*) and ex-position of that actual in which a mere possible could find its fulfilment, in which the possible as intention could find its goal, time is the claim of the unfinished and failed, of the broken and thwarted for its completion and rescue in happiness. Time is always the time of the unfinished and itself unfinished time, time that has not reached its end. It is the time of that which is not yet and perhaps never will be. It is therefore the dimension of the possible as the claim to become actual. For Benjamin, the addressee of this claim is not an instance that precedes this claim – it is not an already constituted subject that perceives such a claim, united in itself and in control of itself. The claim's addressee is rather fundamentally a function of this claim, 'thoroughly coloured by the time', and of the possibilities that assert their demands towards this claim, not only *in* its time but *as* its time. Therefore, 'our coming was expected on earth'.[7] What is said here is that we are first of all and primarily the ones that were expected by the missed possibilities of the past. Only *qua* expected have we been given 'a *weak* messianic force'.[8] This messianic force is the intentional correlate of the claim that calls upon us from the missed possibilities of the past, not to miss them a second time, but to perceive them in every sense: cognisingly to seize and to actualise them. In this force, those possibilities and the time in which they survive search for the telos of their intentions. Messianic force is therefore nothing other than the implicit hypothesis of the missed possible that there has to be an instance to correct the miss, to do the undone, to regain the wasted and actualise the has-been-possible. This force therefore is not one that is our own, independent of this claim. It is not 'ours', something we can have at our disposal by our own means, but it is the force which we have been 'endowed with' by others, it is the force of the claim itself and of the expectation that the claim is met. This force is never messianic in the sense that we ourselves are enabled by it to direct the hope for our own redemption towards the future or, to be more precise, to future generations, but only in the entirely different sense that we have been 'endowed with' it by former generations, even by all former generations, as the compliance with their expectations. The messianic force is, in short, the postulate of fulfilability and, in this sense, of redeemability that is immanent in each missed possibility and distinguishes it as a possibility. Regardless of whether this force of fulfilment and redemption of the possible is ever actually proven or not; regardless thus also of whether there has ever been a single case where this 'messianic force' was indeed active in the actualisation of the possible. It is, as this force, *given*, and we have been 'endowed with' it by the simple givenness of what has been and, because it did not reach its goal, did not stay. The possible – possible happiness – is that which demands actualisation – actual happiness – and in which the telos of this demand remains inscribed, even if there has never been and will never be this actualisation. 'We' – independent of whether 'we' presently exist or not – are the intentional complement destined to fulfil the postulate of realisability of this possibility, insofar as it is possibility. The messianic force that 'we' have been 'endowed with' by all that is past is weak because it is not an ability that springs from ourselves but it is the vanishing point of missed possibilities and of their demand for fulfilment. But it is a *weak* force also because it has to become extinguished in each future by which it is not perceived and actualised. Thesis five thus apodictically but consistently pronounces the finiteness of this messianic force: it is an irretrievable 'image of the past that threatens to disappear with every present that does not recognise itself in it as of its own concerns'.[9] The '*weak* messianic force' is therefore the expectation of others towards us, the undischarged remains of possibility that are transferred from former generations to the future ones. It is the rest of time that remains in order to meet those demands – a rest that *is* not as substantial existence but is given as time and passes with it. The '*weak* messianic force' in us is time as mere possibility of happiness.

By determining the relationship of the past to the respective present – towards *us* – as an essentially linguistic relationship: as an *agreement* between former generations and ours, as 'echo of now silent voices that we lend our ear to', as the 'claim' of the unused possibility that we 'could have talked to' certain people,[10] Benjamin explains historical time, if only implicitly, as a time made out of language. History presents itself as the afterlife of unused linguistic possibilities, which demand their redemption by other languages and finally by language itself, as temporal extension of intentions on to language, as imperative claim, which the forfeited possibilities of language raise in view of their realisation, and as an expectation that invests every single word with the '*weak* messianic force' to transform the missed possibilities into fulfilled ones. *Awaiting* (*Erwartung*) is to be understood as a-wording (*Erwortung*); language as the demand of a language that did not become one, for there to be one. And similarly history, which for Benjamin ever since his 'The Task of the Translator' is bound up inextricably with language and even identical with its history: it is the claim of the history that never became one, for there to be history and with it language.[11]

The theology of language and history that Benjamin outlines in his second thesis is a theology of wilted possibilities and thus an essentially wilted, dwarfed and hunchbacked theology. To be more precise, it is a theory that there could only be an unfinished and therefore an anatheology of the *weak* possibility of theology. The formulation '*weak* messianic force' talks about the weak, the insubstantial and thus genuinely historical possibility of historical cognition and historical action. If theology assumes the necessity, constancy and certainty of a God and historiography assumes that there already has been history and there will be history in the future, then both of them assume essentially unhistorical concepts of deity and history. Historicism's concept of history is thus the simple counterpart to the concept of God of substantialist theology. As the latter relies on the constancy of God, so does the former on the positivity of historical facts. The historicity of such facts, however, does not have its origin in their steadiness (*Ständigkeit*), much less in their standing on their own, their autonomy (*Selbständigkeit*). Historical is that which only can be recognised as historical from its contingent possibility to yet have been different and to yet become different, and thus from its after-history. Historical is only ever that which it is not yet – the always other, open possibility. Only that *can* become historical that is not yet historical. This however also means: as it is, namely as a possibility given and subject to actualisation, in principle, this possibility is equally exposed to the danger of being missed. Insofar as it is mere possibility, insofar as it is not grounded in a substantial actuality, historicity is always also the possibility of becoming impossible and expiring. Facts would last if they existed as facts outside any intentional relation; only possibilities can be missed; historical facts, which constitute themselves as having-been only within the space of their possibilities, ensue solely from the dimension of their capacity to be missed. They are insubstantial, singular, finite. Even if facts have the structure of referring and furthermore of intention and tendency (and Benjamin suggests that they do have this very structure: 'The past carries with it a hidden index by which it is referred to redemption'), they are still constitutively designed for their expiration: expiring either in the redemption, fulfilment and resolution of their intention or expiring in the miss of this redemption. The historical is historical only because it manifests itself in the span between these two possibilities of intention, these two possibilities of possibility: that the possibility expires in its fulfilment, or that it passes away if it is not seized. Thus it follows that each possibility is a possibility of its actualisation only if it is at the same time the possibility of the missing of this possibility. Only those possibilities are historical possibilities that can always also not be seized. They are fleeting possibilities, not possibilities that as a substantial stock in the archive of potentialities could be grasped at any time. Because there is no reservoir fixed for all time, in which the treasures of possibility for ever accumulate, but only a reservoir whose stock dissolves with every missed chance, history is no progression where given possibilities, one by one, one out of the other, are actualised, so that in the end all possibilities will have been exhausted and all possible actualities established. Where there is history, there is no continuum between the possible and the actual. Any continuum between them would de-potentialise the possible and turn it into an in principle calculable necessity. Only where its possibility is contingent possibility – namely one that can be another possibility, the possibility of something other or even no possibility at all – only there is the possible historical. As a fleeting, non-archivable, contingent possibility, as one that is just now given and is now already gone – and thus as always singular, as the solitarily leaping out of every pre-stabilised formation – it concerns the one who would have to lapse into lethargy in the face of the automatism of the actualities unfolding homogeneously out of possibilities, and demands of him his grasping intervention: a grasping without which there would be no history, but a grasping which would not exist without the corresponding possibility that it fails to appear or is unsuccessful. Only because Benjamin thinks of history from the point of view of its possibilities, from the point of view of its possibility of being other or of not being, can he view history not as a mechanical series of events, but as act. Only because he does not view historical possibilities as a constant and freely available resource for series of realisation does he have to view each historical act as the always singular answer to an always singular possibility. Only because this answer can be missed can it also succeed.

.

History, as it is thought by Benjamin, is never the history of facts, incidents and developments without initially being the history of their possibilities; and never the history of these possibilities, without being the history of their continued unfulfilment. The redemption to which the past in its 'hidden index' is referred is redemption only because it can be missed. When Benjamin talks about a '*weak* messianic force' and highlights the word *weak* by the use of italics (one of the few such words in his 'Theses') he does not do so because there would be for him also a strong messianic force or even one that would overcome with certainty any conceivable opposition, and not because a force in general would under certain circumstances be reduced to a weaker one. '*Weak*' denotes not so much the quantum of this force in relation to a larger one – be it a demanded one, or even an ideal one – but rather the susceptibility, on principle, to its failure.

There is a messianic force only where it can fail: anything that may be called messianic force is therefore a *weak* one. To imagine that it could be strengthened through vigour or that it could be sufficient to possess it is equally nonsensical. It is enough to perceive and activate it – nothing else is possible to turn it into a historical force and into the only genuine force of history; but nothing else is necessary either.[12] If that which has been and each present that can become past carries with it a 'hidden index' through which it is referred to a '*weak* messianic force' that would realise its possibilities of happiness, then all historical existence has an irreducible – and irreducibly weak – messianic structure. When Benjamin first touches upon the referentiality to redemption in historical existence in his second thesis, the reason he does not talk about 'the Messiah' as a historically determined religious figure is that each singular historical moment, of whatever epoch or religious observance, has to be structured with reference to the messianic and thus as a messianic imperative if it is to fall into the domain of historical existence at all. If the 'index' of a 'messianic force', which 'we have been endowed with like every generation that preceded us', marks every historical possibility, then messianic referentiality is the structure of the possible and of the historical time in which it lives on. Benjamin attributes weakness to this structural messianicity not in order to note an accidental defect, which, under ideal circumstances, could be remedied, but in order to emphasise a structural element of this messianicity, through which it, in turn, is referred to its possible failure. The possibility of happiness is only indicated together with the corresponding possibility of its failure. The messianic index is crossed a priori by its reference to a possible failure and thus to a possible impossibility. There is, in short, no referring (*Verweisung*) to a 'messianic force' that should not at the same time indicate, as Paul Celan used the word, its orphaning (*Verwaisung*); no index that would not have to reach the borders of its indexicality and become an ex-index; no messianicity that does not emerge from its non-messianicity. The weakness of the 'messianic force' lies in its structural finitude. The Messiah, who is supposed to rescue the missed possibilities of history into actual happiness, can himself be missed. Any messiah – and each moment in which he should be able to enter, each Now – is essentially finite. That is to say, he can only be messiah because there is a possibility of his not being messiah.

In early drafts of his *Arcades Project*, which are dated to 1927, Benjamin took up the Kantian metaphor of the 'Copernican turn' and considered it in relation to the 'historical perception': it was thought that a 'fixed point had been found in "what has been", and one saw the present engaged in tentatively approaching the forces of cognition to this solid ground'.[13] This characterises the historicist conception of history. The turn Benjamin wants to bring about – analogous to Kant's – intended to indicate the conditions of the synthesis under which that which until now appeared as a 'fixed point' can only be brought to a 'dialectical fixation'.[14] This fixing in the synthesis between what-has-been and the present that Benjamin called dialectic does not assume a definite past – in that respect it follows the Kantian turn; nor, however, does it assume a fixed instrumentation of the cognitive apparatus that could pre-form its results – in that respect it goes beyond the Kantian assumption of a transcendental form of time. In the realm of 'historical perception' neither object nor subject and its forms of cognition can be substantial. Because both can only become effective as genuinely histori-cal functions, the theorist of history will have to free himself not only from the traditional idealism of the constancy of objects, but also from the transcenden-talism of the forms of the perception of these objects. Kant had fixed a continu-ity of time in the *a priori* form of perception, a continuity of time which cannot be historical because as mere form it has to be established prior to any historical content. For Kant, history moves in time, it does not constitute time and does not form specific historical times that are distinguishable from time's empty form. The 'Copernican turn in historical perception' that Benjamin wants to bring about is thus more than a transcendentalist turn. For this Copernican turn, what-has-been no longer offers any fixed point, nor can 'historical perception' be considered as substantial quantity or as a continuum founded upon transcen-dental forms. History can be missed. That means, however, that it, and therefore also the happiness to which it refers, are only ever to be experienced through the danger of being missed; and that means, furthermore, that history is only possi-ble at the risk of not being history. What is gained, therefore, is the concept of a radically finite history: history is finite if – in each of its moments – it could as well not be; if at each moment it has to be produced anew; if it is only in view

(*Hinblick*) from the moment of its rescue from disappearance. This is what the following passage in the fifth thesis claims: 'The true image of the past *flits by*. The past can be seized only as an image which flashes up at the moment when it can be recognised and is never seen again.'[15] And the sixth thesis:

> To articulate the past historically does not mean to recognize it 'the way it really was'. It means to seize hold of a remembrance as it flashes up at a moment of danger. The historical materialist wishes to retain that image of the past which unexpectedly appears to the historical subject at a moment of danger. The danger affects both the content [*Bestand*] of the tradition and its receivers ... In every era the attempt must be made anew to wrest tradition away from a conformism that is about to overpower it.[16]

In these passages, Benjamin can combine historical cognition and historical action because – as practical, ethical forms of mindful remembering (*Eingedenken*) – they both point towards the same goal, namely the seizure in the present of the missed possibilities of happiness of the past. The danger that the reign of unhappiness (*Unglück*) might continue illustrates on the one hand that the telos of history could be missed; on the other hand, in this danger the principled deficiency appears which makes it possible that history can be missed. This deficiency, namely, rests on there being no stable form that historical cognition could entrust itself to, and no reliable course on which history heads for its goal. History has to be won over and again, at each singular moment, ever again in a singular way. Neither history nor happiness, which is striven for in the former, is reliable; only the existence of unhappiness is reliable. World-historical unhappiness manifests itself as a continuum of catastrophes. Happiness, however, is never given as a state, it is never embedded in a continuing course of events, but is, at best, offered as a possibility and assigned as the goal of longing, of desire and of demand. There is no form of happiness. The domain of forms belongs to the realm of domination, where permanence of forms can only be secured through the suppression of other possibilities – that is, possibilities of happiness – that rebel against such domination. The danger that threatens historical cognition as well as the politics of happiness therefore originates in the last instance from the forms that are to guarantee the rule of a certain reality over an infinity of possibilities of happiness. If, however, this threat does not only originate from the interest of the current ruling class, but rather from the most enduring instrument of its domination, i.e. from a particular form, then in the realm of history and historical time this danger originates from the time-form of constancy and of persistence. This form of time is the continuum. In this form, one Now-point follows another, uniformly, in linear succession. The historical form corresponding to this continuum of uniform points of time is progress, the equally uniform, steady and inexorable striving towards a pre-given ideal of political life. At the base of the social and political conformism that threatens historical cognition, and thus history itself, lies the transcendental conformism of the form of perception of 'time', through which time is represented as the homogeneous continuum of punctual events. The first and decisive step towards historical cognition that does not join forces with the suppression of possibilities of happiness has to be a step out of the transcendental conformism of the continuum of time and history. A historian and a politician takes a stand for the historically possible and for happiness only if he does not see history as a linear and homogeneous process whose form always remains the same and whose contents, assimilated to the persistent form, are indifferent. Together with the continuum the conformity of each Now with every other Now of the time series has to be broken as well. The possibility of this breaking through, however, must be grounded in the very possibility (*Ermöglichung*) of the continuum itself and thus in relations of discrete Nows that precede their homogenisation.

The political critique of social conformism, the historical critique of the automatism of progress and the philosophical critique of the time continuum join together in the critique of the structural conformity of all forms of experience. All three critiques have to retrace, by means of political intervention, historical cognition and philosophical analysis, the conformisms and their underlying forms to the constitutive movement, and they have to push the constitutive elements of these forms to crisis, to diremption, and to the possibility of another configuration. Only in this way can the political outrage over the ruling injustice, the historical melancholy over the incessant sameness in progress and the philosophical dissatisfaction with already constituted forms become productive. Benjamin's critique of progress – an element of his philosophy of history that currently receives little respect even amongst his admirers – is only adequately understood if it is grasped as a critique of time as a transcendental form of perception and thus of the empty form of experience that progresses in it. And so he writes in his thirteenth thesis:

> Progress as pictured in the minds of Social Democrats was, first of all, the progress of mankind itself (and not just advances in men's ability and knowledge). Secondly, it was incompletable [*unabschließbar*], in keeping with the infinite perfectibility of mankind. Thirdly, progress was regarded as irresistible, something that automatically pursued a straight or spiral course. Each of these predicates is controversial and open to critique. However, when the chips are down, criticism must go beyond these predicates and focus on something that they have in common. The concept of the historical progress of mankind cannot be sundered from the concept of its progression through a homogeneous,

empty time. A critique of the concept of such a progression must be the basis of any critique of the concept of progress itself.[17]

The critique of conformism, a conformism that is at each moment on the point of overpowering this critique, thus has to be founded in a critique of the form of the homogeneous and empty time, which, as the mere form of experience, lies at the foundation of each conformism. Any critique of historical cognition and historical action has to be initially a critique of the transcendental conformism of the continuum of time.

Benjamin's conviction that a 'Copernican turn in historical perception' must be brought about emerges thus from the insight that history would not be history if it merely proceeded in 'time' as a stable form of perception, rather than creating its form in the first place. It will therefore have to be proven that time as a continuum of form can only be generated through a discontinuous historical cognition that is not fixed in any form. According to Benjamin's ultra-Copernican turn there is time only by virtue of history: the latter does not run its course in the former, but time is 'fixed' in history in always different ways, the forms of which are not given beforehand. If, according to Benjamin's formulation, that which has been (*das Gewesene*) experiences its 'dialectic fixation' in synthesis with cognition, then, together with that which has been, the time-form in general experiences its 'dialectic fixation'. The time-form is owed to a synthesis and, thus, is not itself the origin of this synthesis. The reflections collected in the theses 'On the Concept of History' contain only cursory indications of the structure of the genuinely generative historical synthesis, and the relevant notes from the *Convolutes* of the *Arcades Project* are often prone to misunderstanding. In order to grasp how Benjamin understood the genesis of the empty time continuum, it is useful to consult the text in which for the first time he explicitly expresses his critique of the idea of progress and argues for a conception of history that abandons the merely quantitative conception of time. In his dissertation 'On the Concept of Art Criticism in German Romanticism', which he submitted after giving up his original plan for a thesis on the concept of history in Kant, as early as 1919, Benjamin, taking up Friedrich Schlegel's remarks against the 'ideology of progress', contrasts the 'continuum of forms', which is supposed to make up the history of art, against any 'progressing into emptiness', that is, against any empty, homogeneous continuum. This is done in the passage where Benjamin mentions twice 'romantic messianism' and thus the tendency that he, in a letter to Ernst Schoen immediately after the completion of his draft, describes as 'the centre of romanticism' and its 'true nature, well unknown in the literature'.[18] While one should not identify the configuration of messianism and critique of the ideology of progress in this early work with his later outlines on the philosophy of history, it is at the same time evident that the concept of time in the book on Romanticism acquires a precision which benefits the understanding of the later theses. For there, Benjamin writes:

> The temporal infinity in which this process [of poetic forms] takes place ... is a medial and qualitative one. Progredibility is thus clearly not what is understood by the modern term 'progress', not a certain, only relative relation of different stages of culture to one another. It is, like the entire life of mankind, an infinite process of fulfillment, not just of becoming.[19]

What is said here is that the historical process is not a 'progressing into emptiness' and not a progress within a given empty form of time, but the 'medial' process in which a form of time is constituted as 'qualitative', as at each moment determined and substantively fulfilled. Calling 'temporal infinity' 'medial' links it with that 'medium of reflection' in which Benjamin's text brings together the paradoxes of self-positing. Reflection is a medium for the transcendental I, for only in this reflection does it reach the 'point of indifference' of its positing and its knowledge of it. Reflection, however, is a medium not only as the common middle of act and cognition, but rather as that element in which they are indistinguishably and unmediatedly one. The reflection is medial as self-affection. The interpretation of the infinity of time and thus of time itself as 'medial', that is, as having sprung from the reflective medium of self-affection, however, cites the Kantian thought of an original creation of time from pure self-affection. The connection between the original creation of time and the reflective medium can be illustrated with a quote from Schlegel's *Athenäum-Fragmente* and its commentary by Benjamin. Schlegel writes: 'The essence of the poetic feeling perhaps lies in the fact that one can affect oneself entirely out of oneself.' And Benjamin: 'That means: The point of indifference of reflection, where the latter springs from the Nothing, is the poetic feeling.'[20] If the 'point of indifference of reflection', and with it its medium, is self-affection, then the 'medial' time, which Benjamin associates with 'Romantic messianism', is in turn, nothing other than this: 'an affecting entirely out of oneself'. The Schlegelian poetics of self-affection, however, is derived, as Benjamin must have realised, from Kant's doctrine on time as the 'way the mind is affected by its own activity ... and hence affected by itself'.[21] By extending self-affection to history, albeit first of all the history of artistic forms, Benjamin pronounces self-affection to be the fundamental constitutive mode not merely of time, but also of history. Before there can be a continuum, be it of time, be it of history, it has to be produced in the self-touching of the soul. And thus – Kant himself speaks of a 'paradox'[22] – in a self-touching only from which a self emerges. With this self-affection – self-affection of something passive, self-determination of something undetermined – historical time rises as the medium of all elements that enter into a relation in it. With historical time, the historical subject appears. This subject, which is nothing other than time, is in its deepest layer, as the happening of a becoming definite through itself, mere medium.

Benjamin never dissociated himself from the Kantian theory of time constitution. The more determined, however, was his critique of the neo-Kantian ideology of progress of the social democracy of the nineteenth and early twentieth centuries.[23] This ideology of progress is based on the assumption that time arises not only out of a manifoldness of always singular auto-affections of the faculty of understanding – for this could only result in an unsteady aggregate of moments – but also out of self-affections *in successione* as a continuous, linear and therefore also geometrically disaffected time. Such a succession can only exist if it is conditioned by a faculty identical in its unvarying duration. In this case, however, such a succession could not be experienced *as* succession and thus not as time. Only between the contents of the continuum could differences be perceived; differences that, in turn, would be numerical, but not temporal and least of all historical differences. To be experienced as succession, a succession of self-affections must be a constant, directed and inevitable affection between different and diverse self-affections. But as there is nothing in the structure of these affections (even if they are, as for Kant, merely affections of the faculty of understanding) that can work towards constancy, strict orientation and inevitability, there is also nothing in that structure from which a continuous and homogeneous series could emerge from such an affection between self-affections. Time can only ever be a homogeneous series if the sameness of the self that is determined through affection is preserved. If this sameness, like historical time, is not given with certainty, then the relation between the discrete moments of self-affection has to be something other than homogeneity. Heterogeneity as such cannot prevail among the moments of historical time, for only under the condition of an at least possible correspondence can connections between those moments, and therefore history, be experienced. The non-homogeneous, unsteady relation, which alone Benjamin for that reason can accept as historical, has to be a relation between moments of a possible, but not automatically self-realising, history; a relation not preformed, not vouched for by any transcendental schema; a relation that is neither founded in the sameness of self-affection nor regulated through linearity or the privileging of a certain moment or series of moments. Nevertheless it has to be a relation of affection – that is, of determination, no matter what sort – and it has to be one of reference, but of an open one, one that does not automatically fulfil itself. In order for a moment to touch another moment, for a Now-point to enter into a configuration with another Now-point, and in order for a historical time to arise out of this configuration, this moment has to be constituted as a reference (*Verweis*), an indication (*Hinweisung*) and an instruction (*Anweisung*) towards this other moment. A moment is genuinely historical only if it recognises itself as intended by a former one, if it recognises itself as the one intended in the other and only in this intention of the other. For Benjamin, the self is not historical that enters into a mechanical causal connection as succession and nearest cause, nor the self that takes the next step towards the goal of its ideal in the path of progress. Beyond mechanical consequences, directions and consistencies, and also beyond self-assigned ideals and programmes for the future, the self is only historical where it experiences itself affected, determined or intended through another person or something other. History is not a connection of causes, it is a connection of affect and intention. This connection is the medium, in which one affection recognises itself in the other – but does not recognise how it is in the other, rather recognises how it is 'meant' by the other, as an instance of realisation of its missed possibilities of happiness. Only because the present Now recognises itself as 'meant' in a former one, as the fifth thesis has it, has the present been given the '*weak* messianic force' to fulfil the demand for happiness of the previous one. History is structured messianically, for it is the medium of the possibilities of happiness of former times and is therein the medium of the possibility of happiness of the present. The historical moment is a moment not out of auto-affection, but out of a hetero-affection, in which the *autós* – in which the *kairós*, the happy moment – crystallises. This moment has to be medium for itself as other.

In order to fix the relation of reference of one moment to another, a relation, decisive for history, that is difficult to grasp in Kantian or neo-Kantian terms, Benjamin had recourse to the terms of phenomenology and scholasticism. In a paralipomenon to the theses 'On the Concept of History' he writes: 'There is a concept of the present according to which the present represents the (intentional) object of a prophecy. This concept is the (complement) correlate to that of a history that enters flash-like into appearance.'[24] If the prophecy intends the present as messianic, then the only present is the one that fulfils that prophecy as Messiah. Then, furthermore, the only present is the one that was expected. Only as expected present – and thus, from the perspective at least of a minimal historical distance – is its 'flash-like' appearance, which would traumatically blind any unprepared faculty of cognition, recognisable as the appearance of a present. The flash of the historical moment can only be endured and only be captured if it was preceded by an expectation. That is why Benjamin describes the concept of the present as the intentional object of a prophecy, as correlate or complement to the shock-like appearance of this object. Expectation is never a claim without also being a protective measure, never an opening without also being a means of fixing. If – again in the context of his theses – Benjamin writes 'The last day is a present turning backward',[25] what is meant then is that the only present is the present that – as the always youngest, last, decisive and directed – turns backward to all that by which it had been expected in the past. This turning into the past, which gives the past a belated direction, a turning that directs and judges (*richtet*) the past, has, though, a double meaning. First, the present, if it is one, does not make claims on the future, but is present alone as that upon which the past makes demands: present is always present *out of* the past and present *for* the past. And second, the past does not only have in this present its intentional object, but its intention comes in it to a standstill: what-has-been shines in the present, if it is one, and unites with the Now of its cognition. That the present is only a present *for* the past does not just mean that it 'stands in' (*einsteht*) for the past, that it stands in as the goal of the past claims and that it contracts and replaces the past's time in its own time. It also means that the past 'stands in' (*einsteht*) in the present, that it comes to the fulfilment of its intentions and to a standstill. When Benjamin writes about a present 'that is not transition but stands in [*einsteht*] in time and has come to a standstill' in character-ising the moment,[26] he presumably links the concept *Einstand*, which is unusual in German, with the French *instant* and interprets the present as the *Einstand* and pausing of the movement of historical time in the fulfilment of its intention. The Now itself is intentionless, for it is the Now only as that which is intended by the past prophecy. It does not pass over, but stands still – and breaks off the course of history. Therefore it can be said: 'The classless society is not the final goal of the progress of history, but rather its often failed, finally accomplished intērruption'.[27] And, correspondingly: 'The Messiah breaks history off; the Messiah does not ap-pear at the end of a development'.[28] Whether it is interrupted or broken off, his-tory has to come to a standstill, for only in this standstill – an *epochē* – with the relation between at least two disparate Now-points has the minimal form of his-torical time been reached and with its fulfilment it has, simultaneously, stepped out of any further historical course.

When history occurs, it is only in its fixation to a moment and furthermore to an image. Whatever occurs, stands still. History does not have a course, it pauses. If the time-form of historical happening is the present – namely the past contracted and fulfilled to the present – then the present is never a transition in a series of other presents and yet other ones, but that always singular moment in which the possibili-ties and demands of the past are contracted and fixed; the present is not the time-form of waiting for a better or even simply different future, not the state of waiting that precedes the state of redemption, but the standstill where one no longer waits, a standstill into which even waiting itself is drawn and in which the demand associated with the waiting has fallen silent. 'Present' is that which is not embedded in the empty course of an always identical continuum, but that which leaps out of it as different, disparate, in order to 'stand in' (*einstehen*) for another disparate. The site of history is the present as interruption of the continuum of time and as the breaking-off even of the continuum of intentions. Expectation, therefore, cannot direct itself to a certain moment of history; it has to direct itself to every moment, because it does not have to be fulfilled in any one of them, but could be fulfilled in each. The present can only be expected, it cannot be anticipated.

It is not that something happens 'to' the historical objects, and these objects do not 'have' something historical (outside themselves and as a contingent attribute) that dresses them in opportunistic colours; rather they are what they are only through the happening of their history (and thus not *theirs* any more, not *ours* any more). Nothing happens other than the happening itself: this is true for the events as well as for their cognition. History, this eminent happening, however, occurs only where a state of affairs finds its intentional correlate in its cognition and cognition finds its intentional correlate in the political act, and thus what did not happen moves towards the happening, or at least the possibility of happening. Since it does not happen 'to' the objects that could resist its movement, nor is it under the authority of subjects that could be free to resist it, this happening, and even more its mere possibility, can, as a pure happening lacking any exterior determination and thus any measure of its movement, appear in no other way than as motionless.

Benjamin clarifies this relation of the happening of history to its pausing in the seventeenth thesis, which, together with the second, is the most important one. He states that, in contrast to historicism whose procedures additively muster the mass of facts 'to fill homogeneous, empty time', the basis of a materialist historiography is a 'constructive principle'. He continues:

> Thinking involves not only the flow of thoughts, but their arrest as well. Where thinking suddenly stops in a configuration saturated with tensions, it gives that configuration a shock, by which it crystallizes into a monad ... In this structure he [the historical materialist] recognizes the sign of a messianic arrest of happening, or, put differently, a revolutionary chance in the fight for the oppressed past. He takes cognizance of it in order to blast a specific era out of the homogeneous course of history.[29]

It would lead to triviality and further to confusion to understand this passage such that an arrest follows a movement, for then the arrest itself would still lie in the succession of the movement and its originally claimed contrast would be negated. Movement and arrest, and therefore continuum and interruption, stand in a relation other than one of opposition. Where arrest still belongs to movement, movement has to rest in an indissoluble substratum of persistence. Benjamin's reflection is aimed at precisely that gesture of thought through which this substratum is lifted out of the appearance of the mere flowing. The urgency of this reflection can be demonstrated by a simple thought: If the arrest of movement – both of thoughts and of historical events – can neither intervene in this movement from outside (since then it would not be an historical intervention) nor be a mere element of the movement itself (since then it would not be its arrest), then this arrest has to be based within the structure of the movement itself; it has to be based in the structure in such a way that the movement itself essentially stands still. And vice versa: the arrest can be nothing other than the movement, it therefore has to be the movement of the movement. The gesture of thought as Benjamin grasps it thus does not bring to light a rigid image purged of the movement of events, but it is nothing other than the events' movement itself. He continues the train of thought' of the seventeenth thesis:

> [the historical materialist blasts] a specific life out of the era, a specific work out of the lifework. As a result of his method the lifework is preserved and sublated [*aufgehoben*] *in* this work, *in* the lifework, the era; and *in* the era, the entire course of history. The nourishing fruit of that which is historically grasped contains time as a precious but tasteless seed in its *inside*.[30]

What the arrest of the movement of work, lifework, era and course of history brings to light is 'the time', that is, as the last words of the thesis emphasise, time 'in its inside'. By virtue of the arrest the genuinely historical thought preserves in its objects that which makes these objects possible and the preservation and continuation of which these objects contribute themselves – and these objects are not merely works, they are the course of history itself. The essential object and the decisive yield of thinking, as of historiography and politics, is time. The movement of a work, of an era and of the course of history are arrested not in order to present them as a dead thing to sad contemplation, but in order to expose time and make it intrinsically productive, i.e. the movement of movement, the time as time, within it. Only in this standstill, as persisting, is time time; otherwise it would be transition into timelessness, into the everlasting or ever-same, into a *sempiternitas* or *aeternitas*, that covers up finitude. Only in its *Einstand* – in the *instant* – is time the 'preserved' and 'sublated' happening of a time that protects against the empty formalism of a mere form of perception and against the absolutism of a substantial eternity. It is always again anew and in different ways the time that stands in, in each *instant*, in each present, in each Now: a *nunc stans* that indicates within the historical objects their true history and only thus relates history to *objects*: not oppositionals of the idea of positioning or propositional subjects, but *instants*, *Einstände* of history. For these objects are not 'in' time as if in a container merely coloured externally; rather, time is in their *'inside* and they are the fruits and carriers of its seed. When Benjamin talks about time with the unusual word 'standing in' (*einstehen*), then that means that time 'stands' 'in' *for* time – for the time of what-has-been as well as for any time: defends it, preserves it, represents it and fixates it as time in its movement. Without the 'insisting' of time, which is another sense of its *einstehen*, there would not be the course of time. Without instant there would be no moment. Time stands in (*steht ein*) because its discrete moments stand together in a unity and because time stands into the inside, into the nucleus of time in the historical course, and sets it free. The *Einstand* of time is mere time.[31]

If the historian and the politician – and everyone acts like a historian and politician in their own history – are concerned with the rescue and fulfilment of possibilities of happiness, then this is not a rescue *in the face* of time, but a rescue *of* time, redemption is no redemption *from* time, but a redemption *of* time. Happiness would not be to free oneself from time but to free time in oneself.

.

In the First Critique, Kant noted on the principle of permanence of substance: 'All appearances are in time ... Hence time, in which all variation by appearance is to be thought, endures and does not vary'. The fact that time 'endures' qualifies it, according to Kant, 'as belonging to the substratum of everything real, i.e. of everything belonging to the existence of things'.[32] If for him thus – in an enormous overthrow of what was called, until Kant, 'substance' – this substance is now nothing other than time and therefore neither an idea nor a supratemporal being resting in itself, it still remains form, and that is an empty one, and remains continuum, and therefore homogeneous. The insisting of the historical course in the Now that Benjamin has in mind is a persistence as well; however, it is not the persistence of the form of a homogeneous course, but that relation – that restraint [*Verhaltung*] – in which a constellation of heterogeneous moments is formed, moments that are situated neither on a time-line nor in an *a priori* common space of time. The Kantian theorem of innertimeliness (*Innerzeitigkeit*), according to which all changing appearances are *in* time as in something that endures, is thus transformed in a second even more radical overthrow into the theorem of the immanence of time according to which time is persisting *in* the changing appearances. Only its pausing in a particular appearance – a work, a lifework, an era – disposes time to stand out from the homogeneous course and to meet with another time with which it is not homogeneous. The figure formed by the two instances of time is no comprehensive or even universal empty form into which yet other instances could be joined, it is the strict relation connecting these two alone with each other. Since the critique of epistemology in his preface to the *Trauerspiel* book Benjamin calls this relation, probably following Mallarmé, a 'constellation'.[33] The constellation, which is not so much a placing-together (*Zusammen-Stellung*) as a standing-in together (*Zusammen-Einstand*), is as much the result of the relation of the instances as these instances are the result of it. A moment, a Now, a present is always the constellation of at least two presents, moments: Now – that is the Now of the correspondence of such presents or moments, a correspondence that cannot be guaranteed by any pre-stabilised form. Only as a formation from unsecured co-instances can history be the object of a construction. What is said here is therefore that time is tied to a time of time, to a time *for* time, to a time where that Now in which time stands in can evolve. To put it more precisely: the setting free of a particular time nucleus is tied to the time of its recognisability. That is the structure of the 'true image of the past', which thesis five supposes: 'The past can be seized only as the image which flashes up at the moment when it can be recognized to then never be seen again … For every image of the past that is not recognized by the present as one of its own concerns threatens to disappear irretrievably.'[34] The central theme of these sentences is without doubt the uniqueness of each chance for historical insight and therefore also the untenability of the historicist credo that Benjamin finds summarised in Gottfried Keller's phrase 'truth will not run away from us'. This uniqueness, however, is that of a possible correspondence between an 'image of the past' and a 'moment of its recognisability', that is between a time that offers itself to cognition and a time in which this time becomes accessible to cognition. 'The true image of the past *flits by*' – that means: there is only ever one single point where one time and the other touch each other in such a way that there is *Einstand* – that is standing together, constellation – between them, an *Einstand* in which the time of that which is recognised and the time of cognition, the past and the present arise. Without their touching in the *Einstand* of the constellation there is neither an image of the past nor a present in which that image could be recognised, neither a past nor a present time, therefore no time at all that would not be the empty ideality of a mere succession. Time is thus always the doubled, and only in its doubling united, moment in which one time recognises itself in another as 'meant' – intended, indicated, demanded, claimed. Neither of its instances, neither the instance of cognition nor the instance demanding cognition, can be absent if there is to be time. There is time only if the time for which it, and only it, is there seizes it.

Benjamin portrays this minimal structure of historical time in one of the very important notes to an epistemological critique from the *Convolutes* of the *Arcades Project*:

What distinguishes images from the 'essences' instant of phenomenology is their historical index. (Heidegger seeks in vain to rescue history for phenomenology abstractly through 'historicity'.) ... For the historical index of the images not only says that they belong to a particular time; it says above all that they attain legibility only at a particular time. And indeed this acceding 'to legibility' constitutes a specific critical point of the movement in their inside. Every present is determined by those images that are synchronistic with it: each now is the Now of a particular recognizability. In it, truth is charged to the bursting point with time. (This point of bursting, and nothing else, is the death of the *intentio*, which thus coincides with the birth of authentic historical time, the time of truth.) It is not that what is past casts its light on what is present, or what is present its light on what is past; rather, image is that wherein what has been comes together flash-like with the Now to form a constellation. In other words: image is dialectics at a standstill ...[35]

This very complex note that starts with one of the rare but significant references to Heidegger to be found in the *Arcades Project* serves to identify the 'image' in contrast to the phenomenological 'essences', even though not Heidegger's *Being and Time* but Benjamin's own *Trauerspiel* book is the likely precedent. Benjamin reproaches Heidegger's notion of 'historicity' as being an attempt to save history 'abstractly' – and therefore, ahistorically and uncritically – for phenomenology, while only such a concept of history could be seen as historical and critical, where what-has-been carries with it a 'historical index', and thus a critical one, for the present in which it becomes recognisable. Benjamin thus also undertakes, as he suggests, to save history for phenomenology, but, in contrast to Heidegger, concretely and critically through the concepts of *'image'* and *'historical index'*. This index, which Benjamin also discusses in the second thesis, marks a double time: the time of what-has-been and the time of the Now that is directed towards the former's cognition. This index, thus, is a twofold one: it stands in for two times; it is critical: it marks the point at which an internal crisis divides time into a Before and an After, into the time of the past and the time of the present; and it synchronises: it connects both times even in their disjunction. By virtue of its 'historical index' each Now is marked as the Now of another Now, and only by virtue of this internal split of the Now is each Now the 'Now of a particular recognisability'. It would be quite simply unrecognisable, unperceivable, it would not be what it is intended to be, if it lacked the complement of a second Now, a distinct one and yet one that is united with it, it would lack the chance to become encircled as the Now that it is. There is no Now that could qualify as being temporal or even historical if it lacked all tension to another, distinct Now. But there would be no Now either if it were separated by an impermeable barrier from the other Now and were untouchable by that other Now, in which it is supposed to be recognised. In order to be Now and *one* Now, it has to be one that takes itself apart into *two*. This is brought about by the critical point of movement at the inside of time. This 'critical point', or more precisely, the crisis of the Now-point, is what 'rescues' time and the historical phenomena in which it contracts itself: as Benjamin notes, phenomena 'are rescued through the exhibition of a leap within them'.[36] Therefore this 'leap', the discontinuous as such, that which creates clefts in the course of time, is at the same time the 'nucleus', the time nucleus of the phenomenon, time out of which the phenomenon forms itself. The crisis in the Now that disperses and moves it, that turns it into a movement of the Now in the Now, is – as the absolute medium – historical time itself.

The identity of 'leap' and 'nucleus' of the Now and thus the temporalising direction [*Zeitigungssinn*] of its crisis can also be deciphered in another note from the *Convolutes* of the *Arcades Project*: 'The present determines where, in the object from the past, that object's fore- and after-history diverge so as to circumscribe its nucleus'.[37] The present lies in the difference, the leap or the interval, that separates the fore- and after-history of an object, and is thus, in its disjunction, the agreement between it and its cognition. The nucleus of time lies in the cleft that its crisis opens up. Splitting between fore- and after-history, this nucleus lies between object and cognition, and is that in which the two touch each other, not in a positive third, but in the gap between them. About truth Benjamin thus says that it is not merely bound to a temporal function of cognition as Marxism claims but to 'a nucleus of time placed within the recognized and the one who recognizes at the same time. This is so true that the eternal, in any case, is far more a ruffle on a dress than some idea'.[38] The nucleus of time, which is placed 'at the same time' in the recognised and in the one who recognises, can lie in nothing else than in this at-the-same-time. Since the simultaneity of the non-simultaneous, if it is understood as the being-at-the-same-time of positive Now-points, can in no way bring about the nucleus of time – and thus time as time – but, in the collapse of the entire temporal expanse, has to lead to the destruction of time, the at-the-same-time must not determine itself as identity within a single Now, but as leap between discrete Now-points. This leap (*Sprung*) has to be understood in the twofold sense of both rift and leap over the rift (*Übersprung*): the difference between Now and Now has to preserve each instant as discrete and has strictly to refer them to each other as the difference between precisely these discrete points. What is at the same time is only that which is not-at-the-same-time *between* the recognised and the one who recognises and *within* each of them and thus that in them which – as nucleus of a differential time – resists its erasure. Time namely would be erased as soon as different Now-points contracted into a single one or were assimilated into the continuum of an always identical line; time would also be erased as soon as the difference between discrete Nows extinguished any relation between them. The possibility not only of historical cognition but of historical time as well thus has to be based on a third that is neither identity nor inability to relate, but distinction and relation at the same time. This possibility, is, for Benjamin, based in a leap which is not secured, held or founded, it is based in an original leap (*Ur-sprung*) that separates the discrete Nows and – one can say paradoxically, or, as Benjamin puts it, 'dialectically' – joins them in their separation. This leap, and nothing else, is the Now, the nucleus of time, the irreducibly historical happening, which the historian has to bring to experience.

In the leap of time (*Zeit-Sprung*), in the origin of time (*Zeit-Ursprung*), at least two different Nows stand together as one. The leap is *Einstand* of time; in it, the crisis that separates and the difference that relates stand together as one – it is 'critical' movement; in it movement and standstill stand together – it is what Benjamin, using Gottfried Keller's words, calls 'petrified unrest';[39] in it, finally, the dialectical movement between has-been and present, object and cognition, stands still – the leap is 'dialectics at a standstill' and as such, for Benjamin, 'image'. Because the 'image' is the constellation in which one Now meets precisely the other one in which it becomes recognisable, the image alone is the place of historical time, being historical time in contrast to time as a mere flux. 'The image is dialectics at a standstill. For while the relation of the present to the past is a purely temporal, continuous one, the relation of what-has-been to the Now is dialectical: is not progression but image, suddenly emergent.'[40] For Benjamin, the image is the historical relation *kat' exochen*, for it brings about and holds on to the discontinuity of appearances, the leap within them. It appears at that moment when nothing but the medium – the middle and the element – and thus the irreducibly dia-chronical and a-chronical between and in the phenomena is preserved. It is historical time as the crisis in the Now – which only opens space for the times and sets free all times as 'nucleus' of time.

Benjamin's claim that 'every present is determined by the images that are synchronistic with it' will have to be made more precise with regard to the critical point in their movement: this synchrony can only be situated in the critical separation, that is, in an asynchronic difference as the common medium of the 'synchronistic' images. Benjamin can therefore compare the process of determining this medium with the 'method of splitting the atom', i.e., not just with the enclosure of the nucleus of time, but with nuclear fission. If, however, only the fission of the time nucleus sets free its historical forces, then this nucleus with its forces, paradoxically, is situated in the fission. Now is Now always in the leap to another Now and is thus always a Now of the crisis of the Now. In its crisis the Now does not just split, it also becomes recognisable as Now only in its crisis: only by virtue of the fissure of the Now is its *krinein*, its *cernere*, its enclosure and cognition as 'nucleus' and as 'seed' of time possible. If the Now is only Now and knowable in its crisis, then the truth of the Now is only fulfilled in the leap to another Now, the goal of its intention – and it is not only fulfilled, but due to the doubling of the Now it is charged to 'the bursting point'. The fourteenth thesis states: 'History is the subject of a construction whose site is not homogeneous, empty time, but time filled by the presence of the Now [*Jetztzeit*]',[41] and this statement is specified by a note from the *Convolutes* of the *Arcades Project*, namely that the truth is not only fulfilled with time, but fulfilled 'to the bursting point' and thus overfilled because it is charged with another than its own time. Fulfilment – the Paulinian *pleroma* – is the pregnancy of a truth that cannot stay with itself and thus in the bursting becomes the origin – the 'birth', as Benjamin puts it – of the 'time of truth, of authentic historical time'. This bursting, and nothing else, is the 'death of the *intentio*, which thus coincides with the birth of authentic historical time, the time of truth'.[42]

With these formulations, Benjamin takes up again the insights from his critique of epistemology in the preface to *The Origin of German Tragic Drama*, which are dedicated to truth as the 'death of the intention' and where origin is characterised as that which 'springs from becoming and passing'.[43] The 'rhythm' of the original is there characterised as a being open uniquely to a 'double insight: on the one hand, it wants to be recognized as restoration, as re-establishment, and precisely therein as something unfinished, incomplete on the other'.[44] That is to say that in the origin, 'uniqueness and repetition condition each other'. The uniqueness of a moment that has been only comes to light in its repetition, that is, in its recognition; this repetition is nothing, however, if it does not demonstrate uniqueness, if the repeated moment is not itself, and therefore still unfinished, incomplete and open for further repetitions. The Now has precisely this structure of the origin (*Ursprung*), which Benjamin calls dialectic. It is thus the 'Now of recognisability' both as that which has been reaching its recognisability in the present, and as the present Now in which that which has been becomes recognisable. Both the ability of the thing to be known and the ability of the historian to know it have a share in the recognisability as well as in the Now. The one, however, is not restored, re-established or repeated in the other without remaining unfinished and incomplete 'precisely therein'. Just as repetition has to be execution in order to testify to the uniqueness of what is repeated within it, so the Now can only occur in the happening and thus only as incomplete, as present, and cannot exist in the perfection of completeness. The 'Now of recognisability' is thus to be thought of as an in principle incomplete – or over-complete – happening of its crisis, in which the discrete elements overfill each other to the point of bursting and remain in the bursting. Now is its leap. Or, to use a mathematical metaphor that

Benjamin repeatedly employs: Now is the 'time differential'.[45] If the Now, however, establishes in the leap and the differential the immanence of historical time in phenomena, then the path of the historian and of the politician which leads to the Now has to correspond to the structure of this Now and be transcendence in the immanence of time.

The Kantian theorem of innertimeliness (*Innerzeitigkeit*), namely that all appearances are *in* time, is overthrown in Benjamin's theorem of the immanence of time; time stands in (*stehtein*) *in* the appearances, that is, in the 'Now of recognisability' of the appearances. This theorem is made more precise in the theorem of the crisis of time: the Now of recognisability is a 'critical moment' and the moment of the leap in the Now, of the leap between one Now and another exactly corresponding to it.

This leap in the Now is what Benjamin considers when noting in his fourteenth thesis that, for Robespierre, Ancient Rome was 'a past charged with the time of the Now which he blasted out of the continuum of history'.[46] This 'blast' becomes possible only by virtue of a leap, which transports the time of the Now into one that has been and identifies it as the repetition of what-has-been. 'The French Revolution viewed itself as a return to Rome. It cited ancient Rome the way fashion cites costumes of the past.'[47] This citation pulls together Now-time and Now-time in such a way that what has been is 'charged' with present time and overcharged to the point of bursting. The repetition is not a replica, it is the explosion of that which is repeated. For it there are no given historical data analogous to data of the senses. Any datum is datum only if it is marked with the datum of the Now-time that corresponds to it. A datum is only ever the one dated by another datum. For this dating a somersault of data is necessary: a leap that is only possible if it does not only proceed between the two Nows, but rather if it opens up each single Now to the other that corresponds to it. Fashion 'is a tiger's leap into the past. This leap, however, takes place in an arena where the ruling class gives the commands. The same leap in the open air of history is the dialectical one, which is how Marx understood the revolution.'[48] Benjamin prefaces these thoughts with a verse of Karl Kraus: *Ursprung ist das Ziel* (origin is the goal). This sentence is misunderstood if one interprets 'origin' as starting-point and the movement towards it as return. Origin is rather the goal as that leap that tears apart each point and each series of points, it is the moment of discontinuity by virtue of which there is, always for the first time, historical time at all. Any revolution that, unlike the bourgeois revolution, did not take place in the arena of the ruling class, would be such a leap. Not a former Now into which a present Now leaps, but the leap itself is the revolution. Because the Now that has been as well as the present Now are Now only by virtue of this leap, the one that leaps ahead of both of them is the original leap (*Ur-Sprung*). Only *as* such an original leap (*Ur-Sprung*) – that is, original crisis (*Ur-Krisis*) – can it reach what Benjamin in the fragment 'Aus einer kleinen Rede über Proust, an meinem vierzigsten Geburtstag gehalten' calls 'original past' (*Urvergangenheit*),[50] that is: a past which was not there before the remembrance of it. In this sense, the Now is the origin of the historical. And in this sense it is messianic: the rescue of that which was not there before the rescue.

With the notion 'Now of recognisability', which is fundamental for his philosophy of history, Benjamin insists on the transcendental status of that to which it refers. He is not concerned with the Now of cognition, but with the Now which, ahead of every actual cognition, fixes the structural condition of the possibility of cognition. Just as the centre of his early study 'On Language as Such and on the Language of Man'[50] is not communication but communic*ability*, the centre of his studies on historical time is the Now of recognis*ability*. Thus no decision has been made on whether there is actual historical cognition and a corresponding politics. Neither has it been decided whether there is indeed a Now of cognition. The object of Benjamin's analyses is not this Now as it actually – now – is, but rather how it has to be constituted in order to be able to be an actual Now. As little as this says about the existence of actual historical cognition, as much does it say about the conditions it has to fulfil in order to become real as genuine historical cognition. Each actual Now is Now and actual only if it corresponds to the constitution which has been prescribed by this structure of possibility of the Now – by Now*ability* (*Jetztbarkeit*). Historical cognition is cognition and historical only if it fulfils the conditions put forward by the structure of recognis*ability*: in all other cases it is not historical, that is, no cognition that triggers history, and not a cognition that intervenes in history; that means it is, in fact, no cognition at all.

The historico-philosophical *aperçus* that Benjamin noted during his work on the *Arcades Project* and provisionally summarised in the thesis 'On the Concept of History' are both diagnostic and propaedeutic and in both respects critical. Written immediately after the Hitler–Stalin pact, which Benjamin, according to his friend Soma Morgenstern, saw as the total discrediting of the Communists[51] as well as of the social democratic movement, these notes give an explanation for the powerlessness of social-democratic politics with respect to National Socialism: social democracy was powerless because it supported an ideal of a community of work and communication, an ideal that was to be reached on the path of the inevitable progress of mankind in the continuum of a time seen as an *a priori* form. Against this politically as well as epistemologically disastrous ideology, which mechanises history as an automatic progression and neutralises the subject of history to a homogenous mankind that heads for an ideal of universal consent, Benjamin objects as follows (and that is what constitutes the argument's propaedeutic nature): the subject of history cannot be mankind, but only a class, that is, the class of the oppressed, of those deprived of their rights and of the exploited (even if they exploit themselves); and history cannot be an automatic process in an already constituted form of time, but can alone be that movement whose form is not set in advance, that is, not directed towards pre-given goals, but rather a movement that is in principle open to unforeseeable realisations. History is not history as long as it does not happen. It cannot happen if it merely follows a pre-destined form and goal. Therefore, neither a form nor the goals of history can be regarded as historically neutral and established once and for all. The transcendental conformism of the social democratic ideology represents such a fixing of form and goal, which in principle, that is, in its ideal of a consensual homogeneous mankind, joined forces with Nazism and the entire tradition of oppression that preceded it. In this conformism, however, it is not just one particular class that is exploited and oppressed, one that defines itself throughout history in diverse ways and thus not only as proletarian; in it, anything that diverges from the form of the course of history and the ideal of its goal is oppressed and exploited.

The question that must be asked by anyone who is concerned that there be history and not merely a tradition of oppression; the question that, since anyone can become the victim of such oppression we must all ask ourselves, and that Benjamin had to ask himself most pressingly at that moment when he saw himself and all those who were close to him fall victim not just to oppression, but to extermination; the question is simply and necessarily this: what is oppressed and what is exploited in the construction of a homogeneous course of history and of a similarly homogeneous mankind? In Benjamin's writings the answer is as clear as it is often obscured by his readers, namely in the following insight: in this construction the fact of its constructedness, in the homogeneity the necessity of its genesis, in the continuity the structure of its creation is used, but used as a means for another end than that of its creation, that is, exploited, driven out of the result and oppressed. If history is thus to be possible, then it is only possible as a history of all *such* oppressed that has no place in any form and yet is indispensable for its constitution. It is indispensable and a minimal condition for history, however, that it happens; that it is not fixed in unvarying forms, but on the contrary that it happens each time in unpredictable ways, and that it happens between at least two moments that were not previously co-ordinated. History is the un-pre-formable event in which one Now meets another corresponding Now. History – this is Benjamin's finding – is thus founded as happening in the possibility of a Now for a second Now, a possibility that can carry the logical and epistemological title 'Now of recognisability'. Wherever this minimal structure of history is ignored and assimilated to a mere progressive form between equally valid points in time, the formal conditions are in place for the catastrophes of the progress to homogenisation carried out by German National Socialism.

But how, if at all, can this minimal structure of history be observed, realised in historiography and actualised in politics? For as long as this possibility is not secured and these forms are not made more precise, any reflection on the philosophy of history has to suspect that history in Benjamin's strict and emphatic sense cannot be realised and the progress in the destruction of historical possibilities is still under way. Neither this suspicion – one could equally justifiably say concern, doubt, horror or even despair – nor the desire, longing or the hope that such history may exist can be external to the possibility of history and thus its structure. The desire for genuine history as well as the horror that it could be impossible have to be integral elements of the possibility of history itself. With this move, however, the perspective of an analysis in terms of philosophy of history is altered on principle: it is not merely that the conditions of the possibility of history will have to be clarified, they also have to be clarified with regard to their possible failing and thus with regard to a category – an allocategory – which has been regarded within transcendental philosophy, dialectics and phenomenology only as an exclusionary criterion, rather than as a structural threat, one that endangers the constitution of its subject domain as well as its procedure. Philosophy of history can no longer be transcendental philosophy and content itself with exploring the irreducible forms of history's constitution – as happening and as cognition of this happening. In these forms it also has to address their possible failure, the de-constitution of even the irreducible in the register of forms, and thus address that which in history, were it to succeed, yet remains open to that which does not enter any forms, but accompanies each form as that which is its exterior and other. The analysis must not direct itself towards a transcendental, and not towards anything that resembles it somehow: if it did resemble it namely as a quasi-transcendental, then the principles of analogy or of correspondence would still remain within it, which can, however, emerge only with history itself and the synthesis of distinct Nows. The analysis rather has to look for that which cannot be predicated in any other terms than its being *open to history* – be it open to the happening of history, open to its impossibility or to the happening of its impossibility – and as such it belongs to a pre-historical, that is, a non-historical that is nevertheless ready for history. That which is open to form, that which colours every possible form as the unexecutable in it, can be called attranscendental: as ante-transcendental; that is, preceding every transcendental; as ad-transcendental – that is, infinitely open; as a-transcendental – that is, not occupied by any transcendental. If there can be history, then only as that happening in which also its Not happens.

In the phrase of the fifth thesis on the 'irretrievable image of the past that threatens to never be seen again and to disappear with any present which does not recognize itself in it as one of its own concerns',[52] Benjamin characterises history as an in principle singular, that is, unrepeatable, repetition of what-has-been in a present Now. If this repetition is the index for the doubleness – and thus for the crisis – of the Now in historical experience, then the unrepeatability of this repetition is the index for the possibility of its failing. If history is always singular and unique, then it is missed if this one time it is not seized. Not only does every time therefore have a virtually corresponding time, in which it is recognised, and this means recognised as intending the latter; furthermore, this time is only a single one. What follows from this is: time is time only in the danger of not being time. Thus it is noted in the sixth thesis: 'To articulate that which is past historically does not mean to recognize it "the way it really was". It means to seize hold of a memory as it flashes up at a moment of danger.'[53] The moment of remembrance is the moment of a danger for the remembrance as well as for the one who seizes it. For the remembrance there is the danger of not being seized, or, even if seized, of being conformistically assimilated to the goods of the powerful. In both cases there is a threat to that which has been missed – that which is past – that the slim chance to be transformed into happiness slips away. For whatever can enter remembrance is a *promesse de bonheur* which in remembering searches out the door to fulfilment. Since the claim only ever poses itself a single time, the one who could remember is threatened with the danger that the claim of the past is no longer intended for him, that he is no longer the addressee of the claims of the past and that he is no longer the one who has been' endowed with a *weak* messianic force'. That which does not enter remembrance has missed the possibility of finding redemption in remembering: there is no longer a messianic time for it, if the one that was meant in it does not recognise itself as the one that was meant.

If remembering only flashes up in a moment of danger, it is the danger of disappearing 'never to be seen again'. If danger is the index of uniqueness, involuntariness and authenticity of remembering, and thus also an index of the possible failure of remembering and history, then danger cannot be understood as being a mere external threat. On the contrary, danger belongs to the innermost structure of historical cognition to such a degree that it is, in each singular case, not merely cognition *in* the danger, but also cognition *out of* that danger. Whoever remembers, remembers at the risk of not remembering, of not being demanded by a past, at the risk of missing the missed and that which demands completion all over again, and at the risk of missing, together with the claims of the past, their historical possibilities and thus history in general. In order to determine more pronouncedly the relation between the moment of remembering and the moment of danger, Benjamin thus writes, still in the sixth thesis: 'The Messiah comes not only as the redeemer, he comes as the subduer of Antichrist. Only that historiographer will have the gift of fanning the spark of hope in the past who is imbued with the conviction that even the dead will not be safe from the enemy should he triumph.'[54] A historiographer namely has been given a '*weak* messianic force' only if he remembers the danger of not being able to remember, the danger of not being able to resurrect the passed-away times in his remembering, to re-present what-has-been, to wake the dead. Only the one who is 'imbued with' the idea that even the dead could be killed and could stop asserting their claims upon the living, will stand up against this cessation; only the one who remembers the possibility that the past could become silent for him will help to bring up its claim towards language; only the one who is aware of the danger that there could be no history can write history. Thus, only because history is in danger of becoming impossible does remembering set in: for it is not only the remembering of a loss, an omission or a failure that lies in the past, it has to be primarily a 'remembering' of that loss that also threatens it, *hic et nunc*, in the 'Now of recognisability': no longer being able to remember, no longer being equipped with the ability to recognise and the ability for the Now. That is what is remembered by the one who 'remembers', who remembers at the 'moment of danger'; is 'imbued' with that which never has been, is never supposed to be and yet threatens. One 'remembers' Nothing.

In each remembering the not-remembering is remembered: but it is not co-remembered as if it were a second object beside the initial one of the Now that has been; it is not remembered as a mere alternative to the image of the past. In the possible impossibility of remembering the making possible of the remembering is remembered, for only in the danger of not being remembered does remembering emerge. That is the minimal structure of history: that each 'Now of recognisability', in which one time leaps into another one, can also not be this Now, can extinguish its recognisability, and the leap can fail to succeed. There is no messianic claim that could not be missed and could fail to find its Messiah. That is, no messianic structure of history that did not arise only out of the possibility that there could also not be a messianic structure of history. A 'Now of recognis*ability*' is only ever one that can be *devoid* of any cognition and can be not Now.

The minimal messianism Benjamin sketches in the second thesis – namely that the past carries with it a 'hidden index' in which it refers to the '*weak* messianic force' of the present – is connected, at the latest in the sixth thesis, to the internal endangering of its structure. This is rendered more precisely as something that could be called a-messianism: the notion that this '*weak* messianic force' 'inhabits' only those who are imbued with the possibility of its failure; that a force is messianic only if it can fail.

The Messiah could not come if his coming were assured and that means: if the Messiah himself would be certain as the one he is, if he comes. Messiah is only the one who can also not come and can also not be Messiah. Messiah is only he who, even in his coming, might as well not come. Only he, who in his not-coming can still come. Because only the coming of the Messiah can give rise to time and can thus in no way be subjected to the form of a continuous and homogeneous course of time, he has to be the one who can come even before he has come, and who can come after he has already come. The Messiah only comes in a time that is distorted, however slightly, against any linear course. And only *as* distorted in such a way, as an always leaped time (*ersprungene Zeit*), can the messianic time come; it can only come as the distortion of time, distortion of the conditions of experience, distortion of its very possibility. The deepest distortion of the possibility of messianic time, however, the distortion of the messianic ability itself, which Benjamin calls messianic 'force', lies in its being exposed to the inability and thus the impossibility of perceiving itself, acting and fulfilling itself *as* the possibility, ability and power. Because 'messianic force' is not a trans-historical substantial ability that realises itself in history from case to case, but an ability out of which alone history could arise, it is a force that opens history without substantial and without historical assurances. It is only effective under the condition that it remains exposed to its own impotence, that is, under the condition that it includes even this impotence into itself. It is a *'weak'* force because it is the force of weakness, because it is force out of the missing of force. This weakness is not in contrast to force, but lies in its centre. For that force cannot be messianic that rescues only itself; messianic is only the force that rescues even its own failing. A Messiah is only he who rescues even the impossibility of a Messiah. He can only come in such a way that he might also not come, and come as someone other than the Messiah. And his coming – this future expected by all pasts, that Benjamin touches upon in his theses – this coming can only be possible out of that which not only holds back all coming, but also threatens it with the possibility of being for ever impossible. The future of the Messiah would not arise out of the wealth of his possibilities, not even out of the single possibility that something like history and thus world, freedom and happiness could be experienced; it would arise from the complete loss of all possibilities of the future, out of the impossibility of its coming, and out of that alone. This impossibility of the coming, the impossibility of the future would be that which comes. In this coming of something that does not come – and could not come and therefore *can* not come – only therein would the coming be even in its most extreme possibility: that it fails to appear; only therein future itself and thus time would be rescued. What would be rescued is that there is no rescue. And this would be the Now of recognisability, the *'critical'* and only thus messianic Now of recognisability, the Now that constitutes history in the moment

191

of its disappearance and *with* its disappearance: the Now of its Not.

Amongst Kafka's notes the following sentence can be found: 'The Messiah will come only when he is no longer needed, he will come one day after his coming, he will not come on the last day, but on the very last'.[55] Benjamin does not cite this passage, although it can be assumed that he knew it. However distant it may be from the manifest content of the theses on history, it draws out the lines that become visible in Benjamin's reflections. For when Benjamin notes that the past can only find its Messiah in the 'moment of danger' and thus ties the messianic possibility to the possibility of its impossibility, then Kafka's remark brings this possibility into the structure of the messianic future itself. He fixes it in a para-doxical distortion of time. If the Messiah only comes the day after his arrival, that is, only after his coming, then the coming of the Messiah is his coming only in his not-coming and thus it is the arrival of his failing to appear. The Messiah who only comes after his coming is not only the split and twofold Messiah that Jewish tradition knows under the names of the suffering and dying Messiah ben Joseph and the triumphant Messiah ben David. The one who comes after his coming, the Messiah that comes after himself and as another than himself, is the Messiah who is not necessary, who does not rescue and who is no Messiah; and more precisely, he is the Messiah of the Not-Messiah. The Messiah is Messiah of there not being a Messiah. This messianicity of the non-messianic, this messianic without the messianic – this a-messianic – is the last and final crisis of which the structure of the messianic is capable. It is not destroyed by this crisis, but steps into it as into the centre of its force. In it, even the Nothing of the messianic is rescued.

Translated by N. Rosenthal

Notes

1 Walter Benjamin, 'Über den Begriff der Geschichte', in *Gesammelte Schriften*, I:2, ed. Rolf Tiedemann and Hermann Schweppenhäuser, Frankfurt/M.: Suhrkamp, 1991, pp.691–704 (translated as 'Theses on the Philosophy of History', in *Illuminations* [trans. Harry Zohn], London: Fontana, 1973, pp.245–55); all references will be to the German text followed by the page numbers of the translation.

2 Benjamin, 'Begriff der Geschichte', I:2, p.63 [p.245, translation altered].

3 Walter Benjamin, 'Das Paris des Second Empire bei Baudelaire', in *Charles Baudelaire. Ein Lyriker im Zeitalter des Hochkapitalismus*, 'Notes', *GS*, I:3, p.1175.

4 Benjamin, 'Begriff der Geschichte', I:2, p.693 [p.245, translation altered, emphasis added].

5 Benjamin, 'Begriff der Geschichte', I:2, p.693 [p.245].

6 Benjamin, 'Begriff der Geschichte', I:2, pp.693–94 [pp.245–46, translation altered].

7 Benjamin, 'Begriff der Geschichte', I:2, p.694 [p.246].

8 Benjamin, 'Begriff der Geschichte', I:2, p.694 [p.246, translation altered].

9 Benjamin, 'Begriff der Geschichte', I:2, p.695 [p.247, translation altered].

10 Benjamin, 'Begriff der Geschichte', I:2, pp.693–94 [p.245].

11 Walter Benjamin, 'Die Aufgabe des Übersetzers', in *Charles Baudelaire. Tableaux parisiens. Deutsche Übertragung mit einem Vorwort über die Aufgabe des Übersetzers*, in *GS*, IV:1, pp.7–63, 7–21 (translated as 'The Task of the Translator', in *Illuminations*, pp.70–82).

12 In the notes on Kafka, Benjamin similarly addresses revolutionary weakness: 'Revolutionary energy and weakness are for Kafka two sides of one and the same state. His weakness, his dilettantism, his unpreparedness are revolutionary.' Cited in Hermann Schweppenhäuser (ed.), *Benjamin über Kafka*, Frankfurt/M.: Suhrkamp, 1981, pp.118–19.

13 Walter Benjamin, *Das Passagen-Werk*, in *GS*, II, p.1057 (Engl. edn *The Arcades Project* [trans. Howard Eiland and Kevin McLaughlin], Cambridge, MA: Belknap Press of Harvard University Press, 1999, p.883); references are to the German text followed by the page number of the translation.

14 Benjamin, *Passagen-Werk*, V:2, p.1057 [p.883].

15 Benjamin, 'Begriff der Geschichte', I:2, p.695 [p.247, translation altered].

16 Benjamin, 'Begriff der Geschichte', I:2, p.695 [p.247, translation altered].

17 Benjamin, 'Begriff der Geschichte', I:2, pp.700–01 [p.252, translation altered].

18 Letter dated 7.4.1919, in Walter Benjamin, *Gesammelte Briefe*, II 1919–1924, ed. Christoph Gödde and Henri Lonitz, Frankfurt/M.: Suhrkamp, 1996, p.23.

19 Walter Benjamin, *Der Begriff der Kunstkritik in der deutschen Romantik*, in *GS*, I:1, pp.7–122, 92.

20 Benjamin, *Begriff der Kunstkritik*, *GS*, I:1, p.63.

21 Immanuel Kant, *Critique of Pure Reason* [trans. Werner S. Pluhar], Indianapolis: Hacking, 1996, B 67/68.

22 Kant, *Critique of Pure Reason*, B 152.

23 Compare the following notes: 'With the idea of the classless society, Marx has secularized the idea of the messianic time. And that was a good thing to do. Disaster sets in with social democracy elevating this idea to an "ideal". In Neo-Kantian theory, the ideal was defined as an "infinite task". And this theory was the basic philosophy of the Social Democratic party – from Schmidt and Stadler to Natorp and Vorländer. Once the classless society had been defined as an infinite task the empty homogeneous time was transformed as it were into an anteroom where one could wait more or less calmly for the onset of the revolutionary situation. There is, in reality, not one moment that did not carry with it its revolutionary chance – it just needs to be defined as a specific one, namely as the chance of an entirely new solution in the face of an entirely new task' ('Begriff der Geschichte', Notes, *GS*, I:3, p.1231). It will not be necessary to point out that the social democratic ideals, which Benjamin blames for the passivity of the working class in the face of National Socialism, were promulgated as regulative ideas in social philosophy – in particular in Germany – even after the Second World War. They still dominate the discussion today.

24 Benjamin, 'Begriff der Geschichte', Notes, I:3, p.1235.

25 Benjamin, 'Begriff der Geschichte', Notes, I:3, p.1232.

26 Benjamin, 'Begriff der Geschichte', Notes, I:3, p.1250 and 'Begriff der Geschichte', p.702.

27 Benjamin, 'Begriff der Geschichte', Notes, I:3, p.1231.

28 Benjamin, 'Begriff der Geschichte', Notes, I:3, p.1243.

29 Benjamin, 'Begriff der Geschichte', I:2, pp.702–03 [p.254, translation altered].

30 Benjamin, 'Begriff der Geschichte', I:2, p.703 [p.254, translation altered].

31 In particular when reading the seventeenth thesis and its emphatic talk about arrest and monad, one should keep in mind that probably as early as 1913, but no later than 1917, Benjamin had read Husserl's essay 'Philosophie als strenge Wissenschaft' from the journal *Logos* (which was published in 1910–11), and got to know the first major attempt of a

philosophical critique of historicism and at the same time of psychologism and scientific objectivism (see the letter to Franz Sachs, 11.7.1913 and the one to Gershom Scholem, 23.12.1917 which was important for Benjamin's dissertation plans on the philosophy of history [*Briefe*, I, pp.141–44 and 406–11]). On the decisive p.50 of his *Logos* essay Husserl summarises in a few sentences some of his most important thoughts from his 1905 lectures on the 'phenomenology of internal time consciousness', *Zur Phänomenologie des inneren Zeitbewußtseins*, which – edited by Edith Stein – were published for the first time in 1928 by Martin Heidegger. There are indications that Benjamin knew Husserl's lectures when he started making plans for the historico-critical introduction to his *Arcades Project*, from which the 'Theses' later emerged. In the *Logos* essay the psychic is said to be 'an experience [*Erlebnis*] viewed in reflection, appearing as self through itself, in an absolute flow, as Now [and thus enters] into a "monadic" unity of consciousness'. Husserl complemented the motives of absolute reflection, of the Now and of the monadic unity – which will play a most important role in Benjamin's work – by characterising this 'monadic' unity and the limitless flow of phenomena as 'a continuous intentional line, which is, as it were, the index of the all-penetrating unity'. This intentional line – the index – is for Husserl the 'line of the beginning- and endless immanent "time", of a time' – as Husserl stresses – 'that is not measured by any chronometer'. (This 'immanent' time Husserl talks about is, as in the lectures, the time of the internal time consciousness, in contrast to the 'objective' or 'transcendental' time which can be measured by chronometers.) The fact that at this point many more convergences between Husserl's and Benjamin's motives accumulate can hardly be a coincidence. Nor can it be a coincidence that Benjamin's attacks in the 'Theses on the Philosophy of History' are directed at the concept of 'empathy', which is central in the *Logos* essay and is also central to the earlier works of Moritz Geiger, a pupil of Husserl's, with whom Benjamin studied in Munich. At this point, I can only briefly go into the relevant convergence between Husserl's lectures on internal time consciousness and Benjamin's notes from the late 1930s: they are mainly found in the conceptions of the 'image' and of the 'protention of re-remembering'. Husserl writes in §24: 'Each remembrance contains intentions of expectation, whose fulfillment leads to the present.' And: 'The re-remembering is not expectation, but it does have a horizon directed towards the future, the future of the re-remembered' (*The Phenomenology of Internal Time-Consciousness*, ed. Martin Heidegger, The Hague: Nijhoff, 1964).

32 Kant, *Critique of Pure Reason*, B 225.

33 Walter Benjamin, *Ursprung des deutschen Trauerspiels*, in *GS*, I:1, pp.203–430, 215 (translated as *The Origin of German Tragic Drama* [trans. John Osborne], London: New Left Books, 1977).

34 Benjamin, 'Begriff der Geschichte', I:2, p.695, [p.247, translation altered].

35 Benjamin, *Passagen-Werk*, V:1, pp.577–78 [pp.462–63, translation altered]. Heidegger is mentioned several times in the *Convolutes* of the *Arcades Project*, but not even once without Benjamin's massive criticism of his philosophy of historical time – which can be assumed to be the criticism of the philosophy of *Being and Time* and not just that of Heidegger's early Marbach lecture – leaving no doubt that Heidegger's philosophy of historical time is seen as the only serious philosophical competition to Benjamin's planned work. In a letter to Gershom Scholem Benjamin announces that in his introduction to the *Arcades Project*, which would be a critique of historical knowledge, 'je trouverai sur mon chemin Heidegger et j'attends quelque scintillement de l'entre-choc de nos deux manières, tres différentes, d'envisager l'histoire' (letter dated 20.1.1930, *Briefe*, III, pp.501–04, 503). It would be misleading to assume Heidegger's 'influence' on Benjamin's later conception of time and history. This is not just because the vulgar idea of a *influxus physicus* could not do justice to the complexity of both trains of thought, but also because that would leave aside the 'influence' that St Paul, Søren Kierkegaard, Friedrich Nietzsche and Edmund Husserl have exerted

on both authors. The 'influence' is particularly apparent in the conceptions of fulfilment, the fulfilled time and the moment. The distinction between that which is past and that which has been (*Vergangenem und Gewesenem*), which Benjamin tries to respect in some of his notes, may have been taken from *Being and Time* and not from Dolf Sternberger's dissertation *Der verstandene Tod*. It speaks in favour of the deep impression Heidegger's book exerted on Benjamin, perhaps even the threat which he may have felt it posed, that he, together with Brecht, thought of organising a 'critical community of reading' for the 'shattering' of *Being and Time* – as mentioned in a letter to Gershom Scholem on 25 July 1930 (*Briefe*, III). A detailed account of Benjamin's relation to Heidegger, which oscillated between fascination and abhorrence, would have to begin with Benjamin's engagement with Heidegger's habilitation thesis on Duns Scotus' theory of categories and meaning (*Kategorien- und Bedeutungslehre*). Such an account could dig deeper into the problems of the work of both authors than the admirers of the one and the despisers of the other would like.

36 Benjamin, *Passagen-Werk*, V:1, p.591 [p.473, translation altered].

37 Benjamin, *Passagen-Werk*, V:1, p.596 [p.476, translation altered].

38 Benjamin, *Passagen-Werk*, V:1, p.578 [p.463, translation altered].

39 Benjamin, *Passagen-Werk*, V:1, p.402 [p.319]. Keller's verses cited by Benjamin evoke the reflecting shield that paralyses the Gorgon. In 'Verlornes Recht, verlornes Glück', which peculiarly crosses the positions of Medusa and shield, it is said of a sailor: 'War wie ein Medusenschild / Der erstarrten Unruh Bild'.

40 Benjamin, *Passagen-Werk*, V:1, p.577 [p.462].

41 Benjamin, 'Begriff der Geschichte', I:2, p.701 [pp.252–53, translation altered].

42 Benjamin, *Passagen-Werk*, V:1, pp.577–78 [pp.462–63].

43 Benjamin, *Trauerspiel*, I:1, pp.216, 226. In the essay on 'Eduard Fuchs, der Sammler und der Historiker' (*GS* II:2, p.468), Benjamin also quotes this passage from the preface to the book on *The Origin of German Tragic Drama* in the context of formulations that later on contributed to the theses 'On the Concept of History'.

44 Benjamin, *Trauerspiels*, I:1, p.226.

45 Benjamin, *Passagen-Werk*, V:2, p.1038, [p.864]. The concept is derived from the context of neo-Kantianism and the calculus of the infinitesimal and, as an emphatic concept of happening, is here brought up by Benjamin against Hegel's discovery of the dialectical 'thought-time' (*Denkzeit*) – and thus against Hegel's dialectic as well as at another place against Heidegger's phenomenology, which, as Benjamin insists, is unable to set free a strict conception of history, at best a concept of time. Benjamin uses the formula of the 'differentials of time' in another place (*Passagen-Werk*, V:1, p.570 [p.456]) in the sense of a deviation or digression (albeit a minimal one) away from the 'grand lines', and thus, once again, from the linear continuum of tradition. In the note relating to Hegel, the concept of the 'Now of recognisability' is also brought into play. It does so as complement of the time differential and thus is not a 'thought-time' (*Denkzeit*), but an 'event time' (*Geschehniszeit*) – a time of the happening of time. Their relation can be formally characterised such that it is only the time differential that opens up the latitude where a Now of recognisability and thus history can happen. Because 'time differential' and 'Now of recognisability' are two aspects of the same happening, it can be said: the Now is differential.

The concept of the 'Now of recognisability', which gives its title to an extended and important reflection in the context of the theses 'On the Concept of History' (*GS*, I:3, pp.1237–38), finds its most significant exposition in a text dated by Rolf Tiedemann and Hermann Schweppenhäuser to 1920 or 1921. This text asks for the *medium* of being true (*Wahrsein*) and truth (*Wahrheit*) and counters the epistemological dualism (Kant's in particular, it seems) with the constitution of things in the Now of recognisability. The Now of recognisability is the logical time, which has to be reasoned for in the place of timeless validity. 'Logical' time, however, is the time of truth which in the Now contains 'in an unbroken way only itself'. That means however: the Now of recognisability, which contains itself, is its own *medium* – it is Now as that which is recognisable and Now, in which cognition is possible, only because it is the point of indifference of both. As such, however, it is the medium in which both move. With this concept of 'logical' time, that is, a time of language that can be characterised as time of pure mediality in the sense of the essay on language from 1916, Benjamin on the one hand opposes – over a period of twenty years – the denial or levelling of time in theories of validity and within the Kantian and neo-Kantian epistemology. On the other hand, he also opposes the uncritical assimilation of the concept of history to the concept of time in Hegelian dialectics and Heideggerian phenomenology. With the 'Now of recognisability' Benjamin did not only achieve a theory of genuine historical cognition that is independent of the historical doctrines. With the 'Now of recognisability' he also managed to lead the motives of transcendental and dialectical phenomenology – while remaining loyal to them – to the point where they leap over into the motive of the possibility of the Now of historical cognition. This is a possibility which does not just contain the resources of any reality, but also determines these resources according to the measure of this possibility, insofar it is mere possibility. As mere possibility it determines this cognition, however, as a cognition that can be missed.

In a text from *Zentralpark*, cognition is therefore characterised as missable, and even unrescuable if it is reachable only under the conditions of mere *'recognisability'*. This text can be read as a predecessor of the fifth thesis: 'The dialectic image is one that flashes up. In such a way, as an image flashing in the Now of recognisability, the image of that which has been is to be held on to. The rescue that is carried out in such a way, and only in such a way, can only ever be gained as on the perception of that which is unrescuably losing itself' (*GS*, I:2, p.682). As incomplete as this sentence is, it is clear at the same time: only that which is unrescuable is rescued – and even in its rescue it remains unrescuable. This can only mean: the Now of recognisability is the crisis, in which alone the crisis can be rescued and not its positive basic data. The crisis – the medium – is messianic.

46 Benjamin, 'Begriff der Geschichte', I:2, p.701 [p.253, translation altered].

47 Benjamin, 'Begriff der Geschichte', I:2, p.701 [p.253, translation altered].

48 Benjamin, 'Begriff der Geschichte', I:2, p.701 [p.253, translation altered].

49 Benjamin, 'Aus einer kleinen Rede über Proust, an meinem vierzigsten Geburtstag gehalten', *GS*, II:3, p.1064.

50 Benjamin, 'Über Sprache überhaupt und über die Sprache des Menschen', *GS*, II:1, pp.140–57.

51 In the letters dated 21.12.1972 and 12.1.1973 to Gershom Scholem, in Gershom Scholem, *Briefe III, 1971–1982*, ed. Itta Shedletzky, Munich: Beck, 1999, pp.299 and 300–01.

52 Benjamin, 'Begriff der Geschichte', I:2, p.695 [p.247, translation altered].

53 Benjamin, 'Begriff der Geschichte', I:2, p.695 [p.247, translation altered].

54 Benjamin, 'Begriff der Geschichte', I:2, p.695 [p.247, translation altered].

55 Quoted from Franz Kafka, *Hochzeitsvorbereitungen auf dem Lande*, Frankfurt/M.: Fischer, 1980, p.67.

Notes on Contributors

Andrew Benjamin is Professor of Philosophy and Director of the Centre for Research in Philosophy and Literature at the University of Warwick. His publications include *The Plural Event* (1993), *Present Hope* (1997), *Architectural Philosophy* (2000) and *Philosophy's Literature* (2001).

Geoffrey Bennington is Professor of French and Director of the Centre for Modern French Thought at the University of Sussex. His publications include *Sententiousness and the Novel* (1985), *Lyotard: Writing the Event* (1988), *Dudding: des noms de Rousseau* (1991), *Jacques Derrida* (with Jacques Derrida) (1991), *Legislations* (1995), *Interrupting Derrida* (2000) and *Frontières kantiennes* (2000). He has also translated many works by Derrida and Lyotard. He is currently working on Stendhal and Kierkegaard.

Karl Heinz Bohrer is Professor of Modern German Literature at the University of Bielefeld. He is co-editor of the journal *Merkur* and author of numerous books, including *Plötzlichkeit* (1981, English translation *Suddenness: On the Moment of Aesthetic Appearance* [1994]), *Das absolute Präsens: Die Semantik ästhetischer Zeit* (1994), *Der Abschied: Theorie der Trauer: Baudelaire, Goethe, Nietzsche, Benjamin* (1996), *Die Grenzen des Ästhetischen* (1998). He has edited *Sprachen der Ironie – Sprachen des Ernstes* (2000).

Simon Critchley is Professor of Philosophy at the University of Essex and Directeur de Programme at the Collège International de Philosophie, Paris. He is author of *The Ethics of Deconstruction* (1992, 1999), *Very Little ... Almost Nothing* (1997), *Ethics–Politics–Subjectivity* (1999), *Continental Philosophy: A Very Short Introduction* (2001) and *On Humour* (2001).

197

Notes on Contributors

Maurizio Ferraris is Professor of Theoretical Philosophy and Head of the Department of Philosophy at the University of Turin as well as Directeur de Programme at the Collège International de Philosophie, Paris. He is editor of the *Rivista di Estetica* and author of numerous books including *Storia dell'ermeneutica* (1988), *Mimica: Lutto e autobiografia da Agostino a Heidegger* (1992), *Analogon rationis* (1994), *L'immaginazione* (1996), *Il gusto del segreto* (with Jacques Derrida, 1997), *Estetica razionale* (1997), *L'ermeneutica* (1998), *Experimentelle Ästhetik* (2000), and *Nietzsche y el nihilismo* (2000).

Heidrun Friese is currently Fellow at the Kulturwissenschaftliches Institut, Essen. She has published widely on the social constructions of time and the images of history, the anthropology of the sciences and on social imagination. Her book publications include *Der Raum des Gelehrten: Eine Topographie akademischer Praxis* (with Peter Wagner, 1993), *Lampedusa: Historische Anthropologie einer Insel* (1996), *Identitäten* (ed. with Aleida Assmann, 1998), *Identities* (2001, forthcoming).

Werner Hamacher is Professor of German and Comparative Literature, Goethe University, Frankfurt am Main, and has taught at the Free University Berlin, Johns Hopkins University, Yale University, the University of Amsterdam and the Ecole Normale Supérieure. Most recent publications include *pleroma: Reading in Hegel* (1998), *Premises: Studies in Philosophy and Literature from Kant to Celan* (1996, 1999), and *Maser* (1998). He is editor of the series Meridian: Crossing Aesthetics (Stanford University Press).

Peter Poellner is Lecturer in the Department of Philosophy at the University of Warwick. He has published on a variety of topics, including Nietzsche, phenomenology, and modernism.

Index

Index

Index

Index